COMPUTING
THE
ENVIRONMENT

ISBN 978-1-119-09789-1 (cloth);
ISBN 978-1-119-09790-7 (pdf);
ISBN 978-1-119-09791-4 (epub);
ISBN 978-1-119-09792-1 (O-bk)

A catalogue record for this book is available from the British Library.

Executive Commissioning Editor: Helen Castle
Project Editor: David Sassian
Assistant Editor: Calver Lezama

Page design by Emily Chicken
Cover design and page layouts by Karen Willcox
Printed in Italy by Printer Trento Srl
Front cover image © BIG - Bjarke Ingels Group

COMPUTING THE ENVIRONMENT

Digital Design Tools for Simulation and Visualisation of Sustainable Architecture

WILEY

Brady Peters & Terri Peters

CONTENTS

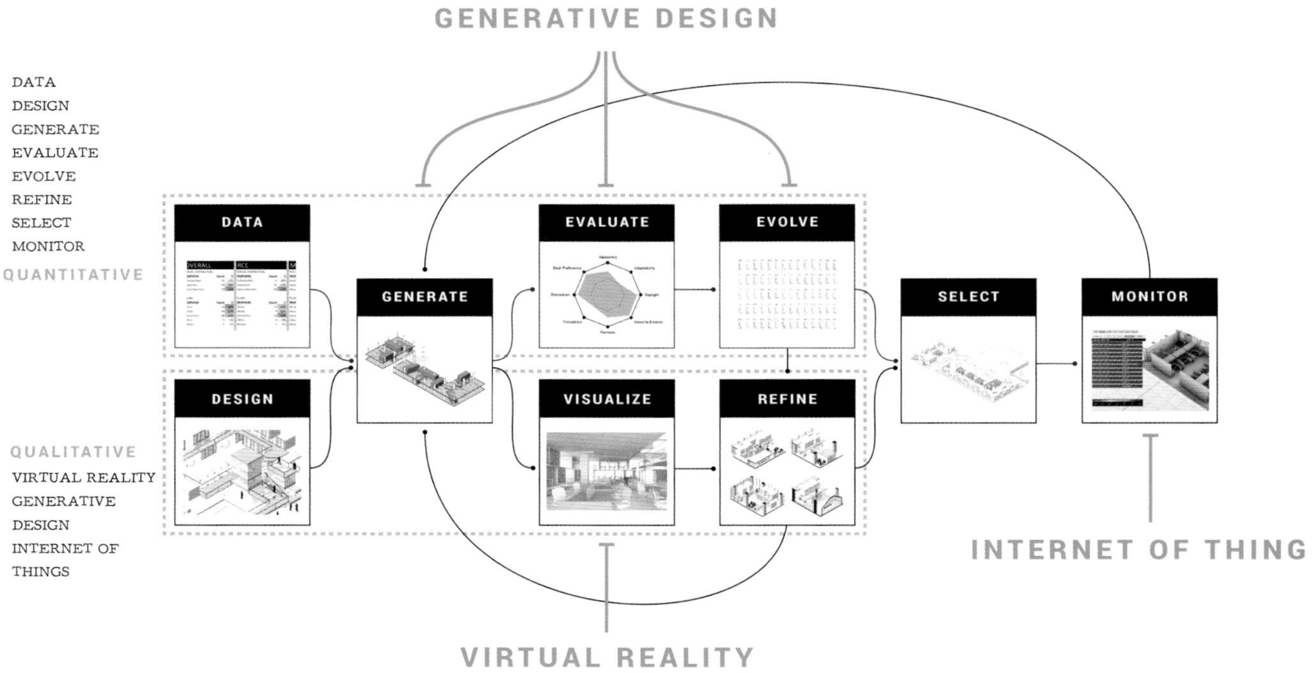

GENERATIVE DESIGN

DATA
DESIGN
GENERATE
EVALUATE
EVOLVE
REFINE
SELECT
MONITOR

QUANTITATIVE

DATA

GENERATE

EVALUATE

EVOLVE

SELECT

MONITOR

DESIGN

VISUALIZE

REFINE

QUALITATIVE

VIRTUAL REALITY
GENERATIVE
DESIGN
INTERNET OF
THINGS

INTERNET OF THING

VIRTUAL REALITY

FOREWORD
COMPUTING THE ENVIRONMENT

PHIL BERNSTEIN

Today functional problems are becoming less simple all the time. But designers rarely confess their inability to solve them. Instead, when a designer does not understand a problem clearly enough to find the order it really calls for, he falls back on some arbitrarily chosen formal order. The problem, because of its complexity, remains unsolved.

In the case of a real design problem, even our conviction that there is such a thing as fit to be achieved is curiously flimsy and insubstantial. We are searching for some kind of harmony between two intangibles: a form which we have not yet designed, and a context which we cannot properly describe.
— Christopher Alexander in *Notes on the Synthesis of Form* (1964)

Having defined the system known as 'pattern language' more than 60 years ago, Christopher Alexander, the seminal mathematician and architect, seems to have anticipated the challenges facing today's building designers as we struggle with an increasingly complex array of constraints, parameters, performance requirements and compositional options. The design harmony he asserts in the quote above perfectly characterises the challenge that Peter Rowe (via design theorist Horst Rittel) described as the making of architecture as a 'wicked problem (that) requires … the use of heuristic reasoning'.[1]

The digital age has certainly changed those heuristics, and we are only now beginning to understand the implications of those changes. Where the architectural design process in the pre-digital age was one of careful contemplation, limited calculation, experienced intuition and, ultimately judgement, today's designer can rely on an array of analytical, simulative and visualisation tools that enhance understanding of an emergent design and predict its ultimate performance.

As hand drawing gave way to computer-aided design (CAD), and CAD to building information modelling (BIM), we now have much of the informational infrastructure and data fidelity needed

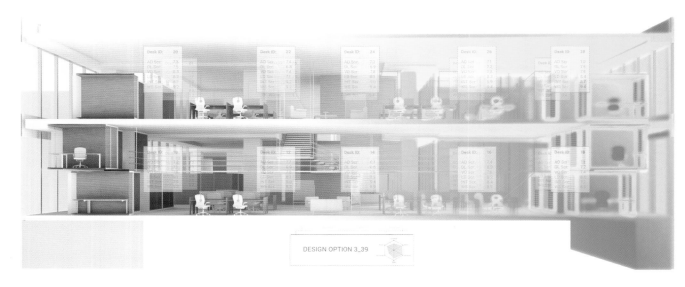

DESIGN OPTION 3_39

to bring on the next technological era in design, characterised by algorithmic design combined with big data. Digital tools can now help designers to reason and optimise their designs with measurable results, changing the design process itself, as well as the roles and responsibilities of architects and engineers, in the systems of delivery of building.

Thus this text by Terri and Brady Peters comes at a critical juncture in the history of the evolution of design methodology in the digital turn. If we are now moving from the era of BIM to that of connected design information, generated not simply by authorial but also analytical tools, both practitioners and tool creators need the theoretical framing, exemplary practices and speculations about the future that *Computing the Environment* offers. At a time when the explosion of software solutions—commercial platforms and bespoke algorithms—presents a bewildering array of procedural options and, with it, a cornucopia of data, the authors offer a lens through which to organise and understand the emergence of computational analysis and evaluation. The methodologies and trends so skilfully described and unpacked here will lead the way for the next generation of designers to find, to paraphrase Alexander, a non-arbitrary formal order'.

The mile markers of the digital turn that *Computing the Environment* represents are just the beginning of this journey for the building industry. Architects will always search for the 'form which we have not yet designed', but will increasingly do so in the context of analytical and predictive insight anticipated by the authors, a context that is, at least in part, now describable. The search for solutions will be informed and enhanced by these systems, giving designers not a new set of constraints, but rather new, greater degrees of freedom to search, iterate, evaluate, select and then synthesise answers to the challenges of our increasingly complex environment. As these methods and tools establish data-rich predictions of building performance across a spectrum of parameters that will soon evolve beyond energy conservation or daylighting, a knowledge base will emerge— the collective insight of predicted behaviour versus actual performance—that will further amplify the power of performance-based design.

The text quotes my colleague Michelle Addington describing buildings as 'in constant negotiation with their surrounding environment'. This has always been true, but integrating an understanding of that relationship with a design strategy has fallen into the realm of Alexander's arbitrary order. Much of the text that follows represents the best attempts to remediate the relationship of the building to the environment and the processes of design that anticipate those relationships. The resulting insights will inspire architects and engineers to create and perfect a new collection of heuristics that should lead to the next generation of high-performance design solutions.

Yale School of Architecture
New Haven
March 2017

REFERENCE

1. PG Rowe, 'A Priori Knowledge and Heuristic Reasoning In Architectural Design', in *Journal of Architectural Education*, vol 36, no 1, 1982, pp 18–23.

IMAGES

© Sean Ahlquist, Achim Menges, Institute for Computational Design, University of Stuttgart

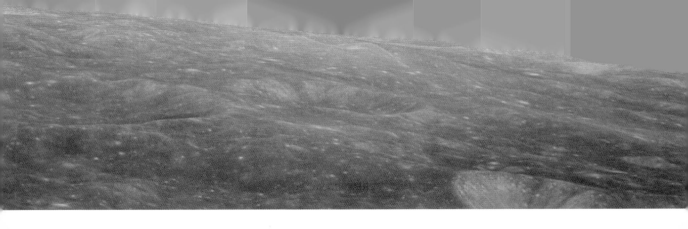

1. INTRODUCTION— COMPUTING THE ENVIRONMENT:

DESIGN WORKFLOWS FOR THE SIMULATION OF SUSTAINABLE ARCHITECTURE

BRADY PETERS AND TERRI PETERS

That's here. That's home. That's us. On it everyone you love, everyone you know, everyone you ever heard of, every human being who ever was, lived out their lives. ... There is perhaps no better demonstration of the folly of human conceits than this distant image of our tiny world.[1]
—Carl Sagan

1 Earthrise image of Earth, photographed by astronaut Bill Anders during a 1968 Apollo mission, the first manned voyage to orbit the Moon

This photograph is renowned as an influential environmental image, sparking people's impression of Earth as vulnerable and small in a large expansive universe. Looking back on Earth, it seems potentially fragile, a finite, closed-loop system.

Architects design for the future. The act of drawing is a predictive act of experimenting with possible futures. The buildings architects design today form the cities of the future. Necessary optimists, architects design to achieve better ways of living—turning 'existing situations into preferred ones'.[2] In architecture, the vast majority of projects are now designed in virtual environments; and, beyond architecture, in almost all sciences, we are seeing the rise of computer simulations as more and more experiments are carried out 'in silico'.[3] Simulation is a way in which designs can be tested for their future performance. In architecture, 'while simulation once pertained to modes of presentation, it now connects architecture to the natural sciences and to a methodological and strategic instrument, a tool of knowledge'.[4]

A 'model' is an approximation of the real world, and following the building of models, simulations are repeated observations of models that enable analysis and visualisation of behaviour.[5] Architects have always used simulations—tools to forecast a range of behaviours in buildings. Yanni Loukissas suggests that this way of working is not new in architecture—Filippo Brunelleschi invented linear perspective to simulate the perception of space, Pierre Patte used ray diagrams to simulate sound and Antoni Gaudí used graphic statics to simulate structural performance. While in today's practice, numerical methods have overtaken graphical techniques in the domains of visualisation, sound and structural performance, what remains constant is the notion of simulation—the desire to get feedback from the design environment. [6]

Like many architects, Bjarke Ingels designs by imagining a whole new world from scratch. Discussing the work of science fiction author Philip K Dick, Ingels says: 'the whole story is a narrative pursuit of the potential of the idea or innovation; he writes about

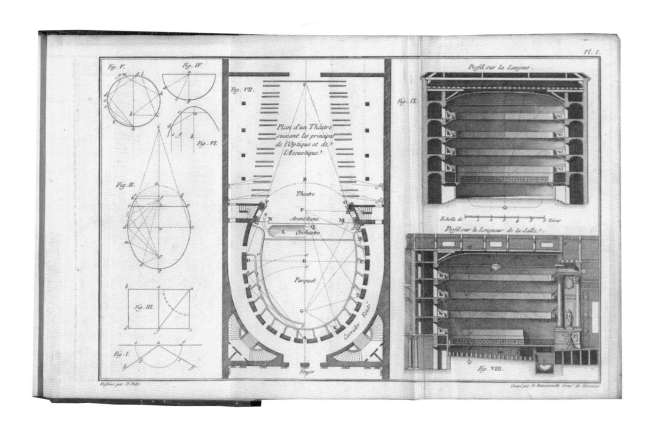

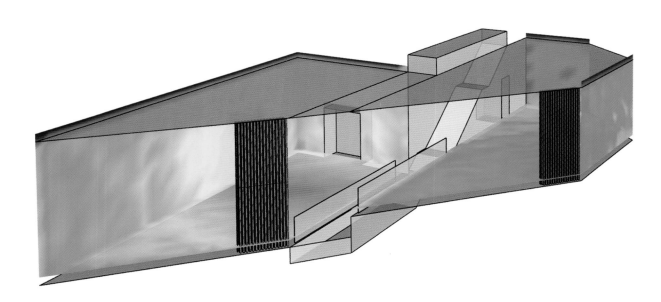

what unfolds as a result: problems, conflicts, possibilities, freedoms … it's almost like unleashing a whole new universe based on a single triggering idea'.[7] Ingels describes his design process in a similar way: 'as soon as I discover some kind of innovation that has altered the game, making the project is like pursuing the consequence of these changes—at that point, I don't have to come up with lots of new ideas; I just have to work with the consequences of a single innovation'.

Simulation is what allows architects to 'work out the consequences' of their innovations.

DATA, DRAWING AND SIMULATION

Now these simulations are carried out using computers— and have become part of the (almost) everyday practice of architecture. Simulations transform quantitative models of building physics into qualitative sensory experiences. Internally, these simulations are purely numerical, but through visualisation (and auralisation) can create convincing sensorial events for architects and clients to consider. 'In sustainable terms, the complexity and inefficiencies of buildings present the most challenging environmental problem. Simulation remains the primary tool for the designer to develop intuitions and analysis of performance,' Azam Khan and Andrew Marsh explain. The software developers say: 'simulation is about complex relationships and time. Complexity can be defined in many ways, however, put most simply it describes a system in which unspecified emergent behaviour can be observed'.[8]

The digital has been accused of 'losing its materiality' and it has been said that it 'edges out the real' by the psychologist Sherry Turkle.[9] However, this book can be seen as an extended argument that the use of computational design tools now enables critically important aspects of environmental performance to become part of the architectural design process; and that through computation designers can better predict what is real and measure the impacts of materials and energies. Aspects of design that were previously impossible or difficult to design for, can now be incorporated into the architectural design process.

Designers are adopting a new generation of accurate and specific simulation tools. Khan and Marsh predicted in 2011: '[the] future of simulation lies in three areas: more detailed modelling, building integration and becoming an indispensable part of any design process; that is, simulation as a design tool'.[8] Through the use of design simulation, building performance can be predicted. Early geometries can be compared for energy use, daylight, shading, airflow, comfort, sunlight and other parameters. Kjell Anderson writes: 'simulations provide immediate feedback about the consequences of design decisions, continued use of simulation software validates and hones an individual's intuition'.[10] He further explains that simulation itself can be a highly creative act, it helps designers develop intuitions on real performance, as 'play leads to understanding'.

2 Pierre Patte, acoustic ray-tracing theatre design diagrams, 1782
This drawing of sound paths and their reflections off interior surfaces was used as a way of understanding acoustic performance. This is an early example of performance analysis. Architects have always been interested in this, but digital simulation tools offer more sophisticated and precise options for computing performance, including sound, light and airflow.

3 BIG, Mexico City Villa, 2016, acoustic simulation
This simulation uses Pachyderm, developed by Arthur van der Harten, a plug-in for Rhino that is used for acoustical analysis and simulation. Simulation can be used to understand how material and geometry impact acoustical performance, and this study looks into how the main stair could work as a sound absorber.

COMPUTATION IN PRACTICE

The contemporary concepts and workflows in *Computing the Environment* have roots in earlier design experiments and technological advancements, and a path can be traced from early parametric modelling to current advances in custom tool development. In 1963, Ivan Sutherland created the first computer program to design architecture. He created a program that could not only draw geometry, but also create relationships between different elements in the design (associative modelling), and compute basic structural performance analysis.[11] However, when design software was introduced to architectural practice, it only functioned as a virtual drafting board; the important 'computed' aspects of parametric relationships and performance were not included. Starting in the early 1980s, 2D drafting continued the practice of representing buildings as multiple 2D drawings. 2D drafting technology could be retrofitted to existing design practice, using existing skills without challenging established professional methods and conventions.[12]

Robert Aish sees the history of computer-aided design (CAD) as being divided into three eras: the 2D drafting era, the building information modelling (BIM) era and the design computation era. The BIM era actually started before the 2D drafting era in the 1980s, and is based on the idea that buildings are assemblies of components, but that does not necessarily imply that a designer conceives of a building in terms of such assemblies. This 'component' assumption forces the designer to think about micro ideas (the components) before macro ideas (the building form). The design computation era introduced the distinction between a generative description of a building and the resulting generated model, and introduced a process where the designer no longer directly models the building, but instead develops an algorithm whose execution generates the model. There are two ways in which this enables a completely different kind of architecture to be created: first, it enables a move away from manual modelling and encourages the adoption of generative design tools; and second, it allows the designer to create his or her own components and, more importantly, to define a building and its components in terms of its behaviour.[12]

A DEEPER WAY TO THINK

In the late 1990s, in response to the lack of functionality in available programs, a few architects began to borrow technology from other industries: physics engines in game software, and parametric and fabrication abilities in industrial and aerospace software. Perhaps now we are beginning to re-establish the vision of the original innovators (such as Sutherland), that CAD is not a better way to draw, 'but a deeper way to think'.[12] Designers are 'moving away from employing computational design as a means to produce conventional architectural representations towards something more', according to Volker Mueller and Makai Smith. They are searching for ways in which to expand the scope of what may be represented computationally: material properties, energy flows and other informational aspects.[13] People movement, solar performance, daylight and glare, acoustic performance, airflow, thermal comfort and energy use can now be accurately simulated. The barrier to entry has been lowered to such an extent that all practitioners and students can now use advanced tools. Simulation software, which was only decades ago the domain of specialists and highly expensive, is now freely available on the internet and fully customisable to project demands. It appears that it is architects' new ability to 'compute the environment' that will reconnect the architectural design process with 'real-world' performance issues. This is largely to do with the widespread popularity of Rhino and Grasshopper. Using an 'open innovation' concept, Robert McNeel enables people to create their own 'plug-in' design software, and this has spawned a whole 'ecosystem' of new and innovative computational design tools for architects. Architects are increasingly the authors of their own design environment.[14]

ENVIRONMENTAL IMPACTS AND THE HUMAN DIMENSION

> We lack even basic things like data calculation methods and basic knowledge about sustainable building design. … We have no methods for the design and construction of truly recyclable buildings. … The list of missing knowledge is long.
> —Werner Sobek[15]

Human actions are changing our climate. Climate change and extreme weather events are having an undeniable impact on our built environment, with new regulations, mindsets and timeframes for sustainable design and development emerging from multiple sectors. The building industry uses a tremendous amount of energy, creates pollution, material use. The construction, operation, maintenance and demolition of buildings have an enormous impact on the environment and our shared resources. Renewable energy, passive environmental design strategies, low-energy techniques, life-cycle assessment, and integrated neighbourhood and community designs will become increasingly important topics for simulation and digital design. Computational design tools and workflows are a wide topic area, and we chose to focus on those particularly relevant to environmental design, such as energy use, daylighting, life cycle, thermal comfort and other design topics, rather than structural design or other parameters. There is a need for more research into how digital tools can advance sustainable architecture.

There are areas of tremendous potential for architects to positively affect humans' impact on the environment. Architects must synthesise broader societal concerns of climate change, energy and resource use together with the site specific and local environments of architecture. There now exists, with computational design tools, the ability to design better performing buildings using more accurate simulation tools. New functionality in industry standard tools such as Revit is making it easier for architects to design for and manage environmental parameters. For

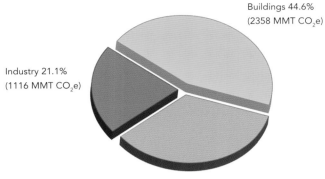

Buildings 44.6%
(2358 MMT CO_2e)

Industry 21.1%
(1116 MMT CO_2e)

Transportation 34.3%
(1816 MMT CO_2e)

US CO_2 Emissions by Sector

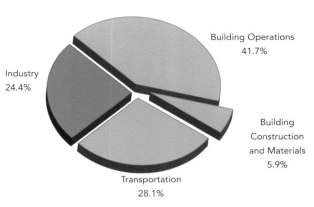

Building Operations
41.7%

Industry
24.4%

Building
Construction
and Materials
5.9%

Transportation
28.1%

US Energy Consumption by Sector

4 United States CO_2 emissions by sector, 2012
Buildings are a significant source of emissions
and the 2030 Challenge is a global architecture
and building industry initiative that aims to
incrementally lower building-related emissions
and energy use by 2030, so that they use no
fossil fuels and greenhouse gas-emitting energy
to operate.

5 United States energy consumption by sector,
2012
To make the largest impacts on energy
consumption in buildings, the focus should be
on building operations. The 2030 Challenge
seeks to transfer the building industry's focus on
fossil fuels to renewable energy sources.

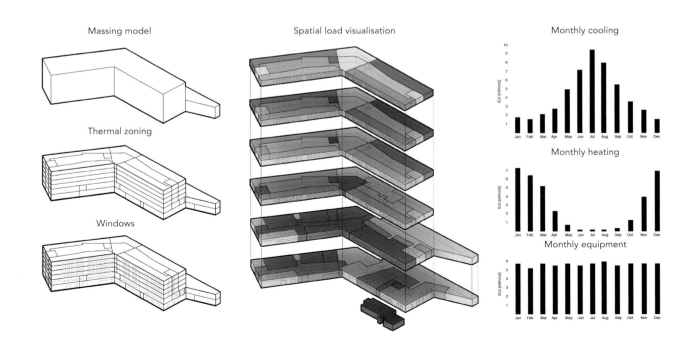

Massing model

Thermal zoning

Windows

Spatial load visualisation

Monthly cooling

Monthly heating

Monthly equipment

example, the Insight 360 tool includes an automated workflow for understanding photovoltaic energy production and the impacts on building costs. The tool creates a graphic dashboard for the design of renewable energy sources, so users can adjust settings such as panel type, percentage of roof coverage and payback period, and then see the impacts of these decisions in the Energy Cost Range of the model. Another example is the Tally tool, which runs within the Revit BIM design environment. It was developed by KieranTimberlake, which offers a life-cycle analysis tool to quantify embodied energy along with other environmental impacts and emissions to land, air and water.

The book relates to leading green rating systems, including Leadership in Energy and Environmental Design (LEED), and the principles of the 2030 Challenge pertaining to lowering building emissions, focusing on how new digital simulation and modelling tools are integrating with these systems. However, there are aspects to building that are not so easy to predict, and those aspects have to do with buildings' interaction with people, and with the environment, over time.

Architects can compute the environment in terms of material use, energy consumption and carbon footprint but also relating to the intimate experienced qualities of light, heat, sound or airflow. The exploration of all of these invisible terrains offers new potentials for the definition of architectural space, enclosure and meaning in architecture. Beyond the critical importance of designing buildings that are sympathetic to the ecosystems in which they operate, these are also fundamental aspects of health and wellbeing. Not only are these aspects of architecture important physically, but also perceptually and spatially.[16] Sean Lally argues for an 'architecture of energies' that is much more than the building of an object on a site: 'it is a reinvention of the site itself. The microclimates of internal heating and cooling, outdoor shadows and artificial lighting, vegetation, the importation of building materials, and the new activities that will occur there create new places in time on site'.[17] Aspects of design that were previously impossible or difficult to design for, microclimates, gradients of experience, responsive controls, can now be incorporated into the architectural design process using new computational tools.[18]

THE STRUCTURE OF THE BOOK

In contemporary practice, there are now designers who specialise in sustainability. It has been observed that often these specialist designers are situated in research and development groups, and that these individuals and groups, have tended to specialise in technology and the use and development of digital design tools and simulations as primary methods for research.[19] There is a need for a more in-depth discussion of the inner workings and workflows of how architects are 'computing the environment' and how they define the environment, and how they use computation and digital design workflows. Instead of profiling buildings, we have profiled practices, documenting how designers work, and how they engage with computation and environmental design. This

6 Architectural energy calculation using Archsim

Archsim was developed by Timur Dogan as an energy simulation plug-in for Grasshopper and has now become a part of DIVA 4.0. Archsim links the EnergyPlus simulation engine with a powerful parametric design and CAD modelling environment.

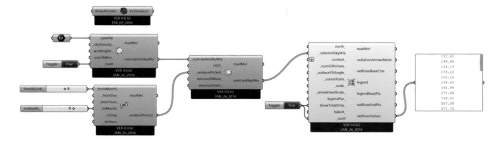

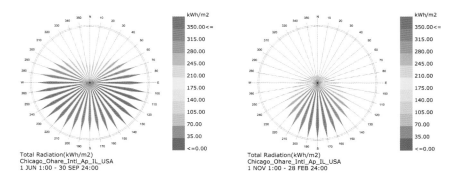

7 Thornton Thomasetti, solar analysis tools

Ladybug and Honeybee are two open-source environmental plug-ins, developed for Grasshopper3D by Mostapha Sadeghipour Roudsari. Ladybug allows designers to analyse and visualise EnergyPlus weather data and Honeybee connects to various simulation engines, including EnergyPlus and OpenStudio, for feedback on energy, daylight and lighting simulations.

Total Radiation(kWh/m2)
Chicago_Ohare_Intl_Ap_IL_USA
1 JUN 1:00 - 30 SEP 24:00

Total Radiation(kWh/m2)
Chicago_Ohare_Intl_Ap_IL_USA
1 NOV 1:00 - 28 FEB 24:00

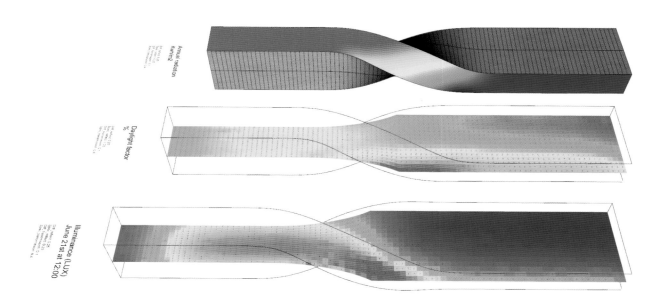

book offers a new generation of architects and designers a sense of direction in how to contextualise their work and see a history of ideas, how to meaningfully apply the framework and concern of architecture within sustainable design practice. It is about architectural design, in particular computational methods and tools for sustainable design.

The book is structured into three sections: themed theoretical chapters, practice profiles and a concluding chapter on the future outlook. Following this introduction, five chapters outline key concepts in environmental design and focus on the associated computational design tools and workflows. These chapters begin with the large scale: we discuss issues of climate and energy, and the tools and workflows that are impacting global and local contexts; then explore the siting, massing and exterior envelope of buildings; move into an investigation of designing for the interior environment and how simulations can improve design for human comfort; and finally look at workflows and processes for life cycle and materials and at various measurement methods for quantifying sustainability. A chapter on smaller scale 1:1 prototypes and pavilions follows, which allows us to showcase more experimental approaches that are not yet found in mainstream practice, to reveal near future directions in the field.

The practice profiles are the second major section of the book. We selected a range of larger design-led offices that see their designs realised in built works. We initially intended to feature a series of exemplary singular buildings by these offices, but quickly realised that few built projects incorporate enough computation of environmental parameters and that the real story is in the design of workflows relating to computation and environmental design. We interviewed researchers and computational design specialists at eight architecture offices: Foster + Partners (UK), BIG (Denmark), KieranTimberlake (USA), 3XN (Denmark), White (Sweden), Thornton Thomasetti (USA), Zaha Hadid Architects (UK) and Woods Bagot (Australia) with a particular focus on how they integrated feedback from simulation and computational tools at early stages of the design process. We profiled engineers BuroHappold (UK), Max Fordham (UK) and Transsolar (Germany), and computational designers at the real estate company WeWork (USA) to gain an understanding of data and simulation in the design process and how this contributes to the design concept.

The final chapter is based on a series of interviews with some of the most prominent, influential and creative sustainable design theorists and educators in the world. These six are conceptually advancing the field through their thought leadership, authoring the most architecturally relevant books and papers relevant to themes in this book: Timur Dogan (Cornell University and lead developer of Archsim Energy Modeling, UMI and Urban Daylight simulation software), Werner Sobek (founder of the engineering practice Werner Sobek), William W Braham (University of Pennsylvania), Kiel Moe (Harvard Graduate School of Design), Neil Katz (Skidmore, Owings & Merrill) and Mostapha

8 BIG, solar analysis of Kistefos Museum bridge, Norway

Early design stage simulations done in Honeybee of Annual Radiation (kWh/m^2), Daylight Factor (%) and Illuminance (LUX) to determine how much of the facade would be open, if the facade would need external shading and if the twist would allow for a skylight as it goes from vertical to horizontal.

9 Weathers, proposal for a new energy landscape
Sean Lally explores a speculative series of designs for what he calls 'new energy landscapes'. He argues that energy is 'more than what fills the interior of a building or reflects off its outer walls. Instead, energy becomes its own enterprise for design innovation: it becomes the architecture itself'.

10 Sean Lally, energy shape diagram
Sean Lally of Weathers argues that architecture in the future will be the design of energies and microclimates.

Sadeghipour Roudsari (University of Pennsylvania and creator of Ladybug and Honeybee). Their expertise and critical abilities to imagine new universes for sustainable design help to situate this book beyond current practice, to begin to imagine, design and influence architecture of the future. We hope that readers will gain a critical overview of important environmental parameters and tools, learn key references and gain a further understanding of the state of the art in practice, and find inspiration to develop their own tools and workflows.

NEW POTENTIALS FOR ARCHITECTURE
Computation is redefining the practice of architecture. It can amplify a designer's ability to: simultaneously consider multiple options; connect to vast databases; analyse designs in relation to many performance parameters; create their own design tools;

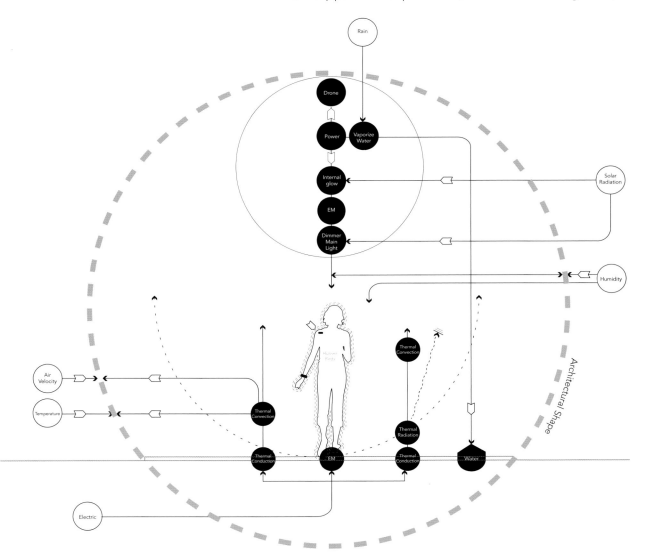

and, through digital fabrication and robotic assembly, engage in the processes of building construction. Architectural practice is defined by the tools we use; as Jonathan Hill writes: 'the [modern] architect and the architectural drawing are twins ... they are representative of the same idea ... that architecture results not from the accumulated knowledge of a team of anonymous craftsmen but from the individual artistic creation of an architect in command of drawing who conceives a building as a whole at a remove from construction'.[20] So, if the practice of architecture involves the imagining and predicting of future scenarios relating to the built environment, then by probing the boundaries of new computational and simulation techniques, new potentials for architecture can be discovered, and new scenarios for how life will be in the future can be predicted.

REFERENCES

1. Carl Sagan, *Pale Blue Dot: A Vision of the Human Future in Space*, Ballentine Books (New York), 1997, pp 8–9.
2. Herbert Simon, *The Sciences of the Artificial*, third edition, The MIT Press (Cambridge, MA), 1996.
3. Eric Winsberg, *Science in the Age of Computer Simulation*, University of Chicago Press (Chicago and London), 2010.
4. Georg Vrachliotis, 'Flusser's Leap: Simulation and Technical Thought in Architecture', in Andrea Gleiniger and Georg Vrachliotis (eds), *Simulation: Presentation Technique and Cognitive Method*, Birkhäuser (Basel), 2008, p 8.
5. John Sokolowski and Catherine Banks, *Principles of Modeling and Simulation: A Multidisciplinary Approach*, John Wiley & Sons (Hoboken, NJ), 2009.
6. Yanni Loukissas, *Co-Designers: Cultures of Computer Simulation in Architecture*, Routledge (New York), 2012.
7. Bjarke Ingels, 'Unleashing New Universes', interview by Terri Peters, in *Mark Magazine*, no 36, 2012, pp 194–9.
8. Andrew Marsh and Azam Khan, 'Simulation and the Future of Design Tools for Ecological Research', in Terri Peters (ed), *Experimental Green Strategies: Redefining Ecological Design Research*, Architectural Design (AD) series (John Wiley & Sons, Chichester), vol 81, no 6, November/December 2011, pp 82–91.
9. Sherry Turkle, *Simulation and Its Discontents*, The MIT Press (Cambridge, MA), 2009.
10. Kjell Anderson, *Design Energy Simulation for Architects: Guide to 3D Graphics*, Routledge (New York), 2014, p 9.
11. Ivan Sutherland, 'Sketchpad, a Man-Machine Graphical Communication System', Massachusetts Institute of Technology, 1963.
12. Robert Aish, 'First Build Your Tools', in Brady Peters and Terri Peters (eds), *Inside Smartgeometry: Expanding the Architectural Possibilities of Computational Design*, John Wiley & Sons (Chichester), 2013.
13. Volker Mueller and Makai Smith, 'Generative Components and Smartgeometry: Situated Software

Development', in Brady Peters and Terri Peters (eds), *Inside Smartgeometry: Expanding the Architectural Possibilities of Computational Design*, John Wiley & Sons (Chichester), 2013, pp 142–53.

14. Daniel Davis and Brady Peters, 'Design Ecosystems: Customising the Architectural Design Environment with Software Plug-ins', in Brady Peters and Xavier de Kestelier (eds), *Computation Works: The Building of Algorithmic Thought*, Architectural Design (AD) series (John Wiley & Sons, Chichester), vol 83, issue 2, March/April 2013, pp 124–31.

15. Werner Sobek, 'Architecture Isn't Here to Stay: Toward a Reversibility of Construction', in Ilka Ruby and Andreas Ruby (eds), *Re-inventing Construction*, Ruby Press (Berlin), 2010, pp 34–45.

16. David Orrell, *The Future of Everything: The Science of Prediction from Wealth and Weather to Chaos and Complexity*, Thunder's Mouth Press (New York), 2007.

17. Sean Lally, *The Air From Other Planets*, Lars Müller Publishers (Zurich), 2014, pp 11–12.

18. Juhani Pallasmaa, *The Eyes of the Skin: Architecture and the Senses*, John Wiley & Sons (Chichester), 2005.

19. Terri Peters (ed), *Experimental Green Strategies: Redefining Ecological Design Research*, Architectural Design (AD) series (John Wiley & Sons, Chichester), vol 81, no 6, November/December 2011.

20. Jonathan Hill, *Immaterial Architecture*, Routledge (London), 2006, p 33.

IMAGES

1 Max Fordham, energy modelling and
simulation, Fiera Milano District, Milan, Italy,
2012
The engineers used energy modelling
extensively in these projects, and this is a
screenshot of an EnergyPlus whole building
analysis. The study shows how the two
buildings, one by Studio Libeskind and the
other by Zaha Hadid Architects, perform
independently and in relation to each other
on the site.

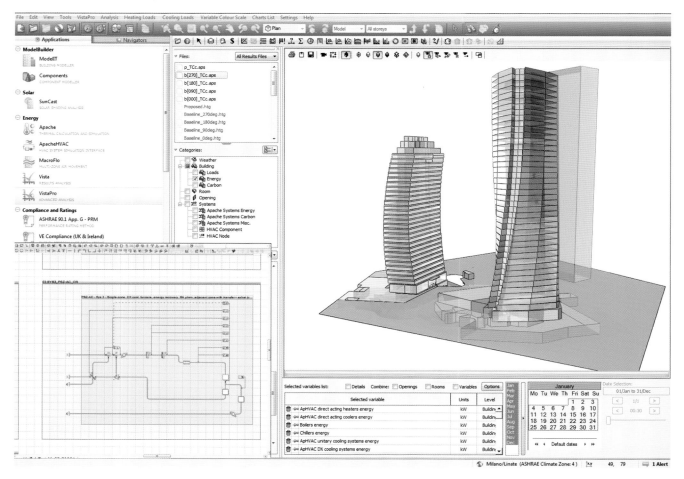

2. NEW DIALOGUES ABOUT ENERGY:

PERFORMANCE, CARBON AND CLIMATE

TERRI PETERS

We live in an era where data is abundant, yet very little of this data is used to effectively inform the early design of buildings … early geometries are rarely compared for energy use, daylighting, shading, or airflow potential, since there are many other issues for architects to consider.[1]
—Kjell Anderson

Architects are largely excluded from performance evaluations of their building designs. Even with the best intentions, most decisions in this realm remain difficult to significantly impact (or measure) at the building scale as architects, engineers or urban planners. New tools and workflows are being developed in trying to address this issue. For example, predicting energy consumption is an important aspect that can be effectively studied using simulation, and until recently was largely the domain of engineers and specialised consultants. New tools and workflows are being developed by and for designers, not with the aim of competing with certified energy analysis specialists, but to have a better dialogue with them, and to explore design issues. This chapter begins by introducing the concept of performance-based design and then considers energy, carbon and climate, three important parameters relevant to sustainable design, in terms of new computational approaches and tools, and what new directions are being explored by computational designers and theorists.

PERFORMANCE-BASED DESIGN

The concept of performance-based design is not new, but in the last decade architects and theorists have increasingly discussed this term in connection to digital tools and workflows, and more recently to sustainable design. Greg Foliente describes performance-based design as the practice of thinking and working in terms of ends rather than means, where designers are concerned with what a building or building product is required to do, rather than prescribing how it is to be constructed.[2] Foliente argues that performance-based approaches encourage innovation, optimisation and the exchange of products and ideas between domains. Especially in the context of this book, an important point about performance-based design is that it is centred on the concept of the building being defined by and meeting human requirements rather than by some sort of abstract dimensional or material specification.

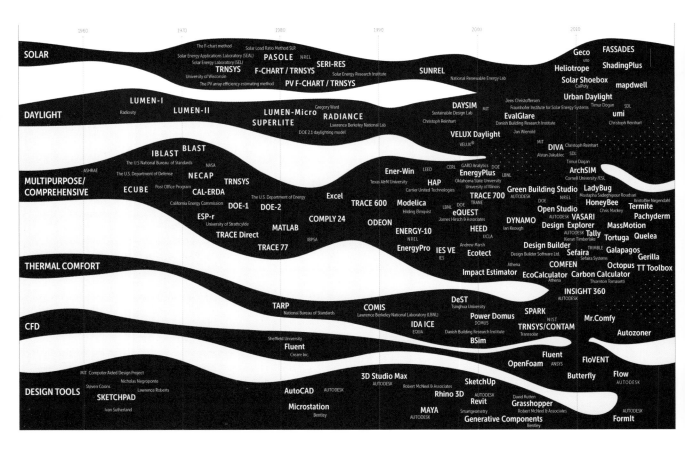

2 A selected history of building performance tools, 1960–present

This diagram, inspired by Charles Jencks's 1973 graphic chart of architects and movements, illustrates the recent history of building performance simulation tools for designers. The chart lists the year in which they were introduced, and in many cases the creator of the tools. The diagram reflects the diversity of tools available and the large number of new tools developed in the past five years.

Does performance-based design mean better buildings? The answer is not necessarily.—It is a different workflow and decision-making process, so it depends on the designer and how success is measured. Yehudi Kalay's research into performance-based design finds that improvement in the design process will be brought about through feedback via performance evaluation. He argues that performance-based design should be a bi-directional design process, in which both form and the evaluative functions inform each other, and are modified throughout the design process until the designer reaches a solution when form and function come together to achieve an acceptable performance. He suggests that this leads to a new design paradigm for architecture, that of true performance-based design. Kalay argues that the design process is a confluence of three important factors: form, function and context; and these three factors combine to determine the behaviour of the proposed solution.[3] What are the implications and possibilities for computing the environment?

RETHINKING ENERGY

> A study of humanity and nature is thus a study of systems of energy, materials, money, and information. Therefore we approach nature and people by studying energy systems networks … The small areas of nature, the large panoramas that include civilization, and the whole biosphere of Earth, and the miniature worlds of ecological microcosms are similar. All use energy resources to produce, consume, recycle, sustain.
> —HT Odum 1971[4]

Energy is a fundamental consideration in life and in sustainable design. In the 1970s, HT Odum conducted pioneering research in environmental systems. Using a systems approach that connected energy, materials, money and information over time, he defined ecological economics in terms of the interrelations between energy and environment and their importance to humans and our planet.[4] Energy is defined as the ability to do work by moving matter; however, our relationship to energy is directly influenced by the values we place on nature and natural resources. Therefore, in defining and measuring energy in the design of a building element or structure, the systems boundaries are debatable. To design for energy—does an architect need to calculate for an interior zone, a building, the whole site or a larger area? What kind of energy is being considered—for example renewable or non-renewable—and how can it be compared? As a designer, it is hard to know the best scale to consider and what the inadvertent impacts are on the larger system. Designing for a desired end-goal using performance-based design, rather than to meet a standard or requirement, allows designers to think about what they are really trying to accomplish.

Digital energy modelling is standard practice in order to predict and measure energy use before a building's construction. Energy modelling is required for Leadership in Energy and

Angle/grid controlled points

Floor-plan build-up

Window geometry

Thermal zones

Floor build-up

Automatic adjacency detection

Shading system

Full geometric model

Results

3 Timur Dogan, energy modelling in Archsim, showing fully parametric energy and daylight model

Archsim Energy Modeling is a plug-in developed in 2014 by Timur Dogan that links the EnergyPlus simulation engine with a powerful parametric design and CAD modelling environment. Designers can create complex multi-zone energy models and then simulate them and visualise results within the Rhino/ Grasshopper environment.

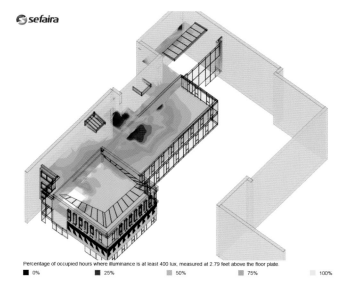
Percentage of occupied hours where illuminance is at least 400 lux, measured at 2.79 feet above the floor plate.
0%   25%   50%   75%   100%

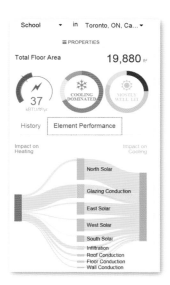

Environmental Design (LEED), International Energy Conservation Code (IECC), International Green Construction Code (IgCC) and many other environmental standards. Depending on the quality and level of detail as inputs, and when in the design process it is carried out, the energy model can be a highly useful tool for comparing design options and predicting performance. Energy models are typically carried out by engineers and external consultants, and typically usually compare modelled performance between the building design and that of a baseline design. This is the basis for point allocation for the primary energy credit under LEED and the modelling software must meet the minimum performance requirements set by ASHRAE 90.1.[5] To set up a digital energy model, a calculation engine accepts inputs such as building geometry, system characteristics, operations schedules to produce outputs such as performance comparisons and compliance reports. The most commonly used base algorithm for whole building energy simulation is EnergyPlus, created by the United States Department of Energy as a free, open-source and cross-platform program that outputs to text files.[6] It is not a standard practice for designers to use this software due to its complexity and non-graphical interface. However, it is the underlying engine behind a range of other programs that are increasingly being used by designers, such as Sefaira, Honeybee, IES, Termite and Archsim.

PREDICTING ENERGY USE

> *There is no energy crisis – we have solved it.*
> —Thomas Rau[7]

Projected energy use is a satisfying parameter for evaluating sustainable design in systems such as LEED, but focusing on 'low energy' is difficult as it only applies to non-renewable energy and its meaning is relative to the building type, location and programmatic benchmark. There are many kinds and hierarchies of energy that need to be considered in building design and operation. Embodied energy, or the energy expended in the production and transportation, plus inherent energy at a specific point in a life cycle should be considered. This is often poorly conceptualised in the design process (see Chapter 5 for more information on embodied energy and life cycle). Operational energy or the ways in which people use the building once it is built, is the energy consideration that is the hardest to accurately estimate, and yet the most important because it relates to how people use and adapt the building over time. The energy that people use in operating a building over its lifetime is the largest aspect of energy consumption, far more than the energy required to build it in the first place.

Designers with a knowledge of history, culture and aesthetics should be ideally placed to predict how people will use a building—and setting up a model and simulation of how people behave and how they engage with buildings is a huge area of potential growth for designers and programmers. Emboldened

4 Sefaira energy modelling tool
Sefaira is a daylighting and energy simulation plug-in for SketchUp and Revit. It is designed to be easy to use and to be quick to calculate and visualise results, so that it can be used in the early stages of a design.

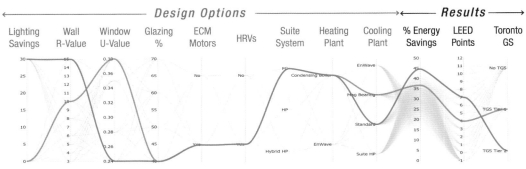

Design Options ————————————→ ← Results —→

Lighting Savings	Wall R-Value	Window U-Value	Glazing %	ECM Motors	HRVs	Suite System	Heating Plant	Cooling Plant	% Energy Savings	LEED Points	Toronto GS

Modeling results generated using EnergyPlus Version 8.4

MORRISON HERSHFIELD

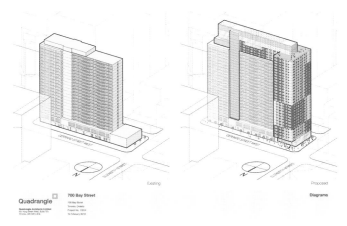

Existing

Quadrangle   700 Bay Street
Quadrangle Architects Limited
901 King Street West, Suite 701
Toronto, ON M5V 3H5

700 Bay Street
Toronto, Ontario
Project No. 13014
16 February 2016

Proposed

Diagrams

5a Building energy optimisation tool, created by engineers Morrison Hershfield, showing 700 Bay Street renovation, Toronto, Canada, 2016
This building energy optimisation tool is a way in which to visualise results and options of energy modelling within a project.

5b Quadrangle Architects, 700 Bay Street, Toronto, Canada, diagram of existing and proposed renovation
The designers incorporated energy modelling feedback at early stages of the design to assess trade-offs and opportunities to meet performance targets. The project is a renovation of a 1970s tower to include retail and housing while offering a public plaza at ground-floor level.

6 Insight 360, a building performance analysis tool, developed by Autodesk in 2015
Autodesk developed this tool for use with FormIt 360 Pro and Revit. The dashboard allows users to interact with key performance indicators, benchmarks and ranges, and to make comparisons to the 2030 Challenge.

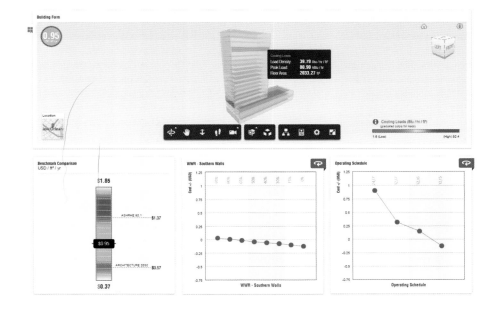

and empowered with inexpensive sensor technologies, some designers are facilitating advances in digital communication workflows, devices like apps, new ways of collecting and sorting data and new interdisciplinary ways of working (see Chapter 6). These strategies are challenging the prescriptive, rule of thumb-based, conservation paradigm and continuing the shift towards a performance-based, results-oriented and potentially more effective paradigm.

SO WHY DON'T DESIGNERS MODEL ENERGY?

Energy modeling is a no-brainer for HOK … It's like reading the MPG (miles per gallon) rating before you buy a car. It's basic information every building investor should know.[8]
—HOK

A survey by the American Institute of Architects (AIA) in 2014 found that 12 per cent of architecture firms used energy modelling software for projects completed in 2013, with 61 per cent of firms reporting no immediate plans to purchase energy modelling software.[9] Most energy models produced by engineers and consultants are used quantitatively to prove performance compliance with various codes and regulations, not as a design tool. However, energy modelling can be a useful feedback tool in other ways. If it is carried out at early design stages, before the design is fixed, it could lead to design iterations that lower energy use. It could also make renewable energy seem like a more attractive option, and offers designers and clients more options when considering trade-offs and compromises.

HOK tracked energy modelling costs and predicted energy savings for several projects, and found that energy modelling payback is typically one or two months.[8] Some of their findings were that energy modelling revealed unnecessary designs or systems built into the model, such as oversized heating, ventilation and air conditioning (HVAC) systems. Their experience shows energy modelling as a part of an iterative design process has the potential to enable design teams to make informed energy decisions for trade-offs and cost savings addressing a range of design issues.[9]

Often building codes and construction guidelines use a prescriptive approach—the opposite of a performance-based

7 Termite tool, developed by Kristoffer Negendahl in 2015 Termite is a parametric tool for Grasshopper3D/Rhino3D that uses the Danish building performance simulation engine Be10, the standard engine for building energy calculations required by Danish law when constructing new buildings.

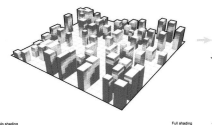

No shading — Full shading

< 40 kwh/m²/year — > 120 kwh/m²/year

< 40 kwh/m²/year — > 120 kwh/m²/year

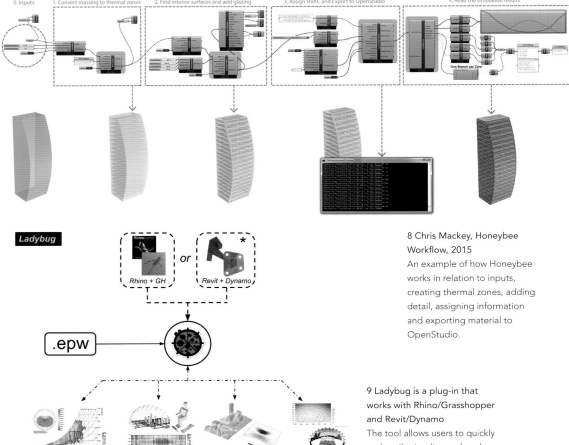

0. Inputs   1. Convert massing to thermal zones   2. Find interior surfaces and add glazing   3. Assign HVAC and Export to OpenStudio   4. Read the simulation results

One Branch per Zone

Ladybug

Rhino + GH   *or*   Revit + Dynamo *

.epw

Visualize Weather Data   Analyze Weather Data   Analyze Geometry   Estimate Renewables

* Dynamo connection has been partially released at the time of publication and is undergoing development to match the features of Grasshopper

8 Chris Mackey, Honeybee
Workflow, 2015
An example of how Honeybee
works in relation to inputs,
creating thermal zones, adding
detail, assigning information
and exporting material to
OpenStudio.

9 Ladybug is a plug-in that
works with Rhino/Grasshopper
and Revit/Dynamo
The tool allows users to quickly
and easily visualise and analyse
weather data during the
design process.

10 Honeybee, a plug-in that
works with Rhino/Grasshopper
and Revit/Dynamo
The tool allows designers
to produce a range of
environmental analyses,
including daylight, glare
and visual comfort by using
Radiance, and to model
energy use with EnergyPlus
and visualise the results with
OpenStudio.

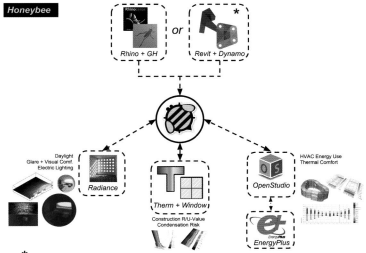

Honeybee

Rhino + GH   *or*   Revit + Dynamo *

Daylight
Glare + Visual Comf.
Electric Lighting
Radiance

Therm + Window
Construction R/U-Value
Condensation Risk

OpenStudio
HVAC Energy Use
Thermal Comfort

EnergyPlus

* Dynamo connection has been partially released at the time of publication and is undergoing development to match the features of Grasshopper

approach outlined above—to focus on meeting specified targets, for example a maximum percentage of glazing or a minimum amount of insulation, reducing opportunities for creative trade-offs and flexibility. The prescriptive approach focuses on using a particular set of materials or building techniques that, if implemented properly, should provide the required performance. Energy modelling promotes a performance-based method as it provides an objective way of assessing the design at various stages. However, the challenges of energy use in buildings are rarely technical, they are social and behavioural. How people use buildings, the intensity of use, people's habits, building maintenance, workmanship during construction, microclimates on sites, are rarely modelled and make or break the final building performance. Assumptions made about the building and its uses by the person doing the energy modelling and simulations, as well as the stage at which the modelling was undertaken, have a large role in determining the accuracy of the output.

According to the AIA's energy modelling guide, architects are the most qualified members of the project team to lead the energy-modelling process, given their expertise in integrating program, space and building systems.[5] The often non-integrated design process in the building industry, the unwillingness of professionals to communicate across disciplines or use similar tools, and the perceived expense and difficulty of using energy modelling tools has contributed to many architects believing that energy modelling is the domain of engineers. This can lead to architects designing a building or system and then the engineer applying a generic sustainable strategy that the architect does not fully understand. Skilful design simulation can help in this regard, to allow options to be quickly tested to achieve shared design and sustainability goals. Results can also prompt designers to ask more informed questions, and to focus resources and time on fine-tuning certain aspects. Until the process of energy modelling and energy budgeting is seen as an iterative, easy and trusted part of the workflow, it will be slow to gain traction. Some designers are finding the benefits extend beyond a singular project leading to a more effective design process, for example energy modelling data can be used to track building performance of similar projects in an office connecting to actual performance over time (see Chapter 5 for the approach undertaken by Canadian office Diamond Schmitt Architects).

VISUALISING ENERGY, CLIMATE AND CARBON
Simulation often produces more data than can ever be read by a human, so data about energy or climate typically needs to be abstracted in a human-readable form. This can take the form of charts, graphs, images and videos. The art of data visualisation (for sense-making and communication) makes this possible (or impossible). For example, to facilitate communication about projected energy use, engineers Morrison Hershfield developed their building energy optimisation tool to visually show the trade-offs between design options (see Figures 5a and 5b). They found this visualisation tool was useful in discussions with clients and

consultants to identify shared design and performance goals. Carbon emissions are slowly becoming included in computational design tools. For example Autodesk's new Insight 360 tool performs a range of environmental analyses including: carbon emissions, whole building energy performance and costs, heating and cooling, daylighting and solar radiation. The tool offers a dashboard showing how a design compares to initiatives such as the 2030 Challenge, which targets carbon emissions in buildings. Insight 360 allows designers to compare and visualise energy costs for a project, using statewide averages for electricity and gas rates or nationwide averages outside the USA. It allows users to visualise solar radiation on mass or building element surfaces in Revit, and the solar analysis function includes an automated workflow for photovoltaic (PV) energy production. The tool's settings include PV panel type, percentage of coverage and payback period, and this makes it simpler for designers to compare and communicate performance expectations and feed this information back to the energy cost range. PV energy production is accessible in Revit as well as through the Insight 360 web interface.

Many new digital design tools allow designers to quickly and accurately predict how climate and local weather and site conditions will influence their designs. The pioneering early stage design program Ecotect, created by Andrew Marsh—which became Autodesk Ecotect Analysis in 2008 and was discontinued in 2015—has inspired many of the new analysis tools for architects. Ecotect had a wide-ranging functionality, as it was able to perform a range of analyses, including solar-energy analysis, sun-path diagrams, shadow displays, acoustic analysis, daylighting and a range of other environmental analyses quickly and visually. The graphic output and ease of use made it popular with designers and students, although it was never intended to replace more accurate building simulation and modelling like EnergyPlus. Some new tools are addressing the need for Ecotect's functionality. Ladybug is a new environmental analysis tool that works as a plug-in for Grasshopper. Developed by Mostapha Sadeghipour Roudsari (see Chapter 19), Ladybug allows designers to import and analyse standard weather data in Grasshopper and draw diagrams such as sun path, wind rose and radiation rose. These can be customised in several ways to run radiation analyses, create shadow studies and carry out view analyses. Another tool by Roudsari is Honeybee, a plug-in that connects Grasshopper3D to validated simulation engines such as EnergyPlus, Radiance, Daysim and OpenStudio for building energy, comfort, daylighting and lighting simulation. These open-source tools are increasingly becoming more well-used and powerful (see Figures 8–11).

While there remains a gap between research-based digital tools and commercially available programs for computing the environment, there have been advances allowing these two realms to be brought together. DIVA is a successful example of how research is getting the word out to practice. DIVA enables quick dissemination and integrates well with existing design workflows. More offices are experimenting with modelling and simulation, as seen in the rise of computational design specialists focused on environmental issues in practice (see Chapter 10 about GXN/3XN and Chapter 15 about CORE/Thornton Thomasetti). In the last five years, there have been a wealth of new open-source and commercially available environmental simulation tools that are easy-to-learn and designer-friendly, such as Ladybug, Honeybee and DIVA. These tools plug in to familiar computer-aided design (CAD) software and respond to the increasing pressure on design teams to carry out early-stage environmental simulations.

Energy models require a range of inputs, including local weather files and geographical location data in order to output climate- and site-specific results. In Chapter 9, KieranTimberlake's use of local weather stations to augment standard weather files is discussed. As the costs for this kind of infrastructure decrease, it can be expected that the availability of nearly real-time local weather and climate data is going to become increasingly practical. Satellite data for use in climate analysis is improving in resolution. Remote sensing using satellite data, such as the data collected by NASA, is not dependent on ground stations, and it allows terrain to be taken into consideration.[10] The most common standard files used in digital models, typical meteorological year (TMY) files are not designed to represent current or future realities. TMY files typically used as data for programs, such as EnergyPlus, are collections of average weather data, including temperature and humidity readings averaged over 15 to 30 years of data based on selected weather station locations (typically airports). Wind readings at airport sites are used but since wind speed and direction varies from site to site, the best way to assess wind conditions for natural ventilation strategies is to measure these on site. TMY files are suitable for comparing options and standards, but there is no provision for extreme conditions and therefore they are typically not accurate enough for low-energy building design. In considering 15–30 year data, it was assumed that the

11 Urban modelling workflows
These urban modelling workflows integrate data from public databases, such as Geographic Information Systems (GIS), and inputs from modelling tools for single buildings to create dynamic simulations.

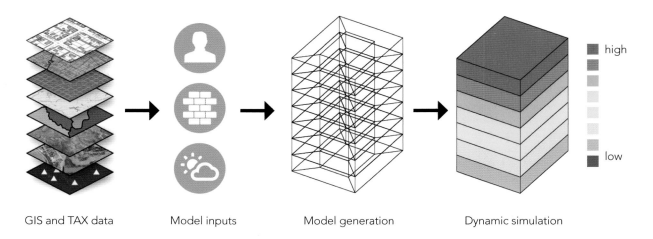

GIS and TAX data   Model inputs   Model generation   Dynamic simulation

high

ENERGY COST ($/yr)

< 1000
1001 - 1500
1501 - 2000
2001 - 2500
2501 - 3000
3001 - 3500
3501 - 4000
4001 - 4500
> 4501

climate and weather would not change rapidly from decade to decade. But as climate change is occurring, new strategies are needed. With climate change and extreme weather, there is a need for projections of future conditions. The IPCC climate change scenarios represent four emissions 'pathways' and four climate models, so there are 16 climate prediction scenarios.[11] These have been modelled and used in global climate models and updated weather data to reflect changing climate can be obtained and used in simulations.[12]

FUTURE CHALLENGES: SCALE, SKILLS AND ACCURACY
Reconsidering system boundaries and specific contexts relating to energy is necessary and the urban scale presents new challenges for energy modelling. Urban heat islands (UHI) present another challenge with regard to weather data, as an increasing number of urban sites have microclimate conditions that elevate air temperature by up to 5 degrees celsius, and taking this into consideration means augmenting the TMY files at airport locations with measured on-site data. In dense urban settings, buildings interact with each other and heat emitting buildings and hot surfaces are reflected and intensified. The results of taking into consideration many buildings rather than modelling individual ones are that buildings shade each other, urban heat islands are created, wind patterns are redirected, and these impact an area's energy use and carbon emissions. Urban building energy models

12 Mapping energy costs, South Boston, MA, USA, 2014 By combining urban data sets including costs of energy and building types and performance, visualising energy use and costs can be used in the design process.

(UBEM) combine several data sets including climate data, building geometry, construction standard and usage schedules.[13] Increasingly, incorporating specific energy goals, like creating a design that uses renewable energy or utilising low-energy design strategies for non-renewable energy use, are part of the designer's responsibility. There are many challenges in developing new digital tools and workflows to simulate energy performance. As noted above, one of the main ones relates to the typically inaccurate assumptions that designers make about how people use buildings. Another challenge is that, as demonstrated throughout this book, there are no industry standard modes of working or collective approaches to how these new simulation and visualisation tools are to be used by designers. In fact, as illustrated in the later chapters of this book, there is an extremely broad range in how well, how accurately, and how often, these tools are used in practice. But how inaccurate does a model have to be before it is no longer useful? Workflows and tools vary from project to project as does how they are used within projects at different stages and from office to office and within different specialist groups in firms. There is an emerging and thriving ecology of digital design tools and approaches. How designers use emerging computation and simulation workflows is increasingly dynamic.

There are urgent environmental reasons why designers need to re-examine our relationships to energy, carbon and climate, and to incorporate accurate data, more quickly and skilfully at early design stages, where decisions matter most. Will future tools be plug-ins or bespoke tools? Judging from the last few years, there will be many of both and increasingly they will run natively, be accurate and quick to use, and many of them will be open-source. Renewable energy is becoming more mainstream, affordable and critically considered and there will likely be a range of new digital tools and workflows to address this. There remain issues of accuracy and cost—for example some designers will wonder why it is necessary to predict and simulate energy use if the engineers will do the final simulations anyway—despite increasing studies on the benefits of early stage simulation, even if they are not completely accurate. In addition, these new tools and workflows offer significant challenges of established disciplinary boundaries. But if designers do not better and more consistently engage with the parameters, such as energy, carbon and climate, then other professionals will control the time and cost calculations, climatic considerations, design trade-offs and ultimately the design decision-making.

REFERENCES
1. Kjell Anderson, *Design Energy Simulation for Architects: Guide to 3D Graphics,* Routledge (London), 2014, p 1.
2. Greg Foliente, 'Developments in Performance-Based Building Codes and Standards', in *Forest Products Journal,* vol 50, no 7/8, pp 12–21.
3. Yehuda E Kalay, 'Performance-Based Design', in *Automation in Construction*, vol 8, no 4, 1999, pp 395–409.

4. Howard T Odum, *Environment, Power, and Society for the Twenty-First Century: The Hierarchy of Energy*, Columbia University Press (New York), 2007, p 1.

5. American Institute of Architects' Energy Modeling Working Group, 'Architect's guide to integrating energy modeling in the design process', 2012, online at https://www.aia.org/resources/8056-architects-guide-to-integrating-energy-modeling (accessed 21 July 2017).

6. US Department of Energy's Building Technologies Office, EnergyPlus, online at https://energyplus.net (accessed 21 July 2017).

7. Terri Peters, 'Ecology Beyond Buildings – Performance-Based Consumption and Zero-Energy Research: RAU Architects', in Terri Peters (ed), *Experimental Green Strategies: Redefining Ecological Design Research*, Architectural Design (AD) series (John Wiley & Sons, Chichester), vol 81, no 6, November/December 2011, pp 124–9.

8. HOK Architects, 'HOK Case Studies Reveal Short Payback Period of Energy Modeling', 26 May 2016, online at http://www.hok.com/about/news/2016/05/26/hok-case-studies-reveal-short-payback-of-energy-modeling (accessed 21 July 2017)

9. Wanda Lau, 'The Case of the Missing Energy Model', in *Architect*, 31 May 2016, online at http://www.architectmagazine.com/technology/the-case-of-the-missing-energy-model_o (accessed 21 July 2017).

10. NASA Earth Observatory, 'NASA Remote Sensing Accomplishments', online at http://earthobservatory.nasa.gov/Features/RemoteSensing/remote_09.php (accessed 21 July 2017).

11. RK Pachauri and LA Meyer (eds), *Climate Change 2014: Synthesis Report. Contribution of Working Groups I, II and III to the Fifth Assessment Report of the Intergovernmental Panel on Climate Change*, IPCC (Geneva, Switzerland), 2014.

12. CIBSE Weather Data Sets, 'New Sets Released 2016', online at http://www.cibse.org/knowledge/cibse-weather-data-sets#3 (accessed 21 July 2017).

13. Carlos Cerezo Davila, Christoph F Reinhart and Jamie L Bemis, 'Modeling Boston: A Workflow for the Efficient Generation and Maintenance of Urban Building Energy Models from Existing Geospatial Datasets', in *Energy*, vol 117, part 1, 15 December 2016, pp 237–50.

3. PARAMETRIC ENVIRONMENTAL DESIGN:
SIMULATION AND GENERATIVE PROCESSES
BRADY PETERS

A COMPLEX LANDSCAPE OF TOOLS

The design of a building is a highly complex problem. Architects and engineers must negotiate an endless series of constraints—physical, social, economic, spatial and environmental. It is only in the last 10 years that the profession has seen the emergence of computational software, enabling associative parametric design, data integration and performance simulation. Today, building designers must be able to navigate a constantly changing landscape of digital tools for many tasks, such as document creation, communication, graphics, drawing and design, software development, data management and performance simulation. For example, the Building Energy Software Tools index lists 147 software packages for environmental design.[1]

The invention of new technology often happens because a designer is searching for a better way to work, in some cases to improve an existing workflow, or to find a fundamentally new solution to a currently intractable problem. This search prompts the adoption and development of new techniques, and this book offers many examples of this search, invention and application. Once successes are visible to others, they may adopt the same or similar technologies. The recent adoption of computational and simulation techniques is not only changing the range of the technically possible, but also altering the social structures that architects operate within. The use of modelling and simulation predicts a future state or behaviour, and there is an inherent risk that there are errors or inaccuracies. This is a common argument against the use of simulation, and in particular architects' use of simulation. However, architecture has always borrowed technics from neighbouring disciplines, and to assume that architects cannot learn new techniques does not give them enough credit, and suggests a static disciplinary state in which change does not occur. Kjell Anderson writes that while design simulation is often seen as a specialist's tool for predicting energy performance, the greatest value for architects is the freedom to play with design ideas and receive timely feedback'. Anderson recognises that, 'while there are risks in including architects in the design simulation process, the risk of continuing to exclude them is far greater'.[2] Following on from the discussion in Chapter 2, the architect's role is to question and probe and evolve. It is

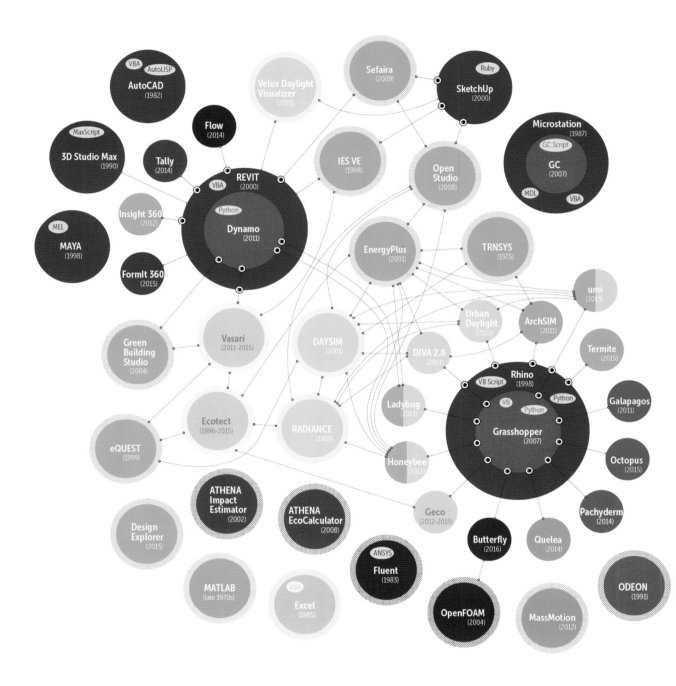

- Design
- Parametric Engine
- Energy
- Daylight/Solar
- Fluid Dynamics
- Acoustics
- Agent Based Modeling
- Life Cycle Analysis
- Optimization

1 Design tools for simulation and design: geometry, generation and analysis
A selection of currently available computational tools for architectural performance analysis: red – acoustics, dark red – materials and life cycle, orange – energy, yellow – solar/daylight, green – people movement, blue – fluid dynamics, purple – CAD, pink – parametric plug-ins to CAD, grey – software used but no longer supported.

2 Ecotect solar radiation analysis and text file of exported analysis results
Using Rhino, a double-curved surface was generated using Kangaroo structural form-finding software and then discretised into panels and then analysed using Ecotect. The results of this analysis are then exported as a simple text file that links the panel geometry to its solar performance. This data can then be used as input into a computational algorithm running on a wide range of platforms.

important that the architect remains critical of the tools they use in their quest to find better solutions.

TOOL MAKERS AND TOOL USERS

In the last 20 years, there has been a shift in architectural design techniques from the use of software, to the development and customisation of software. As tools have literally defined the profession of architecture[3], this shift from tool user to tool maker is profound. The first computer-aided design (CAD) software—Sketchpad—was introduced to the world in 1963, but it wasn't until AutoCAD was introduced in 1982 that architects had access to CAD, and it did not become widespread until the early 1990s, when Microsoft and Intel released fast and affordable personal computers with 32-bit operating systems and Pentium chips. However, early CAD software did not have the data integration, parametric capability or simulation potentials that were promised by Sketchpad. In 1995, SolidWorks was released, demonstrating that 3D parametric CAD systems could now be developed and released on start-up budgets in less than a year. However, SolidWorks was not designed for architecture projects. Designers adopted tools from other disciplines, for example Frank Gehry's office used CATIA from the aerospace industry and Greg Lynn's office used Maya from the field of animation. Or architects needed to program their own software, as seen in the works of John Frazer, Paul Coates and Christian Derix. The work of some in-house research groups, such as Foster + Partners' Specialist Modelling Group, and emerging communities such as Smartgeometry, inspired the creation of parametric design software, as well as numerous techniques and theories.[4] In 2003, Generative Components, a plug-in for CAD software MicroStation, became one of the first free and widely available types of parametric software designed specifically for architects. Around this time, scripting interfaces in MicroStation and Rhinoceros empowered architects to author and share custom design tools. The development of the programming tool Processing offered another alternative environment in which algorithmic design could be explored, and shared with an interested community. There is a trend in architecture towards parametric design—in which

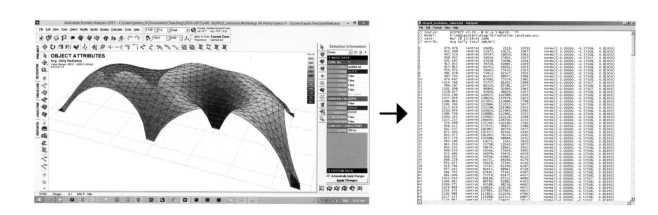

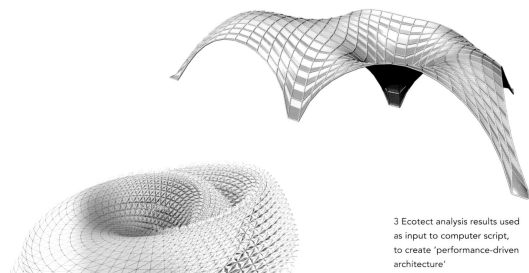

the designers focus their attention on the creation of generating algorithms rather than specific instances. In this paradigm, variants of the design are produced through varying the parameters of the underlying algorithm, and it is in the evaluation of design variants where computer simulation can play a significant role.

2007 saw the introduction of Grasshopper, a new visual scripting plug-in for Rhinoceros. Similar to the popular visual programming language Max/MSP, first introduced in the late 1980s, functional components are represented as graphic nodes and are directionally wired together to create an algorithmic logic. The architectural community was ready for an algorithmic design tool, so Grasshopper rapidly gained in popularity. It is financially accessible, it has a vibrant online community and it makes it easy for designers to create their own design tools. A visual scripting environment and online community are now being developed in Dynamo—a plug-in for Revit software for BIM (building information modelling). Crucially, in the context of introducing simulation to the digital design environment, what Rhino/Grasshopper has offered is the ability to easily create custom plug-ins. This ability has resonated with a growing community of architect/engineers and has resulted in a new 'eco-system' of plug-ins.[5] Through the combination of CAD, parametric plug-ins and custom simulation programs, architects are now able to realise some of the potential that Ivan Sutherland hinted at with Sketchpad. This is significant as it gives architects access to simulation tools that did not exist even a decade ago. The rapid adoption of Grasshopper and its suite of simulation plug-ins demonstrates designers' interest in computing the environment. As simulation is now accessible within

3 Ecotect analysis results used as input to computer script, to create 'performance-driven architecture'
A script written in RhinoScript (VB) that uses the Ecotect analysis text file as input to generate a detailed facade geometry that is responsive to local performance, in this case where panels receive more sun, the percentage of glass is lower.

4 [uto] (Ursula Frick and Thomas Grabner), research study, Innsbruck, Austria, 2014
The GECO software enables the user to export complex geometries, evaluate the design's performance in Ecotect Analysis and import the results back into Grasshopper, without reworking the model repeatedly. The colours in this image show the total incident solar radiation from 0% (blue) to 100% (yellow).

the architect's everyday design environment, it can be customised and integrated into various design tasks. Designers have gone from being tool users to tool makers.

INTEROPERABILITY—NAVIGATING THE SOFTWARE LANDSCAPE

In general, there are two ways of structuring a CAD software tool: as a monolithic application that can do everything, or as a diverse collection of applications that connect to each other, whereby the action of individuals collectively contributes to the larger community. Traditionally, CAD and BIM systems have been monolithic applications, but increasingly there is pressure to connect. The promise of a single piece of software to carry out all design tasks and be used from conception through to operation is still not realised, and may not be the best strategy anyway. While in the past, only a few design tools, a drawing board, pencil and paper, were used to design a building, now many pieces of software with many different commands and sub-programs are used, and these form complex design processes. This results in a complex web of digital and analogue processes, influenced by what tools are used, the order in which they are used, and how well they communicate with each other. Interoperability between software systems, and in particular between simulation and design environments, has justifiably received a lot of attention. Interoperability may take the form of a mix of methods: integrated, run-time interoperable, file exchange and stand-alone.[6] One way to connect is through file exchange, and scripting tools can facilitate this through customisable data output mechanisms. An increasingly popular way in which to connect is through run-time interoperable programs. Many of the plug-ins for Rhino's Grasshopper are building performance simulation software tools. These enable the connection of CAD geometry to simulation software natively within the architect's design environment, offering the ability to simulate designs during the design process. This method is faster and easier for architects to integrate into their workflow. It is easier to visualise and to understand the results, and the coupling of design and analysis enables formation processes to be linked to analysis routines.

It is well known that most decisions that impact a building's environmental performance occur during the early stages of the project. The effort required to implement those decisions at the beginning of the design process is small in comparison to the effort that would be necessary later on. This means that architects have great potential to affect passive strategies in their designs, but they need to have the means to evaluate their design decisions. The ability to add several different simulation plug-ins could be a feasible way in which to facilitate holistic simulation support. Michael Wetter, from the Lawrence Berkeley National Laboratory, predicts that much of the innovation in building science is likely to happen at the interface between different disciplines, and that the need to collaborate more effectively will require new tools, more integrated systems, immersive simulation and visualisation, and increased modularisation of code, which enables users to participate in program development.[7] TRNSYS (TRaNsient SYstems Simulation program) has been around for 35

SW   SE   NW

years and provides a suite of tools for the simulation of energy and solar. Wetter points out that it is the modular design of TRNSYS simulation components that facilitates a large user community to develop simulation components that extend the scope of the program. Similarly, with the lighting simulation software, Radiance, it is the fact that the software is a customisable series of components that has inspired building designers and engineers to create custom tools, share knowledge and create a cohesive community around the software. However, the customisation of these tools requires high-level specialist knowledge. It is the creation of applications that link programs like Radiance, to Grasshopper, such as DIVA and Honeybee, which is making simulation accessible to a greater number of designers.

MODELLING AND SIMULATION

Simulation is now a fundamental aspect of contemporary scientific knowledge and discovery, and building simulation is a key tool to quantify building performance; it is the method by which designers can predict how buildings will perform in the future. But what is simulation? The concept of simulation assumes that knowledge of the real world can be obtained by reproducing reality in a substitute medium—and in most cases now that medium is the computer. In computer simulation, a typical approach is to take a mathematical model that depicts the time-evolution of a system. The mathematical model is constructed from a mixture of well-established theoretical principles, some physical insights and some clever mathematical tricks. The model is transformed into a computable algorithm, and the computation of the equations over time is said to simulate the system under study.[8] In simulation, drawings are not simply expanded to models, but multiplied through time to create time-based situation-specific experiences. The epistemological nature of the architectural drawing is changing as many more layers of information are exposed and this is apparent in many aspects of architectural practice.

Unlike a model, a simulation is not wholly descriptive—when a simulation is begun, the outcome or result is not necessarily known. Also, unlike models, simulations do not prescribe to the view that, given a sufficient amount of detail, everything can be

5 BIG, ST7 Stettin project, Sweden
Views and access to sunlight were important in this project. The form of the project reacts to local site conditions. The architect's simulation software enabled iterations to be quickly studied for the amount of solar radiation on the facade.

predetermined. When simulations are not accurate, their inaccuracy is often attributed to the amount of randomness in the environment. However, it has been shown that errors in the description of models that are used to describe systems, rather than the random nature of the environments, account for more inaccuracies in prediction techniques.[9] Simply put, the better the model of the system, the more likely it is to get accurate simulation results.

NEW PARAMETERS

The computational nature of the design environment has the potential to include far more than geometric visual description. The conceptualising of new environmental performance ideas involves more than the creation of new ways of generating geometry; it involves fresh ways of quantifying performance, of measuring design success, of representing and communicating and constructing models, and the use of new mediums of design feedback. A computer simulation produces a vast amount of numerical data. However, this data is meaningless to humans until it can be visualised. As Yanni Loukissas explains, computer simulations transform quantitative models of building physics into qualitative sensory experiences.[10] The choice of instruments is influenced by what questions the designer needs to answer; not only can geometric generation and data exchange be customised, but the manner in which simulation is integrated. With simulation, design tools are changing, design tasks are shifting and so is the nature of knowledge we gain from architectural drawing. The techniques of design, the subject of design, and the perception and interpretation of the results of design are changing.

As the awareness of climate change and its impacts grows, architects are increasingly concerned with imagining, depicting and calculating the future environments their buildings will occupy and create. As demonstrated by the famous 'hockey stick graph', it is not necessarily a graphic or representational strategy, but

6 Central Park shadow study
This example shows how to use Ladybug's sun-path and sunlight hours analysis to identify which parts of the buildings around Central Park need to be removed, so the park can see more than four hours of sunlight on 21 December, which is often the date of the winter solstice.

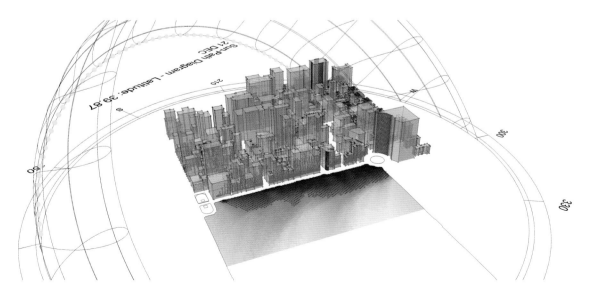

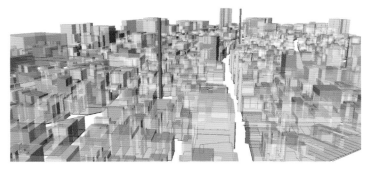

7 Comfortable coffee shops in New York, USA
This example shows the solution for finding the most comfortable outdoor places for coffee shops in the West Village, New York City. Using the @it plug-in for Grasshopper, it was possible for the designer to create these geometries.

sometimes an entirely new way of conceptualising a situation that can reveal new information or a potential solution. The ways in which simulation results are displayed, interpreted and mapped onto drawings and models play a crucial role in their effectiveness in influencing the ultimate building design. Up until recently, Ecotect was the most widely used building performance simulation tool used by architects.[11] Developed by Andrew Marsh, Ecotect offered a wide range of types of environmental simulations, produced clear visualisations of performance and enabled designers to simulate projects with a minimal amount of additional modelling effort. A designer could take a design from CAD, export it as a DXF file, import it into Ecotect and perform a simulation, visualise the results and export the results as a text file, which could then be used as input into a generative script that produced geometry based on the simulation result. One of the main reasons for Ecotect's popularity was because of its exceptional graphical user interface (GUI)—it enabled designers to easily explore and communicate environmental data.

BUILDING FORM AND SURFACE
The simultaneous adoption of a parametric design agenda and an integration of simulation into the architects' design workflows suggests a linking of the generative schema of architects to

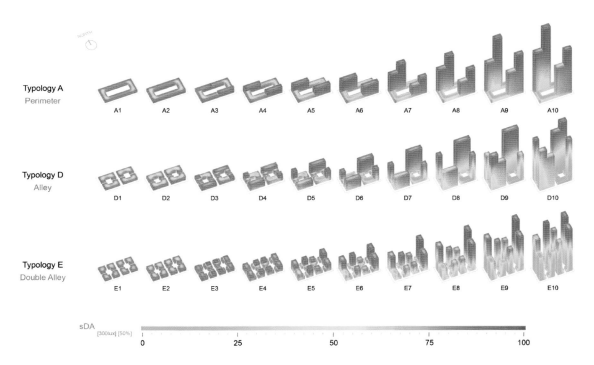

Typology A
Perimeter

A1　A2　A3　A4　A5　A6　A7　A8　A9　A10

Typology D
Alley

D1　D2　D3　D4　D5　D6　D7　D8　D9　D10

Typology E
Double Alley

E1　E2　E3　E4　E5　E6　E7　E8　E9　E10

sDA
[300lux] [50%]

0　25　50　75　100

8 An illustration of the UrbanDaylight tool
With this UrbanDaylight tool, options can be explored in a design by using a block typology evolution matrix with daylight availability mapped onto floor plates.

performance simulation. The examples from practice in the later chapters in this book demonstrate that architects and engineers are incorporating performance simulation, material knowledge, tectonic assembly logics and the parameters of production machinery in their design drawings. They are creating custom digital tools, enabling performance feedback at various stages of an architectural project, creating new design opportunities. Using these tools, structural, material or environmental performance can become a fundamental parameter in the creation of architectural form. Designer and MIT professor Neri Oxman explains that architects working with digital design are now facing an 'expressionist crisis of formalism' which, 'conceals a deep vein of complexity and contradiction between form and formation'. Oxman suggests that concepts such as parametric and performance-based design can be considered 'form without formalism' and promote 'new ways of thinking about form and its generation'. As designers adopt approaches that are more material-, construction- and environmentally focused, new design theory and new building forms will emerge.[12]

The professionals interviewed in this book seem keen to use technology to apply disciplinary knowledge to create buildings that better achieve their aspirations for better architecture and better cities. They have very specific ideas about what will make better architecture, and the digital environment is enabling the modelling and simulation leading to forms that more closely will perform to their conception of the future that they design for. The site of much of their design effort is in the geometry and materiality of the building envelope. The form of a building,

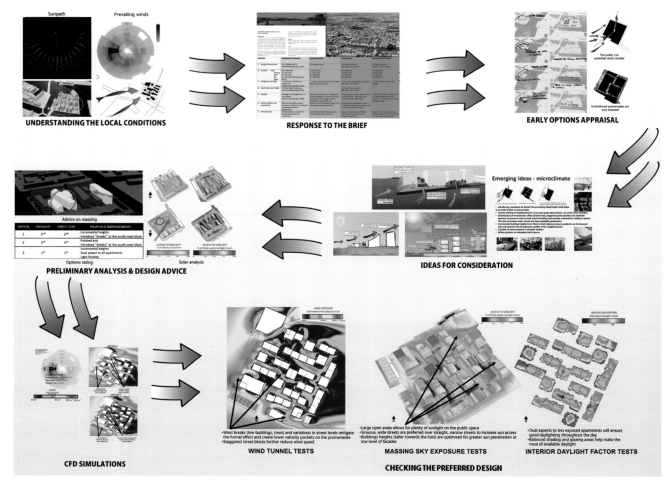

UNDERSTANDING THE LOCAL CONDITIONS

RESPONSE TO THE BRIEF

EARLY OPTIONS APPRAISAL

PRELIMINARY ANALYSIS & DESIGN ADVICE

IDEAS FOR CONSIDERATION

Emerging ideas - microclimate

Advice on massing

CFD SIMULATIONS

WIND TUNNEL TESTS

MASSING SKY EXPOSURE TESTS

INTERIOR DAYLIGHT FACTOR TESTS

CHECKING THE PREFERRED DESIGN

9 Max Fordham, urban combined analysis
This analysis focuses on computational fluid
dynamics (CFD), sky exposure and interior
daylight.

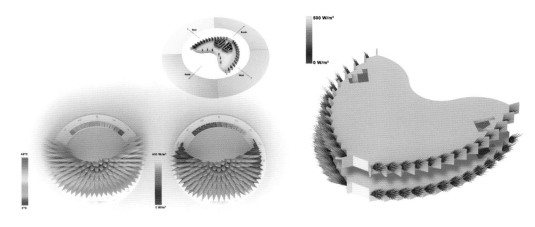

its apertures, the materials it is made from, have a significant impact on its performance and how it modifies the surrounding environment. In terms of environmental performance, architects and engineers focus a significant amount of design decisions on the envelope. The building form and orientation allows access to sun and wind for internal and external spaces, impacting heating, cooling and ventilation, and lighting requirements; the building envelope is the site of numerous performance characteristics and so envelope elements are often designed to perform multiple functions. To address the multitude of issues surrounding the performance of facades, from technical construction to the mathematics of simulation to the experiential design intent, requires knowledge from many disciplines, and so the teams dealing with these designs have within them a broad spectrum of skills and abilities.

The designers and programmers interviewed for this book articulate attitudes, which can be broken down into three large conceptual arenas: algorithmic thinking, simulation and measurement, including real-time data and post-occupancy studies. All the groups featured in this book use computational design approaches, and all use a wide variety of software. For parametric studies, Rhino/Grasshopper appears to be the current industry favourite, while other examples of parametric design platforms include Dynamo/Revit, CATIA and Maya. The creation of custom computer scripts, which was a predominant mode of computational design prior to the development of Grasshopper and Dynamo, is still widely in evidence, but is now an approach that is used when the limits of visual programming are reached. However, in all of the offices studied, the creation of custom software is still an essential part of the design process. There are some designers who primarily use custom parametric software that they write themselves, as this gives ultimate control, scalability and the incorporation of unique performance analyses. There are different ways in which algorithmic thinking is applied and often, different algorithmic techniques are used within the same group or even within the same project. Parametric variation can be driven by the designer, in response to simulation results or aesthetic concerns. But the generation of design options can also be driven computationally through optimisation or other heuristic techniques. For simulation, the interviews and research conducted for this book have found that there are three areas of performance analysis that feature prominently in innovative digital design workflows: sun, wind and sound. A decade ago, the majority of designers were using Ecotect. However, now it is the plug-ins for Grasshopper that offer the first tool of choice for many practices. Members of the design team sometimes write custom simulation software, and sometimes they write custom front-ends to connect parametric CAD to existing simulation engines.

THE FUTURE OF SIMULATION
While building simulation emerged as a discipline in the 1960s, it was not until the 1990s that architects began to use building performance tools in a more intensive way. There are many

10 Foster + Partners, National Bank of Kuwait, Kuwait, 2007–
Foster + Partners used innovative three-dimensional graphing techniques to understand the amount of solar radiation incident on the facade from different directions.

Air Velocity (m/s)

0.0   3.5   7   10.5   14 15.0

11 Foster + Partners, National Bank of
Kuwait, Kuwait, 2007–
Computational fluid dynamics (CFD)
simulation was used to understand wind
velocity effects of different form and facade
options.

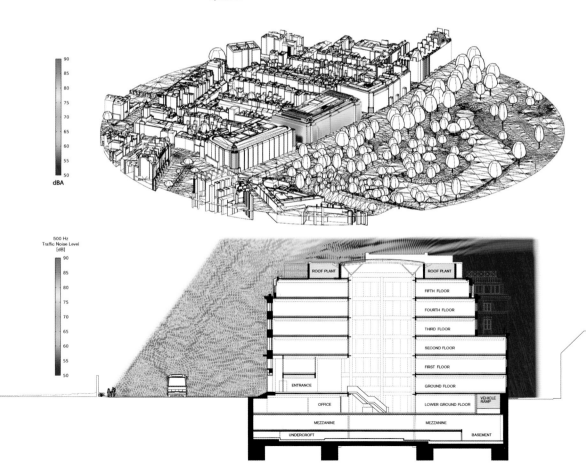

90
85
80
75
70
65
60
55
50

dBA

500 Hz
Traffic Noise Level
[dB]

90
85
80
75
70
65
60
55
50

ROOF PLANT   ROOF PLANT

FIFTH FLOOR

FOURTH FLOOR

THIRD FLOOR

SECOND FLOOR

FIRST FLOOR

ENTRANCE   GROUND FLOOR

OFFICE   LOWER GROUND FLOOR   VEHICLE RAMP

MEZZANINE   MEZZANINE

UNDERCROFT   BASEMENT

benefits to the use of simulation, with the major benefits being improved performance and customised interior environments in our buildings. Anderson has identified several advantages of performance simulation by architects: first, that it enables architects to gain an intuitive understanding of how their designs can affect light, heat and airflow; second, that analyses can be done in a matter of hours, enabling more evaluations and better designs to evolve; third, that the use of simulation makes designers think about performance, and enables them to engage in higher-level discussions with engineers; fourth, that it enables designers to answer questions about a design's performance and enables a comparison of design options in real time while designing; and fifth, that architects will often graphically map results onto a 3D model, creating clear communication devices that offer proof of design concepts.[2]

Jan Hensen[13] identifies the current issues with building performance simulation as being: that most simulations are applied to the final processes of building design yet they have the most impact in early design phases; that simulation tools are largely used for single designs and not for the analysis of multiple alternatives; that simulation is mostly used for envelope design and testing of its compliance to codes and standards; that simulation needs to incorporate multi-objective decision-making including optimisation; and, that users need to be able to combine simulation tools. Although accessibility to simulation may have improved greatly, even now, with all architects working in a digital design environment, many still find it difficult to use even basic tools. Shady Attia suggests that a reason for this may be that these tools have been developed by technical researchers who forget that, 'building simulation is a human, psychological and social discipline because it involves man-computer interaction and human knowledge processing, while enriching human experience'.[11]

The integration of simulation engines with design software has the potential to address many current issues that have been identified with building-performance simulation. Recent developments in simulation software and its application in practice, as shown by the case studies in this book, demonstrate that digital design with its computational customisability through various programming interfaces enables a flexible modular computational approach. This is enabling data exchange and interoperability between simulation and design software. The accessibility of simulation engines is encouraging architects to experiment and therefore increase awareness and intuition about building performance. While there do not appear to be common approaches to optimisation, new tools such as Galapagos and Octopus are now available, which can integrate optimisation into design and simulation processes. As algorithmic design is essentially a definition of design space, the exploration of this design space is where future developments seem to lie.

12 Foster + Partners, facade noise elevation and section analysis
To reduce noise on the facade, the designers either use roadway barriers or use the simulation findings to specify noise isolating windows, natural ventilation openings and facade assemblies. For the spaces around the back of the building, the designers could use a barrier on the roof or an overhanging canopy to protect the rear space if necessary.

REFERENCES

1. 'Building Energy Software Tools Index', online at http://www.buildingenergysoftwaretools.com (accessed 18 February 2017).

2. Kjell Anderson, *Design Energy Simulation for Architects: Guide to 3D Graphics*, Routledge (London), 2014, pp 3–5.

3. Jonathan Hill, *Immaterial Architecture*, Routledge (London), 2006.

4. Brady Peters and Terri Peters, *Inside Smartgeometry: Expanding the Architectural Possibilities of Computational Design*, John Wiley & Sons (Chichester), 2013.

5. Daniel Davis and Brady Peters, 'Design Ecosystems: Customising the Architectural Design Environment with Software Plug-Ins', in Brady Peters and Xavier de Kestelier (eds), *Computation Works: The Building of Algorithmic Thought*, Architectural Design (AD) series (John Wiley & Sons, Chichester), vol 83, issue 2, March/April 2013, pp 124–31.

6. Torben Østergård, Rasmus L Jensen and Steffen E Maagaard, 'Building Simulations Supporting Decision Making in Early Design – A Review', in *Renewable and Sustainable Energy Reviews*, vol 61, August 2016, pp 187–201.

7. Michael Wetter, 'A View on Future Building System Modeling and Simulation', in *Building Performance Simulation for Design and Operation*, Spon Press (London), 2011.

8. Eric Winsberg, *Science in the Age of Computer Simulation*, University of Chicago Press (Chicago), 2010.

9. David Orrell, *The Future of Everything: The Science of Prediction from from Wealth to Weather to Chaos and Complexity*, Basic Books (New York), 2008.

10. Yanni Loukissas, *Co-Designers: Cultures of Computer Simulation in Architecture*, Routledge (New York), 2012.

11. Shady Attia, Liliana Beltrán, André De Herde and Jan Hensen, 'Architect Friendly: A Comparison of Ten Different Building Performance Simulation Tools', in proceedings of the 11th IBPSA 'Building Simulation' conference, International Building Performance Simulation Association, Glasgow, Scotland, 27–30 July 2009, pp 204–11.

12. Neri Oxman, 'Per Formative: Towards a Post Materialist Paradigm in Architecture', in *Perspecta: The Yale Architectural Journal*, no 43, 2010, pp 19–30.

13. Jan Hensen and Roberto Lamberts, 'Introduction to Building Performance Simulation', in *Building Performance Simulation for Design and Operation*, Spon Press (London), 2011.

IMAGES

4. DESIGNING ATMOSPHERES:
SIMULATING EXPERIENCE   BRADY PETERS

CREATING ATMOSPHERE

Through light, sound, space, air, temperature and material, designers choreograph user experience. As architect and theorist Juhani Pallasmaa writes, 'every touching experience of architecture is multi-sensory; qualities of space, matter and scale are measured equally by the eye, ear, nose, skin, tongue, skeleton and muscle … an architectural work is not experienced as a collection of isolated visual pictures, but in its fully embodied material and spiritual presence'.[1] This characteristic property of buildings to have emotional effect is something that Swiss architect and Pritzker prizewinner Peter Zumthor terms as 'atmosphere', which is perceived through emotional sensibilities and produced as people interact with objects in the real world.[2] Architects affect the creation of atmosphere through their building designs. Architect and professor Farshid Moussavi suggests that it is through surface articulation and overall form that buildings affect users and elicit multiple interpretations. Moussavi calls for an expanded approach to materiality—to understand material not exclusively as physical and tangible, but also to include the non-physical, such as climate, sound or economics.[3] The notion of atmosphere can be considered to be part of our definition of ecology. Philosopher Gernot Böhme sees current definitions of ecology as insufficient to explain the qualities of an experienced environment, and so has sought, through his 'new aesthetics', to introduce aesthetic viewpoints into ecology. Böhme suggests that 'perception is basically the manner in which one is bodily present for something or someone or one's bodily state in an environment' and that 'the primary object of perception is atmospheres'.[4] This chapter investigates current efforts by designers to turn these sensory experiences into computable form, enabling them to become part of the predictive act of architectural drawing/modelling.

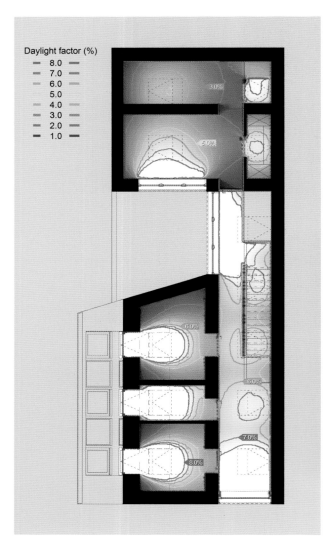

Daylight factor (%)
- 8.0
- 7.0
- 6.0
- 5.0
- 4.0
- 3.0
- 2.0
- 1.0

3.0%

5.0%

6.0%

6.0%

7.0%

8.0%

cd/m²							
	68.1	37.9	33.1	84.2	329.9	64.2	71.1
360	102.8	96.1	38.8	55.0	50.5		131.4
315	108.0	109.7	103.5	122.6	70.9	51.6	87.8
270	110.1	103.9	92.8	87.9	73.1	55.3	75.3
225	110.5	98.3	79.7	37.2	7.9	50.8	72.5
180	107.9	89.0	41.4	48.2	53.1	39.0	68.5
135							
90							
45							

1a, b and c Velux daylighting tool

The Velux Daylight Visualizer is a lighting simulation tool that accurately simulates and quantifies daylight levels in interiors, enabling architects to make informed decisions about daylight performance. Featuring excellent visualization functionality, the tool makes it possible to transform the large amounts of numerical data into comprehensible and communicable information.

DESIGNING ENVIRONMENT AND ATMOSPHERE

Shelter is one of our essential needs as humans and one of the primary aims of architecture. However, architecture aims to do more than merely shelter, but also to create space that has cultural meaning, social significance and is comfortable. Architectural design should not merely sustain, but enable humans to flourish. The goal of high performance buildings must be to improve indoor environmental quality rather than simply meeting minimum standards. While there are established techniques used by professionals that ensure that buildings will meet building codes, what if designers wish to achieve more? Kjell Anderson writes:

> Architects have relied on engineers to understand and provide building comfort so much that in the middle of the twentieth century they began to abandon the art of designing rational climate responses. Comfort and lighting became the exclusive territory of engineers—their tools for providing comfort using energy have become very sophisticated. The tools to help architects make better passive decisions during early design are embarrassingly less so.[5]

There are four primary areas of comfort that should be considered when designing a building: visual, thermal, air quality and acoustic. Visual comfort largely relates to lighting, whether this is natural daylighting or artificial lighting. Thermal comfort links with air temperature, humidity and speed. Air quality describes clean and fresh air. Acoustic comfort relates to background noise levels, as well as appropriate acoustic characteristics—primarily reverberation time, but also the types of sounds, the loudness and clarity of signals. To capture the experience of building is a nuanced condition that currently simulation tools are challenged to predict and communicate. While current simulation tools can predict daylight and the acoustic soundscapes of unbuilt projects, these are not experienced in 3D, and not together as a complete experience. Temperature, humidity and air speed are often not simulated at all in a way that can be experienced and so comfort can only be guessed at through quantitative predictions. So given the challenges, how can architects engage with design at this level? Building designers must look beyond the drawing to design atmosphere.

HETEROGENEOUS ENVIRONMENTS

With the industrial revolution and modernism, production shifted from the crafting of singular objects to the mass production of identical objects, and assumptions of a preferred homogeneity have been applied to many other aspects of life. However, with the rise of parametric and algorithmic design, there is a move towards mass customisation and a rejection of homogeneity. Many architects and designers are now exploring the concept of heterogeneity, of 'differentiated' geometry, structure and performance. French architect Philippe Rahm sees the potential for changing the focus of architecture away from fixed concepts of program and performance to allowing, and celebrating, spatial

2a and b Foster + Partners, daylighting study of the Thomas Deacon Academy, Peterborough, UK

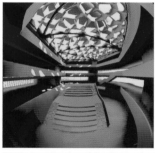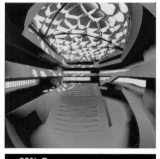

20% Open
69% CDA (500 lux)

40% Open
73% CDA (500 lux)

60% Open
75% CDA (500 lux)

Lux
2000
1800
1600
1400
1200
1000
800
600
400
200
0

3 Analysis of atrium roof openings: continuous daylight autonomy and daylight visualisation

variation in building performance, in terms of air temperature, humidity, sound and smell—what he calls an 'architecture of gradients'. In conceptualising an 'atmospheric' architecture, Rahm states that he likes: 'the idea that space is not defined only by walls, matter and color but also by temperature, relative humidity, and light … a more sensual approach to space, where the body is completely immersed into architecture, through all senses'.[6]

Michelle Addington recognises that 'buildings are open systems in which the energetic inputs and outputs are in often radical disequilibrium; as with all things in the natural world, buildings are in constant negotiation with their surrounding environment'.[7] While building designers may intuitively understand structures and these intuitions can correlate structural forces to building form, Addington explains that when designers try to extend this relationship to thermodynamics, energy systems simply do not map onto a building in the same way. In thermodynamics, the boundary is emergent and determined by phenomena; it is a site of dis-equilibrium and a zone of exchange and transformation. A building's envelope is an arbitrary and ineffective place to make decisions about thermodynamics—architecture is not just about mass, but about energy. Much current environmental design effort and research focuses on the building envelope. Addington says that it is 'incredibly strange to think that every single type of phenomenon taking place out there is somehow magically mediated at the level of the envelope, in order to deliver this homogeneous environment on the inside'.[7]

Sean Lally, an American architect and professor, proposes that architecture is the design of not only physical surfaces, but also the energy systems that are contained within them. These systems are fields in which inhabitants move, changing from one place to another, and involve the engagement with sensory perceptions. Lally sees that architects will explore new territories of design 'when walls and geometry are no longer our primary means of spatial organisation'. Energy systems, whether they are wind, air, sound or something else, can define space—they are what Lally calls 'sensorial envelopes'. Architecture is more than simply the physical materials of building, but includes a consideration of experience.[8]

DESIGN FOR SUN AND LIGHT
The consideration of the effects of sun, and the heat and light it provides, has been a part of the design of buildings, perhaps for as long as there have been buildings. To shelter from the sun yet still maintain day-lit conditions is a primary objective. Until recently, architects approached environmental design by using precedents and by establishing prescriptive rules. However, the adoption of simulation techniques has the potential to change this approach. MIT professor Christoph Reinhart sees that there are two reasons for a growing number of design practitioners using daylight tools. First, there is a strong link between daylight and sustainable design, and the number of practitioners doing sustainable projects is growing. Second, the ubiquity of computer-aided design (CAD) in building design and education promotes daylight simulations due to the fact that three-dimensional building models already contain geometrical detail that can be reused for computer-based daylighting analysis.[9]

One of the key components of designing light is the use of natural light in buildings. The objectives for daylighting a building range from questions of aesthetics, to health, to comfort, to energy savings from natural lighting. Daylight simulations should be combined with simulations of electric light. All models are an abstraction, whether it is a physical model for an architectural presentation, or a mathematical model for a performance simulation; however, the degree of abstraction and what information is retained and how it is constructed depends on the purpose of the model. Different simulations require different modelling strategies. For daylight, the complexity of the 3D CAD model depends on what is being calculated. Modelling the ground plane and neighbouring buildings as simple blocks is important, but it is critical that all surfaces have been assigned meaningful material or optical qualities for daylighting analysis.

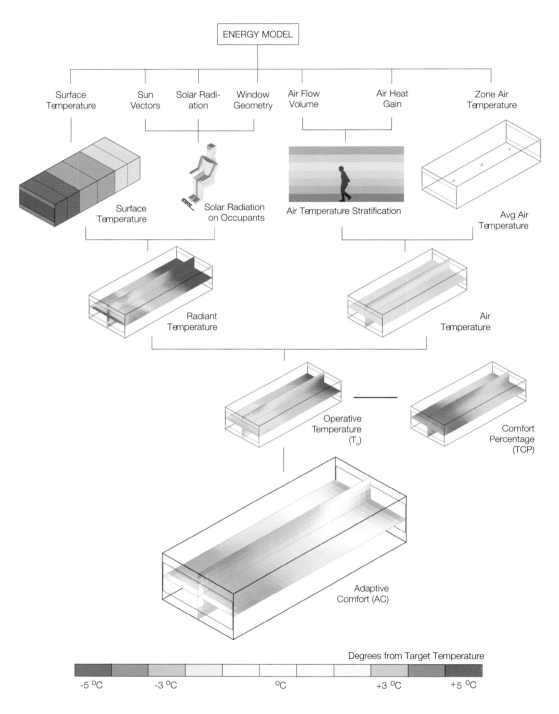

ENERGY MODEL

Surface Temperature — Sun Vectors — Solar Radiation — Window Geometry — Air Flow Volume — Air Heat Gain — Zone Air Temperature

Surface Temperature

Solar Radiation on Occupants

Air Temperature Stratification

Avg Air Temperature

Radiant Temperature

Air Temperature

Operative Temperature (T$_o$)

Comfort Percentage (TCP)

Adaptive Comfort (AC)

Degrees from Target Temperature

-5 °C   -3 °C   0°C   +3 °C   +5 °C

4 How microclimate is
calculated by using Honeybee
and Ladybug

First developed in 1985, Radiance is today the most widely used simulation engine for daylight and solar design. Radiance was made free and open-source in 1989 and has since been embedded in many research and commercial architectural engineering software applications. Radiance has benefited from an enthusiastic, active user group, and it continues to be developed and improved. One of the key goals in the development of Radiance was to produce physically accurate light simulation and visualisation for architecture and lighting design. Radiance uses a backwards ray-tracing algorithm, which provides a profound benefit over other calculation strategies.[9] It includes specular, diffuse and directional-diffuse reflection, and transmission in any combination to any level in any environment, including complicated curved geometries.

The 'sky model' tells the simulation engine how much direct sunlight and diffuse daylight is coming from the different parts of the celestial hemisphere. Within the 3D CAD model, areas of interest should be identified, and key views and sensors should be set up, with ideas as to what required light levels might be desired. The daylight simulation engine combines the sky model with the geometric scene to calculate illuminance and/or luminance values. These values are then translated into a format that can be used to inform design decisions such as visualisations, 'falsecolour' maps and other metrics. Reinhart reminds designers that it is the visualisation and processing of results that is the most important: 'for the analysis to really impact the design, it is important what metrics are calculated … the use of different daylighting metrics may lead to different, if not opposing design conclusions'.[9] The daylighting simulation can be combined with a thermal simulation for an integrated energy assessment; however, the requirements for the CAD models are different as more detail is required in the daylighting model and the division of the model into zones is not necessary. The different requirements of different simulation methods make the concept of a unified building information model (BIM) a challenging one.

THERMAL COMFORT

Air quality and the thermal condition influence both human health and productivity; a well-designed indoor environment helps to increase the mental performance capacity. Thermal comfort is a condition of mind, and a subjective evaluation, which relates directly to our bodies' heat gain and loss, with the goal to achieve some sort of a balance between our own body and its environment. The primary factors influencing it are: metabolic rate, clothing, insulation, air temperature, mean radiant temperature, air speed and relative humidity, although psychological parameters also play a role.

While there are now established computational workflows for the calculation of metrics, such as energy, solar gain and air movement, an emerging trend is to develop simulation routines for more subjective metrics such as thermal comfort. Daniel

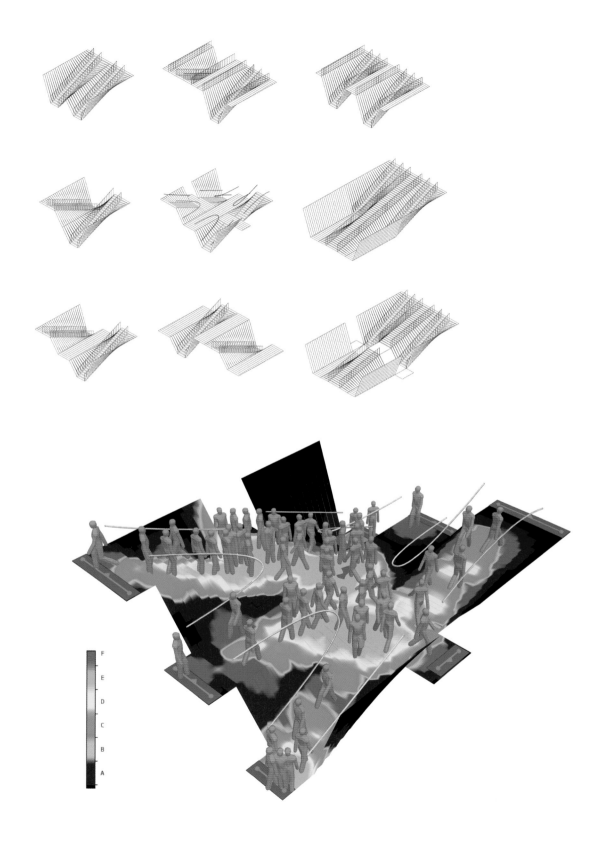

Knott from BuroHappold's Sustainability group uses the Universal Thermal Climate Index (UTCI) as a way to compute comfort, and his goal is to predict metrics for productivity, health and wellbeing. Knott feels that it is these soft metrics that will become increasingly important and that the focus will shift away from energy and carbon. To design for sustainability is to design all aspects of the environment such as air, humidity and temperature (see Chapter 11 on the work of BuroHappold).

USER EXPERIENCE

Drawings and physical models are the traditional tools of architects and have been used to determine how a building will be experienced. These instruments enable designers to predict the spatial, lighting and material effects of architecture on users as they navigate through buildings. In relation to energy modelling and thermal comfort, internal heat gain is an important and sensitive parameter for building simulation, and internal heat gain has a direct relation to user behaviour. However, user behaviour does not currently get a lot of attention in simulation models, it is one of the hardest things to predict, and it plays a large role in current inaccuracies in simulation.

Shrikant Sharma of BuroHappold Engineering maintains that one of his current challenges is to virtualise the operation of a building—to predict performance from a user experience perspective. While user experience is a subjective measure, it can be expressed in terms of measurable parameters, such as journey and waiting times, congestion densities, air quality, view, wind, sunlight and noise. Sharma explains that 'modelling of visitor comfort involves simulating human behaviour which varies with spatial layouts, context, environment and interaction with other users. A vast amount of research and development work is under way in the academic and commercial world to model, visualise and assess the impact of designs on visitor comfort and safety'.[10] In practice today, new simulation techniques are helping designers to predict how people interact with building designs, and how to shape the designs to achieve maximum comfort and experience. Sharma explains that all new designs for airports, stadiums, theatres, schools and hospitals should design for aspects such as: layout, wayfinding, visibility, processes and management. Therefore, there is a need to incorporate user characteristics, such as culture, age, gender, disability and group size (see Chapter 11 on the work of BuroHappold).

BuroHappold has developed its own proprietary software, SmartMove; Woods Bagot's SuperSpace group has developed its own proprietary code; and some firms such as Arup have released their simulation engines as commercial software. Arup's MassMotion simulates pedestrian traffic and crowd behaviour and can predict the movements of hundreds of thousands of people within hours. The software produces various visualisations and evaluations such as: how long it takes people to get from one point to another, the flow rates for doors and stairs and escalators, and the comfort rating in different locations and at

5 David Di Giuseppe, movement analysis

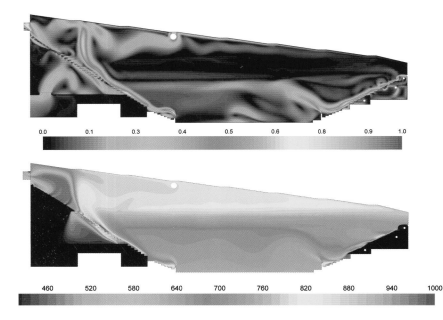

| 0.0 | 0.1 | 0.3 | 0.4 | 0.5 | 0.6 | 0.8 | 0.9 | 1.0 |

| 460 | 520 | 580 | 640 | 700 | 760 | 820 | 880 | 940 | 1000 |

6a and b Computational fluid dynamics (CFD) simulation, showing velocity and CO_2 build-up of interior spaces

various times. This type of user simulation is put into practice increasingly often for transit operations, large event venues, stations, airport terminals, healthcare facilities, office towers and stadiums. Quelea is a plug-in for Grasshopper, created by Alex Fischer, which enables designers to simulate user behaviour through agent modelling.[11] Through the assigning of forces and behaviours to systems of agents to create interaction, designers can create complex simulations and analyses, and generate geometric forms through the combination of simple rules.

COMPUTING FLUID FLOWS

Computational fluid dynamics (CFD) is a technique that enables the study of wind in and around buildings. CFD has been around for decades but has not been widely used by architects or engineers for buildings. CFD is used successfully in design practices among the aerospace, automotive and many product design industries. The testing of physical models in a wind tunnel has been the primary way of simulating air movement around buildings and neighbourhoods. However, now that computers are running faster, and CFD software is more available, designers are more frequently turning to CFD as a way of simulating airflow. Wind tunnel testing is very time-consuming, expensive and offers only a few points of investigation, whereas CFD enables multiple studies, faster, and with greater resolution.

The use of CFD is increasing, and as computers increase in speed, the accuracy and extents of CFD models can increase; however, there are still challenges to its widespread adoption. First, a new model needs to be constructed that is a volumetric meshing of the building and its surroundings. However, if the model requirements are known and planned for, this can be built into a generative computational model. The quality and quantity of the mesh are the two critically important aspects as the quality affects the accuracy of the analysis, whereas the quantity impacts the time it takes to compute the solution.[12] To use CFD, knowledge of the mechanics of fluid flow is necessary for model construction, to set up and run the simulation, and to synthesise the results. While some practices rely on commercial engineering analysis, using CFD software tools such as Ansys, many practices are now turning to open-source computer programs. One such open-source piece of software is OpenFOAM. It has been around since 2004, and has a large user base, an extensive range of features, and is used widely in industry and research. OpenFOAM is being used as the simulation engine for two new software projects that connect to Rhino Grasshopper: Albatross, developed by Timur Dogan, and Butterfly, developed by Mostapha Sadeghipour Roudsari.

Air movement impacts thermal comfort and indoor air quality, and good ventilation can improve health and productivity. Two prediction approaches exist: multi-zone airflow network and computational fluid dynamics (CFD) simulation. These can calculate: airflow rates, temperature and contaminant concentrations. The two most widely used multi-zone models are both available as shareware and have user-friendly interfaces and user manuals. These models can be coupled with energy simulation and CFD to improve the model accuracy and provide the necessary boundary conditions for the energy and CFD models.

ACOUSTIC ATMOSPHERES

Our experience of architecture is influenced by its acoustic qualities. Human activities produce sound and architecture constantly interacts with us through its modification of the sounds we create. The sounds we hear allow us to judge space in several ways: the direction of sound sources, the distance to a sound source or various sound sources, and the dimensions and reflective properties of the walls and surfaces surrounding us. Physically, no sound can be considered separate from where and when it was created and heard. Subjectively, sound is shaped depending on the auditory capacity, attitude, psychology and culture of the listener. Sound communicates social meaning and reminds us of our own presence in the world. Despite the importance, and omnipresence of sound, there are no widely available tools for architects.

Sound enables us to experience architecture in a spatial and temporal way. Unlike light, which is practically instantaneous, the speed of sound is perceptible. The sounds of the past exist simultaneously with the sounds of the present, a phenomenon of echoes we experience as reverberation time. The experience of reverberation time is one of the most critical aspects of our experience of space. For most of the last 2,500 years, architects have used empirical guidance for designing the sound of new buildings. American physicist Wallace Sabine introduced the first design tool that is able to accurately predict the acoustic performance of new buildings; Sabine's formula for the calculation

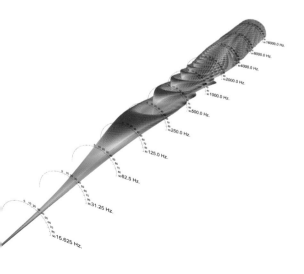

7 Simulating material performance—acoustic absorption

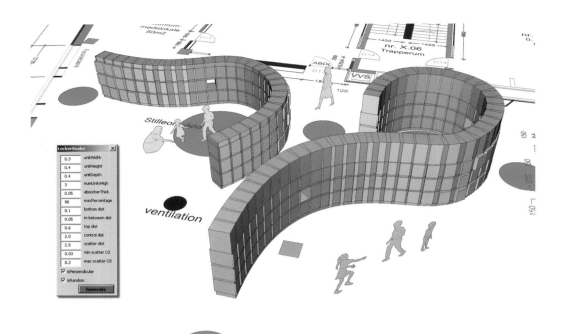

8 JJW Arkitekter, Sydhavn Skole,
Copenhagen, Denmark: perspective view
of locker snakes

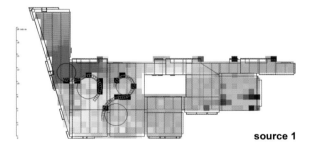

source 1

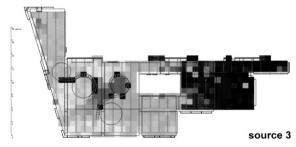

source 3

source 2

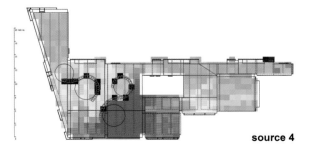

source 4

9 JJW Arkitekter, Sydhavn
Skole, Copenhagen, Denmark:
view of sound levels of study
areas, defined by locker
snakes

of reverberation time gave architects the ability to predict acoustic performance prior to construction. Sabine's study of sound and the dissemination of his research sparked the development of the field of architectural acoustics. Unfortunately, despite advances in acoustic science, this tool remains one of the only tools architects have to predict acoustic performance.

Since 1995, computer acoustic simulations have not only been sufficiently accurate, but efficient in terms of time and cost. Today, the computer simulation of room acoustic performance can be grouped into two approaches: wave-based and ray-based. Wave-based techniques attempt to solve the wave equation numerically. They are more computationally intensive, as they involve the discretisation of either the space of the room or its bounding surfaces and model the interactions between all of the resulting elements. Ray-based techniques assume that sound travels in a straight line and its reflection from surfaces is computed using geometrical methods. These two techniques can be used to study different aspects of architectural acoustic performance. The majority of specialist acoustic simulation software packages provide valid results, and while most of these simulation software packages have limited abilities to actually create geometry, it is possible to export geometry from architectural design software to the simulation software. As designers often already have a 3D model of a space, it can be faster to simulate than calculate. Unfortunately, there are no design software tools that combine sound and geometry. However, there does exist a plug-in to Rhino, Pachyderm, which will perform acoustic simulations.

BEYOND DRAWING TOWARDS ATMOSPHERE
Tom Maver did pioneering research on the use of computer-aided design aids and conceptualised a design workflow that should be familiar to many designers today. First, a designer generates a design hypothesis that is inputted into the computer (the representation); second, the behaviour of the design is simulated and a performance is outputted (the measurement); third, the designer must evaluate the measurement(s) and exercise value judgement (the evaluation); and, finally, the designer must decide on appropriate changes to the design (the modification). Like the designers featured in this book, he saw design as 'an iterative, exploratory human activity'. However, while Maver promoted this performance-based approach, he acknowledged that some aspects under investigation 'defy enumeration'. He felt this was acceptable so long as the models are accessible in a meaningful form to those who should exercise judgements on them. He saw that there would need to be a move towards models that enable an experiential appraisal of the building designs.[13]

To explore notions of atmosphere building, designers need to search out new ways of investigating these phenomena. While the understanding of scientific principles is essential for the modelling and simulation of a building's environment, there are many concepts relating to experience, perception and atmosphere

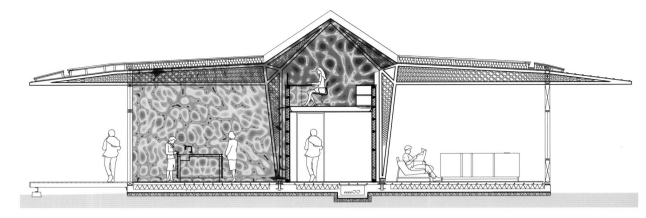

10 Speech privacy study, 500Hz sound waves

that perhaps transcend mathematical formulation. However, perhaps it is insufficient to say that some parts of the design simply 'defy enumeration'. The goal of new simulation methods can be to transform physical phenomena, such as light, sound, air speed, temperature and humidity, into computable models. We can use the multi-faceted potentials of simulation to predict the atmosphere of our future buildings. There are intersections and interdependencies between those who design and those who develop simulations—between tool users and tool makers. Perhaps one of the reasons that this issue is emerging is because of the current intersection where designers are becoming tool makers, creating methods through which their design interests can be explored. As aesthetics can now be considered as a part of ecology, atmosphere must become a part of architectural design. But it is also clear that we are not where we need to be yet—simulations are still largely independent and so a holistic experience is not yet possible. So what is needed moving forward? New tools could visualise, and virtualise, the qualities of user experience in buildings, so that designers could evaluate and react to building design options. This may be seen in new lightweight virtual reality technologies, such as wearable screens combined with real-time lighting simulation and sound auralisation. New attitudes of designers are needed that recognise the importance of experience and see it as a considered aspect of design, something that can be conceptualised and explored. Of course, more accurate, faster simulation would be wonderful. Finally, what is required is the integration of the representational aspects of multi-simulation in the design model—a BIM/SIM model.

REFERENCES
1. Juhani Pallasmaa, *The Eyes of the Skin: Architecture and the Senses*, John Wiley & Sons (Chichester), 2005, pp 41–4.
2. Peter Zumthor, *Atmospheres: Architectural Environments – Surrounding Objects,* Birkhäuser (Basel), 2006.
3. Farshid Moussavi, 'The Function of Form', in *The Function of Form*, Actar Publishers and Harvard Graduate School of Design (Barcelona), 2009.

4. Gernot Böhme, 'Atmosphere as the Fundamental Concept of a New Aesthetics', in *Thesis Eleven*, vol 36, no 1, 1993, pp 113–26.

5. Kjell Anderson, *Design Energy Simulation for Architects: Guide to 3D Graphics*, Routledge (London), 2014, p 3.

6. Philippe Rahm interviewed in Terri Peters, 'Hot/Cold: Philippe Rahm's Architecture as Meteorology', in *OnSite*, vol 21, 2009, p 20–3.

7. Michelle Addington, 'Disciplinary misTranslations', lecture presented at Design Modelling Symposium Copenhagen 2015, Copenhagen, Denmark, at CITA, Centre for Information Technology and Architecture, Royal Danish Academy of Fine Arts, Schools of Architecture, Design and Conservation, 30 September–2 October 2015.

8. Sean Lally, 'Architecture of an Active Context', lecture presented at ACADIA: Synthetic Digital Ecologies, California College of Arts, San Francisco, 2012.

9. Christoph Reinhart, 'Daylight Performance Predictions', in *Building Performance Simulation for Design and Operation*, Spon Press (London), 2011, pp 235–76.

10. Shrikant Sharma and Al Fisher, 'Simulating the User Experience: Design Optimisation for Visitor Comfort', in Brady Peters and Xavier de Kestelier (eds), *Computation Works: The Building of Algorithmic Thought*, Architectural Design (AD) series (John Wiley & Sons, Chichester), vol 83, issue 2, March/April 2013, pp 62–5.

11. Alex Fischer 'Quelea: Agent-Based Design for Grasshopper', online at http://www.grasshopper3d.com/group/quelea-agent-based-design-for-grasshopper (accessed 15 February 2017).

12. Sawako Kaijima, Roland Bouffanais, Karen Willcox and Suresh Naidu, 'Computational Fluid Dynamics for Architectural Design', in Brady Peters and Xavier de Kestelier (eds), *Computation Works: The Building of Algorithmic Thought*, Architectural Design (AD) series (John Wiley & Sons, Chichester), vol 83, issue 2, March/April 2013, pp 118–23.

13. Tom Maver, 'Appraisal in Design', in *Design Studies*, vol 1, no 3, 1980, pp 160–5.

IMAGES

courtesy NASA/JPL-Caltech
megacities.jpl.nasa.gov

1 Los Angeles Megacities Carbon Project,
ongoing research 2014–
This site is one of three urban greenhouse gas
measurement test beds, established by the
National Institute of Standards and Technology
(NIST), an agency of the US Chamber of
Commerce.

5. USE DATA:
COMPUTING LIFE-CYCLE AND REAL-TIME VISUALISATION
TERRI PETERS

*A key difference between a living thing and an object is
predictability: kick a stone, and you know what happens; swat
a bee, and things get more complicated.*
—David Orrell[1]

Overwhelmingly, it is the operation of buildings—how, when, in which ways they are used and by whom—that most affects the environmental performance and impacts of buildings. In fact, for typical standards of building construction, the embodied energy is equivalent to only a few years of operating energy.[2] However, data about how buildings use energy and occupant behaviours at all scales tends to be poorly understood and oversimplified. Usually it is because data about buildings in use is simply not collected, but sometimes this is because of the nature of the design process. In the course of a project, the client may adjust the brief and scope of the project to include new spaces or uses, or reconsider the number of hours that a building will be in use, and this inevitably leads to changes to the layout and size of the building, and also impacts the requirements for equipment and machinery inside. Variable aspects such as the actual efficiency of systems and workmanship during installation among others also impact how a building will perform. So how useful is a model to predict performance? Statistician George Box stated that 'the most that can be expected from any model is that it can supply a useful approximation to reality: all models are wrong; some models are useful'.[3] This does not mean that it is pointless, on the contrary, skilful early stage modelling and simulation is proving too important not to engage with.

At the scale of a building or a room, the interplay between inhabitant and site behaviours can be effectively studied in a variety of ways, including using digital simulation, yet surprisingly given the benefits of this data, this is not yet common practice. At a larger scale, studies of buildings and cities in use and their related environmental impacts and emissions are being informed by real-time data and simulated to show impacts over time. One such initiative, the Megacities Carbon Project, demonstrates new measurement and simulation techniques for urban emissions using computational design tools. Figure 1 shows the Los Angeles pilot study, which simulated and analysed data about emissions and their sources at urban and regional scales.[4]

COMPARING AND SHARING DATA

*A great building must begin with the immeasurable, must
go through measurable means when it is being designed,
and in the end must be unmeasured.*
—Louis Kahn[5]

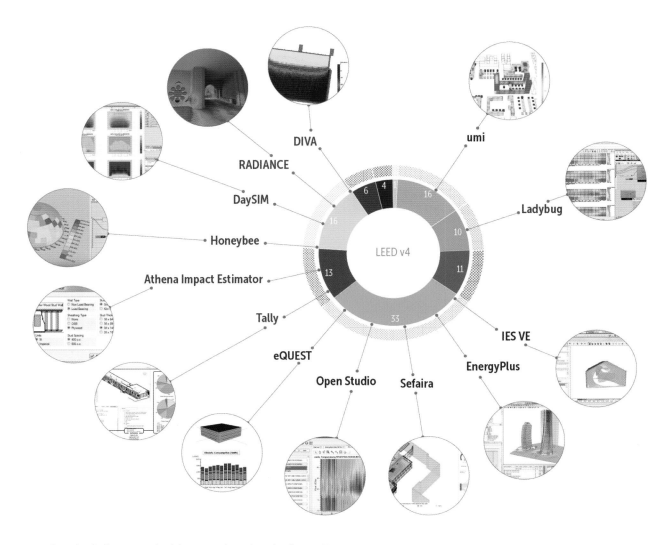

DIVA

umi

RADIANCE

DaySIM

Ladybug

6   4   16

16

10

Honeybee

LEED v4

11

Athena Impact Estimator

13

IES VE

Tally

33

eQUEST

EnergyPlus

Open Studio

Sefaira

Standards for green buildings, such as Leadership in Energy and Environmental Design (LEED), the world's most well-used rating system, are one of the ways in which designers and clients categorise, prioritise and compare their green building design strategies. There are LEED categories for many aspects of green building, including energy and atmosphere, location and transportation, and various other environmental design aspects. Designs are awarded points in each category to achieve different LEED designations.[6] Increasingly, when clients want to have LEED-branded buildings, if an environmental parameter is categorised in LEED, then it is important, otherwise it can be hard to measure and assign value to. It makes sense that there is demand for the range of digital design tools for simulating and predicting performance that align with the LEED categories. For example, designers can measure and simulate energy and indoor environmental qualities, such as daylight and overheating. Figure 2 shows the categories of LEED version 4 and some of the digital tools used by practices featured in this book. Some categories have few tools for designers that are commonly used for measurement and simulation in areas such as water efficiency and integrated design process. Rating systems like LEED have certainly raised awareness of green buildings among clients and professionals, but like all rating systems, in themselves they cannot create more sustainable buildings. Designers, along with clients and the wider community, need to keep focused on systemic, and harder to measure priorities, such as increasing the use of renewable energy, improving quality, and creating inspiring buildings and places that people want to maintain and keep over time.

USING POST-OCCUPANCY DATA

One of the most reliable ways to predict if a building will perform as expected is by studying post-occupancy evaluations (POE) of similar buildings or in the case of a renovation, by comparing the before and after data. Currently neither carrying out nor publishing post-occupancy studies and figures are common practice in architecture offices.[7] There seems to be some interest in understanding pre- and post- occupancy data, but little actual progress in practice. A recent *Architect* magazine editorial[8] reflected on the lack of POEs in the industry, and quoted an architect from a leading practice struggling with how to ask clients to do POEs: 'How do you help a client realise that this is important without looking vulnerable, like you don't know what you're doing?'. Concerns over privacy and legal consequences of what data will be collected during POEs remain, yet some new initiatives and tools are collecting and comparing actual use data to see how buildings measure up. CarbonBuzz is a UK database of buildings that publishes evidence of the 'performance gap' relating to predicted versus actual energy use.[9] The site features in-depth case studies and self-reported data of buildings in use, including several by developer British Land. CarbonBuzz reports that 'on average, buildings consume between 1.5 and 2.5 times predicted values' and that one main problem is that 'designers rarely have operational data and occupants rarely have design data'.[9] The site collects and publishes data anonymously, and offers a unique hybrid research and practice platform for benchmarking and tracking energy use in projects from design to operation. There remains a great need for more sharing of information within offices and between offices to raise the expectations and aspirations of the building industry as a whole.

ECOMETRICS

Some offices are developing their own internal benchmarks, for example the ecoMetrics tool was developed by Canadian office Diamond Schmitt Architects (DSAI) as a searchable database of the firm's energy modelling projects. The architects' idea is to harness the building data that they already have about their buildings to better understand energy use across the projects in the office. To build their database, the team at the office input the energy

- Integrative Process
- Location and Transportation
- Sustainable Sites
- Water Efficiency
- Energy and Atmosphere
- Materials and Resources
- Indoor Environmental Quality
- Innovation
- Regional Priority

2 Tools for building performance simulation
Digital tools for building performance simulation are used by designers to account for many kinds of parameters, including rating systems such as LEED.

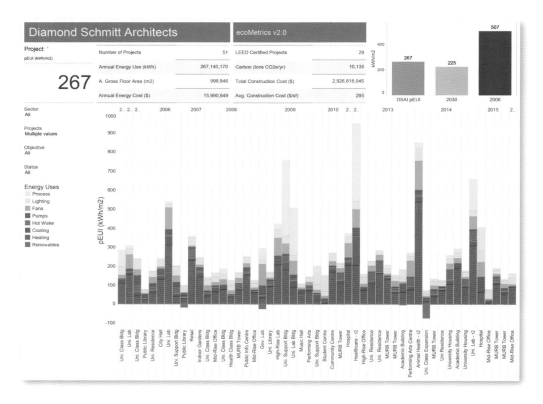

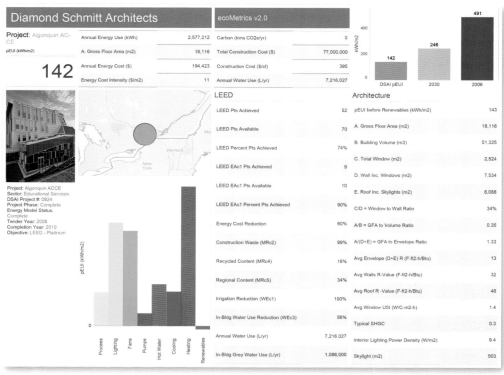

3 Diamond Schmitt Architects (DSAI), ecoMetrics database, 2015
DSAI has developed a database for collecting, comparing and analysing energy use in their buildings called ecoMetrics.

modelling data they have received from their external consultants from more than 50 projects. This data is made useful because it is searchable and graphically communicated. Data can be viewed as individual projects or organised in other ways, such as yearly or by project type. For each project, designers have access to a breakdown of the energy use, construction costs, floor area, annual water use and carbon emissions.[10] Viewing the data across the years, from 2004 to those currently under construction, allows design teams to be able to get a sense of what kind of building performance they should aim for, considering climate, location, cost, building type, client and LEED target.

For example, DSAI's Algonquin Centre for Construction Excellence in Ottawa, Canada, is a LEED Platinum building completed in 2011, which has very low energy costs and use. It also won several design awards, including the 2014 Ontario Association of Architects' Award for Design Excellence. The data input into the ecoMetrics tool considers architectural features, such as building volume, window to wall ratio (here 34 per cent), skylights and other features. Using ecoMetrics, the team could visualise building performance information and make a

4 Thornton Tomasetti/CORE studio, embodied carbon calculator
This tool is one of many developed by CORE studio, the in-house research team at Thornton Tomasetti engineers.

5 Thornton Tomasetti/CORE studio, footprint calculator application
This tool is one of many developed by CORE studio, the engineering office's in-house research team.

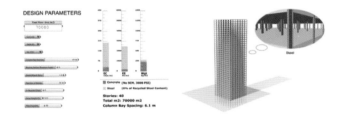

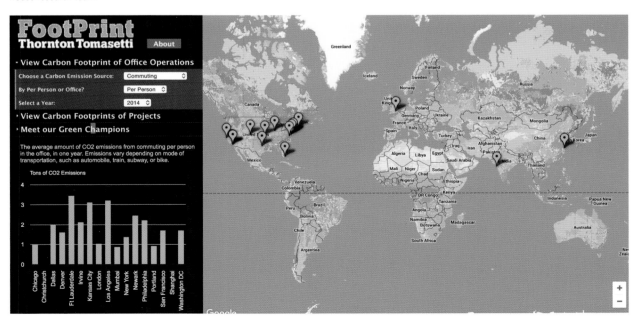

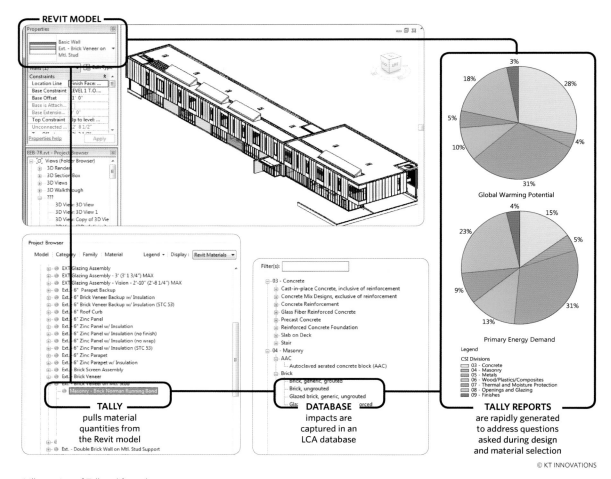

REVIT MODEL

Properties

Basic Wall
Ext. - Brick Veneer on
Mtl. Stud

Walls (1)

Constraints
Location Line   Finish Face: ...
Base Constraint   LEVEL 1 T.O...
Base Offset   1' 0"
Base is Attach...
Base Extensio...   0'
Top Constraint   Up to level: ...
Unconnected ...   2' 8 1/2"

Properties help   Apply

EEB-7R.rvt - Project Browser

Views (Folder Browser)
  3D Render
  3D Section Box
  3D Views
  3D Walkthrough
  ???
    3D View: 3D View
    3D View: 3D View 1
    3D View: Copy of 3D Vie

Project Browser

Model | Category | Family | Material | Legend ▾ | Display: Revit Materials ▾

EXT Glazing Assembly
EXT Glazing Assembly - 3' (3' 1 3/4") MAX
EXT Glazing Assembly - Vision - 2'-10" (2'-8 1/4") MAX
Ext. 6" Parapet Backup
Ext. 6" Brick Veneer Backup w/ Insulation
Ext. 6" Brick Veneer Backup w/ Insulation (STC 53)
Ext. 6" Roof Curb
Ext. 6" Zinc Panel
Ext. 6" Zinc Panel w/ Insulation
Ext. 6" Zinc Panel w/ Insulation (no finish)
Ext. 6" Zinc Panel w/ Insulation (no wrap)
Ext. 6" Zinc Panel w/ Insulation (STC 53)
Ext. 6" Zinc Parapet
Ext. 6" Zinc Parapet w/ Insulation
Ext. Brick Screen Assembly
Ext. Brick Veneer
Ext. Brick Veneer on Mtl. Stud
Masonry - Brick Norman Running Bond

Ext. Double Brick Wall on Mtl. Stud Support

TALLY
pulls material
quantities from
the Revit model

Filter(s):

03 - Concrete
  Cast-in-place Concrete, inclusive of reinforcement
  Concrete Mix Designs, exclusive of reinforcement
  Concrete Reinforcement
  Glass Fiber Reinforced Concrete
  Precast Concrete
  Reinforced Concrete Foundation
  Slab on Deck
  Stair
04 - Masonry
  AAC
    Autoclaved aerated concrete block (AAC)
  Brick
    Brick, generic, grouted
    Brick, ungrouted
    Glazed brick, generic, ungrouted
    Gla...   ...rced

DATABASE
impacts are
captured in an
LCA database

Global Warming Potential
3% 28% 4% 31% 10% 5% 18%

Primary Energy Demand
4% 15% 5% 31% 13% 9% 23%

Legend
CSI Divisions
03 - Concrete
04 - Masonry
05 - Metals
06 - Wood/Plastics/Composites
07 - Thermal and Moisture Protection
08 - Openings and Glazing
09 - Finishes

TALLY REPORTS
are rapidly generated
to address questions
asked during design
and material selection

6 Illustration of Tally, a life-cycle
analysis app
Tally is a digital tool for
calculating life-cycle and
material options during the
design process, developed by
KT Innovations, Autodesk and
thinkstep in 2015.

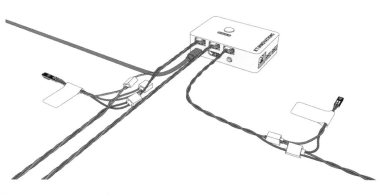

7 KT Innovations, Pointelist, 2016
Pointelist is a high-density sensor network that
allows designers to easily and inexpensively
configure on sites to collect environmental data
on spaces and places.

comparison and even a prediction for other similar buildings. It plans to use this tool and the data about this building to begin conversations with future clients, who may be commissioning a similar building in this climate.

CARBON CALCULATOR

Another comparative tool using a firm's own projects is the Carbon Calculator developed by engineering group Thornton Tomasetti's in-house research team CORE studio (see Chapter 15). CORE developed a tool that was able to calculate the total embodied energy and carbon of any design configuration early in the design phase. [11] The team referenced the Inventory of Carbon and Energy (ICE) database to create an array of Grasshopper components that calculate and visualise embodied carbon in real time with the design process. The tool shows data for the total amount of embodied carbon emissions produced by the structural engineering projects carried out by the firm. While currently only using their own data, this application could be a model for sharing and comparing other data sets. They also developed the FootPrint app that shows the carbon footprint of all of their offices by year, emissions source and office location for easy comparison.[12]

TALLY: CALCULATING AT THE SPEED OF DESIGN

It is difficult for designers to graphically communicate or conceptualise a building's materials and life cycle as part of the design process. Innovative architecture office KieranTimberlake (see Chapter 9) has developed several tools and workflows in the course of its projects, and many of these it has shared with the wider community. KT Innovations, its in-house research group, was part of a collaboration to create Tally, a life-cycle analysis app that enables designers to calculate the environmental impacts of building material selections directly in an Autodesk Revit model.[13] The benefits of this tool are that it runs in a program that architects already use, is freely available and designed to be used at early design stages by architects. Like all tools, it is naturally only as accurate as the information inputted into the model. It can be used effectively to compare options and make decisions based on specific building data, rather than having to consult with life-cycle analysis (LCA) specialists for every option. LCA is not usually part of an architect's workflow and is largely carried out by consultants. Some tools do exist for designers, such as the freely available Impact Estimator for Buildings software tool by the Athena Sustainable Materials Institute[14], but LCA is not part of the normal scope of work or workflow for the practices profiled in this book. Like many of the digital tools and workflows developed by the office, they saw a need for a new tool and set out to make one themselves. They realised their ideal LCA tool would be one that could easily be a part of an architect's workflow so that many options, not only the preferred options, could be analysed. Tally has been designed so that it can be used to conduct LEED-compliant, cradle-to-grave whole building life-cycle assessments. In addition, within LEED 2009, Tally can be used for the LEED MRpc63 credit and it has been approved for the new LEED v4 Building Life-Cycle Impact

8a Skidmore, Owings & Merrill (SOM), Kathleen Grimm School for Leadership and Sustainability at Sandy Ground, New York, USA, 2015
This net-zero-energy school in New York City is one of the first of its kind worldwide, with a two-storey design for 444 pre-kindergarten to fifth grade students.

8b SOM, Kathleen Grimm School for Leadership and Sustainability at Sandy Ground, New York, USA, 2015
The interior spaces are largely naturally lit and the design includes many features designed to use less energy, including energy-efficient light fixtures, day-lit offset corridors and low-energy kitchen equipment. The sloped ceilings reflect light into the spaces.

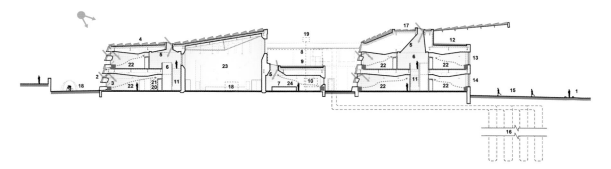

8c SOM, Kathleen Grimm
School for Leadership and
Sustainability at Sandy
Ground, New York, USA, 2015
This section shows the
relationship between indoors
and outdoors, including the
vegetable garden and running
track. Clerestory windows are
situated on the south facade
and the shading system
incorporates photovoltaic
arrays. It has been designed to
use about half of the energy of
a typical school.

1	Walking Track & Sustainability Tour
2	Clerestory Windows at South Facade
3	Displacement Induction Units
4	Photovoltaic Panels (1,900 KBTU Generated Per Year)
5	Sloped Ceilings Reflect Natural Light
6	Double Height Corridors (98% Daylight Autonomy)
7	Low Energy Kitchen Equipment
8	Greenhouse
9	Vegetable Garden
10	Building Dashboard System
11	Open Stairs
12	Green Roof
13	Large Windows At North Facade

14	High Efficiency Envelope (.01% Infiltration Rate)
15	Running Track
16	Geothermal Wells (81)
17	Solar Thermal (For Domestic Hot Water)
18	Energy Bicycles
19	Wind Turbine
20	Occupancy Sensors
21	Aircuity System
22	Classrooms (90% Daylight Autonomy - South Classrooms) Classrooms (60% Daylight Autonomy - North Classrooms)
23	Gymatorium (50 % Daylight Autonomy)
24	Cafeteria (50% Daylight Autonomy)

Reduction credit.[13] Tally is unique because for the first time, there is a design tool that offers LCA calculations at the speed of design, in the same resolution, using tools that architects are using already, in this case within their Revit model.

CREATING USEFUL INFORMATION FROM REAL-TIME ENVIRONMENTAL DATA

Predicting environmental performance is important, as is collecting post-occupancy data, but what about *in-occupancy* data? How can designers collect and make sense of data about their buildings while they are being used, in order to make them run better, fine-tune systems and prepare for future renovations? Pointelist is another collaboration by KT Innovations, in this case a way of collecting and making use of environmental data using sensors.[15] After years of experimenting with low-cost sensor networks on their own projects, they have developed and commercialised a product for designers: a low-cost sensor network of data points that test temperature and humidity that uses existing sensor technologies in ways applicable to designers. The data collected by the sensors is automatically uploaded using Wi-Fi to the online interface every five minutes, and data can be visualised, compared and graphed easily using a desktop or mobile device. Pointelist is new, and so far in beta testing only, but it could have a big impact on how designers are able to gather knowledge about buildings in use.

REAL-TIME MONITORING AND TRACKING OF ENERGY USE

The adage 'you can only manage what you measure' is not strictly true, although having a visualisation of how resources and energy are being used can inspire users to be aware of, or even change, their behaviour. A recent benchmark project in New

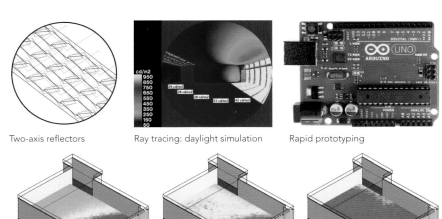

Two-axis reflectors   Ray tracing: daylight simulation   Rapid prototyping

No system   Static system   Dynamic system

9 Timur Dogan, daylight redirection system, diagram connecting digital tools to real-time monitoring, 2015

Light $_B$ Light $_A$ CO_2 Motion

Current $_A$ (Computer)   Current $_B$ (Monitor)

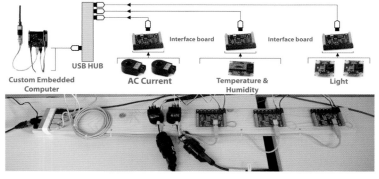

Custom Embedded Computer USB HUB AC Current Interface board Temperature & Humidity Interface board Light

10 Autodesk Research, Project Dasher, 210 King Street, Toronto, Canada, 2011
These diagrams show locations of sensors deployed in the office cubicle and the prototype physical layer. The sensors collect data on temperature, humidity, light, motion, CO_2 and send it via Wi-Fi.

York by Skidmore, Owings & Merrill (SOM) is an inspiring and beautiful building that is highly efficient, exceeds sustainability targets and offers users a chance to understand the impacts of their actions in the building.

The Kathleen Grimm School for Leadership and Sustainability at Sandy Ground is the first net-zero-energy school in New York City and one of the first of its kind worldwide. SOM integrated a range of sustainable design features, including renewable energy generation on site, passive design features and high-efficiency building components. The school has interactive energy dashboards so that students and teachers can see how much energy their building is using and where it is being used. This has impacted how students use the school and they feel invested in the way that it is designed and operated. The real-time monitoring and graphic visualisation of energy use is unique in this type of project. A goal of the project was that not only must the design and construction of the building be in keeping with the project's goals for resource use, but also the operation of the building and the way in which the inhabitants use the building must be designed and managed. The appropriate and interactive real-time data visualisation is highly successful in this project and allows the building's data, too often not shared with or understood by occupants or the design team, to be collected as a source of useful information potentially informing future similar projects.

As programmable hardware becomes cheaper and easier to use, there are new possibilities for embedding climate responsive behaviour into architectural elements. Architect and software developer Timur Dogan (see Chapter 19) and Peter Stec worked with architecture students to develop a workflow for rotating mirrored light shelves that can tilt in two directions based on the sun's direction, using real-time monitoring and rapid prototyping.[16] They used Radiance for daylight simulations and Arduino circuit boards to actuate and control the system. Dogan and Stec credit 'the convergence of rapid prototyping, parametric design and environmental modelling software' as making it easier to 'evolve a dynamic, direct-reflective daylight redirection system' that can be compared against normal static louvre systems.[16]

DASHER
Rather than building occupants being considered passive participants in building environments, researchers at Autodesk Research have carried out ongoing research projects into 'occupant-centric' approaches (rather than typical 'HVAC-centric' approaches) to collecting and visualising fine grain environmental data. Project Dasher (2011–) is a research project in the group's own offices where a range of environmental sensors were employed to collect data in office cubicles and automatically store the data using Wi-Fi.[17] The Dasher project focused on data sensing, data collection and storage, and data representation and visualisation, all of which are critical to actually filter and make sense of the data to inform the design process.[17] The aim of this kind of research is to gather data about aspects of the experience

11 Autodesk Research, Project Dasher, 210
King Street, Toronto, Canada, 2011
Project Dasher is an ongoing Autodesk research
project using a BIM-based platform to visualise
real-time building performance throughout the
life cycle of the building.

12 Delos and Mayo Clinic,
Well Living Lab, Rochester,
Minnesota, USA, 2016–
The Well Living Lab uses
sensors and digital tools for
analysing data and simulating
the interior environments. The
space is a physical test bed for
research into health and indoor
environments, and it is the first
space of its kind to provide
research-grade, human-
subject and environmental-
condition data, that will be
gathered from a wide variety
of simulated settings, such as
homes and offices.

of the user. The Pointelist research by KT Innovations tackles similar issues (see Figure 7)

SIMULATING AND VISUALISING WELLNESS

Links between human health and the interior environment remain understudied areas in terms of computational tools and simulation by designers. Responding to the need for specific environmental and human health-related studies to support early design phases, the Well Living Lab has been designed to offer controlled research settings and reconfigurable lab spaces to allow interdisciplinary researchers to test out ideas and use real-time environmental feedback (see Figure 12). This new 700-square-metre (7500-square-foot) research facility in Minnesota opened in 2016 and has been developed by researchers at Delos and the Mayo Clinic. It was designed to offer controlled research settings and reconfigurable lab spaces to allow interdisciplinary researchers to test out ideas and use real-time environmental feedback. Brent Bauer is the medical director of the Well Living Lab, and in a recent interview he stated that the first experiments are going to focus primarily on light, sound and acoustics, and temperature.[18] To study the relationships between the environment and the people, a volunteer group of Mayo employees will relocate their workstations from another building into the Lab and work there for nine or 10 weeks, and the research team will study their behaviour and responses to modifying the light, the sound and the temperature. Future studies will include collecting data about indoor air quality, looking at particulate matter, volatile organic compounds (VOCs) and CO_2. Bauer and his team will undertake research into if and how CO_2 impacts productivity, and consider possible ways of mitigating these impacts. The studies will relate to the framework of the newly developed WELL Building Standard, created by Delos, which has categories for air, water, nourishment, light, fitness, comfort and mind.[19] The WELL Building Standard is a performance-based system for measuring, certifying and monitoring features of the built environment that impact occupants' health and wellbeing and it works with the LEED green building standard. The facility and the WELL standard are innovative in their multi disciplinary development, and could spur the development of new design processes, tools and workflows to reflect how wellbeing can be a part of sustainable design.

USE DATA: COMPUTING LIFE-CYCLE AND REAL-TIME VISUALISATION

Designers are using computational design and simulation at multiple scales to experiment in order to better understand the human dimensions of comfort and experience as well as energy use. Collecting, sorting and storing data about a building is challenging, and there needs to be more focus on monitoring and evaluating buildings over time. Sustainable design is not a 'solution' or an end state; its meaning is constantly shifting and not the result of any one intervention. The location of the building and its uses, the selection of materials and specifying of construction processes, the designing of interior relationships and sizing of rooms are all among the myriad of decisions that are made during the sustainable design of buildings. The next chapter will continue to examine ways in which designers are seeking to collect, analyse and usefully integrate real-time site and climatic data to improve their designs.

REFERENCES

1. David Orrell, *The Future of Everything: The Science of Prediction from from Wealth to Weather to Chaos and Complexity, Thunder's* Mouth Press (New York), 2007, p 117.

2. IPCC, 'Trade-offs Between Embodied Energy and Operating Energy', in *IPCC Fourth Assessment Report: Climate Change 2007*, online at https://www.ipcc.ch/publications_and_data/ar4/wg3/en/ch6s6-4-14.html (accessed 21 July 2017).

3. George EP Box, J Stuart Hunter and William G Hunter, *Statistics for Experimenters: Design, Innovation, and Discovery*, second edition, Wiley (Hoboken, NJ), 2005, p 440.

4. NASA Jet Propulsion Laboratory, California Institute of Technology, 'Megacities Project', online at https://megacities.jpl.nasa.gov/portal/about (accessed 21 July 2017).

5. Louis I Kahn, 'The Value and Aim in Sketching', in *T Square Club Journal*, vol 1, no 6, May 1930.

6. United States Green Building Council, 'Leadership in Energy and Environmental Design', online at http://www.usgbc.org/leed (accessed 21 July 2017).

7. Julie Hiromoto, 'Post Occupancy Evaluation Survey Report', 2015, online at http://www.som.com/ideas/research/post_occupancy_evaluation_survey_report (accessed 21 July 2017).

8. Elizabeth Evitts Dickinson, 'Why Your Firm Should Embrace the Post-Occupancy Review', in *Architect* magazine, 9 September 2014, online at http://www.architectmagazine.com/practice/best-practices/why-your-firm-should-embrace-the-post-occupancy-review_o (accessed 21 July 2017).

9. RIBA CIBSE, 'CarbonBuzz', online at http://www.carbonbuzz.org (accessed 21 July 2017).

10. Birgit Siber and Mike Williams, 'Demystifying and Democratizing The Energy Use Conversation to Support the Net-Zero Challenge', in proceedings of SBE 2016 Regenerative and Resilient Urban Environments, Toronto, Canada, 19–20 September 2016.

11. Thornton Tomasetti, 'Carbon Calculator', online at http://core.thorntontomasetti.com/carbon-calculator (accessed 21 July 2017).

12. Thornton Tomasetti, 'FootPrint', online at http://core.thorntontomasetti.com/apps/Footprint (accessed 21 July 2017).

13. KT Innovations, 'Tally', online at http://choosetally.com/faq (accessed 21 July 2017).

14. Athena Sustainable Materials Institute, 'Impact

Estimator For Buildings', online at http://www.athenasmi. org/news-item/impact-estimator-for-buildings-version-5-2-build-01-press-release (accessed 21 July 2017)

15. KT Innovations, 'Pointelist', online at http://pointelist. com (accessed 21 July 2017).

16. Timur Dogan and Peter Stec, 'Rethinking The Light Shelf: Prototyping a Two-Axis Indoor Dynamic Daylight Reduction System for Building Facades', in *PLEA 2016 Los Angeles – Cities, Buildings, People: Towards Regenerative Environments,* vol 3, pp 1884–90.

17. Ramtin Attar, Ebenezer Hailemariam, Simon Breslav, Azam Khan and Gord Kurtenbach, 'Sensor-enabled Cubicles for Occupant-Centric Capture of Building Performance Data', in *ASHRAE Transactions,* vol 117, issue 2, 2011, pp 441–8.

18. Wellness Council of America, 'Human Health & Wellness in the Built Environment: What You Need to Know about the Well Living Lab: An Expert Interview with Dr Brent Bauer', online at http://welllivinglab.com/wp-content/uploads/2016/08/WELCOA-EI-dr-brent-bauer-062116.pdf (accessed 21 July 2017).

19. International WELL Building Institute, 'Well Standard', online at https://www.wellcertified.com (accessed 21 July 2017).

IMAGES

6. NEAR FUTURE DEVELOPMENTS:
ADVANCES IN SIMULATION AND REAL-TIME FEEDBACK

TERRI PETERS

Interesting phenomena occur when two or more rhythmic patterns are combined, and these phenomena illustrate very aptly the enrichment of information that occurs when one description is combined with another.
—Gregory Bateson, 1979[1]

It all boils down to this: designers want feedback. It's that simple.
—Billie Faircloth, 2016[2]

1 1:1 prototype of a pavilion, Sensory Detective Cluster, Smartgeometry 2016, Gothenburg, Sweden
Workshop participants visualised a physically simulated thermal environment to question the dynamics of heat, moisture and air within an atmospheric pavilion. Participants interacted with the model and experienced the effects via a network of electronic sensors and an augmented reality interface.

Real-time site and climatic data is necessary to make buildings that respond intelligently to their environment. In theory, integrated design processes are best practice and digital design tools can be used for performance simulation at early stages to design ideal environments. In practice, the nature of the disciplinary boundaries in the design industry, budgets for training, design timelines and infrastructure, are just some of the reasons why it is challenging to use computational design. From project to project, there are changing design expertise, timescales and client needs. The practices profiled in the following chapters in this book are large offices with resources and expertise in building full-scale projects. However, there are some techniques, workflows and concepts that are best tested in small scale, with temporary structures, in many cases with no client at all.

The projects highlighted in this chapter are experimental structures that point to promising new trajectories for 'computing the environment' that offer perspectives not seen in mainstream practice. These projects are part of a larger movement in architecture, both in school and in practice, to design and build 1:1 prototypes and pavilions that serve as influential test beds for new ideas. The impact of these temporary pavilions and pop-ups has been studied in recent architectural essays, for the relevance they hold in relation to larger architectural ideas, in the context of digital design and virtual spaces, and these reveal a plurality of approaches.[3]

Several of the projects featured here were created at Smartgeometry workshops, a unique workshop environment for digital design experimentation that explicitly connects professionals and students from industry and academia.[4] Certain educational settings have become known for innovation in architectural prototyping, such as the Royal Melbourne Institute of Technology (RMIT University) in Melbourne, the Centre for

2 Physical wind tunnel testing and virtual airflow simulation, Private Microclimates Cluster, Smartgeometry 2014, Hong Kong, China
This project was run by researchers from the Spatial Information Architecture Laboratory (SIAL) at RMIT University. Workshop participants used both digital and physical models to test airflow and quality.

3 Digital wind simulation with flow lines perspective, Private Microclimates Cluster, Smartgeometry 2014, Hong Kong, China
This project was run by researchers from the Spatial Information Architecture Laboratory (SIAL) at RMIT University.

Information Technology and Architecture (CITA) in Denmark, the ICD/ITKE annual research pavilion collaborations at the University of Stuttgart, and various research groups at the Massachusetts Institute of Technology (MIT). They are able to operate at a professional level, by integrating emerging applied research and collaborating with leading industry partners, while remaining largely outside commercial pressures.

This chapter discusses three overlapping and multi-disciplinary themes in the architectural design process: real-time feedback; human behaviour as a computational data source; and reconsiderations of comfort and experience to consider gradients of performance. In time, concepts explored in these projects could cross over into larger scale and more mainstream modes of practice.

REAL-TIME FEEDBACK
EXPERIMENTATION AT RMIT

There have been a series of successful experiments, involving 1:1 prototyping and real-time feedback for environmental parameters, by researchers at RMIT in Melbourne. Led by Jane Burry, the Spatial Information Architecture Laboratory (SIAL) at RMIT is a research institute for innovation in transdisciplinary research and education. Both examples discussed here were done in the context of the collaborative Smartgeometry network, during the intensive four-day workshops. At these events, international participants at a range of levels of expertise come together to work on predefined and peer-reviewed research questions with the aim of creating new workflows. The Private Microclimates workshop cluster at Smartgeometry 2014 was led by architects Mani Williams and Mehrnoush Latifi, and aerospace engineer Daniel Prohasky, all from RMIT. They investigated how to gain and visualise environmental feedback for wind and airflows by using hybrid physical and digital methods. A wind tunnel was constructed and used for physical testing[5] and simulations were carried out, using Vasari's wind tunnel tool. Vasari is an easy-to-use computational fluid dynamics (CFD) design tool that is useful for early-stage conceptual analysis of airflow around building site and building form. The workshop participants used parametric modelling, data gathering and data visualisation in both physical and virtual platforms. This work contributes to a larger research project by researchers at SIAL that aims to develop design and simulation strategies that enable architects to understand the relational dynamics between airflow and porous screens for building facades.[6]

In 2016, SIAL researchers carried out another real-time investigation of gaining feedback from digital and physical environmental data sources. At Smartgeometry 2016, the Sensory Detective Cluster was led by Latifi and Prohasky.[7] As with their 2014 workshop, the experiments used both digital and physical models to engage with the complexity of performance-driven design to extract data from multiple sources and scales. The cluster used augmented reality by developing a custom application for Android to visualise their designs and data in real time. Live data feedback was easily used by participants to inform

4 Digital wind simulation using digital tools including Vasari, Private Microclimates Cluster, Smartgeometry 2014, Hong Kong, China
This project was run by researchers from the Spatial Information Architecture Laboratory (SIAL) at RMIT University.

5 David Benjamin, 'Amphibious Architecture'
interactive installation, New York, USA, 2009
The temporary installation, created in
collaboration with the artist Natalie
Jeremijenko, floated in New York's waterways.

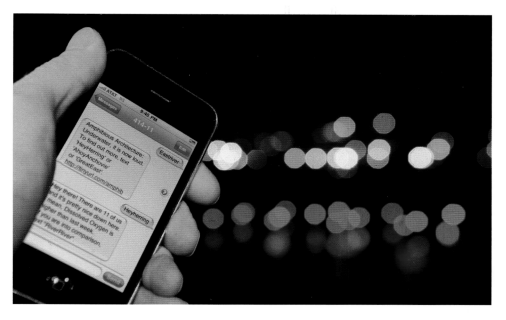

6 David Benjamin,
'Amphibious Architecture'
installation, New York, USA,
2009
The installation created
public engagement through
interaction as visitors could
observe the blinking lights and
changing colours, and send
a query via a text messaging
system, to gain local and
real-time feedback on how
the aquatic and territorial
ecosystems interact.

their design. It allowed them to see the thermal environment
around a pavilion that they constructed while they designed it.
The structure was populated with bespoke fabric panels designed
by participants to test the relationship between form and airflow.
Sensors were attached to the panels and a sensor network
was created so that it could be responsive. A fabric designer
provided expertise in cutting the fabrics and selecting fabrics
with various thermal properties, such as moisture wicking, and
varying levels of absorbency, which impact the thermal behaviour
of the structure. They used digital tools to visualise the data that
they had collected from the sensored physical prototypes. In this
workshop, participants developed a unique process for design
that enabled them to design the modules at 1:1 scale, to make
physical mock-ups and then to add changes to their prototypes in
an iterative process based on the feedback that they had gained
from the visualisation. The installation functioned as an experiential
prototyping platform at full scale with many potential applications
for the building industry, given that every building contains
environmental microclimates.

THE LIVING
The experimental 1:1 material prototypes and new design
workflows by architect David Benjamin of the New York-based
design practice, The Living, use real-time data for feedback into
the design process. The studio has a range of projects and scales,
all of which explore human relationships to our environment in
different ways. Benjamin builds low-cost sensors, develops custom
software and collaborates with artists, material researchers and
software developers in his work to gather and utilise new kinds
of environmental data. He is an architect, and directs his office,
The Living, in parallel with his position as the director of the Living
Architecture Lab and assistant professor at Columbia University's

Graduate School of Architecture, Planning and Preservation. All of The Living's projects are collaborative, multi-disciplinary, and involve making spatial prototypes of computational and ecological ideas. The studio recently joined Autodesk Research to do further experiments with visual interfaces and develop new ways of combining biological and digital information.

SKETCHING WITH PROTOTYPES

Benjamin develops new design workflows, including iterative processes of refining 1:1 models to inform design concepts. His large multi-partner projects often begin with a sketch design strategy that he calls 'flash research', which involves small conceptual projects with self-imposed constraints of being under $1000, taking only a month and resulting in a fully functioning prototype. A recent 'flash research' example is 'Living Glass', a response to a research question that addresses how architecture might be dynamic, and utilises new materials to respond to us in some way.[8] Prototypes have been developed using a thin transparent membrane surface with shape memory alloys, so that the materials contract along its length when electricity is passed through it. The result is a transparent film, and when you breathe into it, it gives the effect of breathing back. He says: 'It is an exploration of technology, of new types of building envelopes, but it is also about an idea that our architecture might register something important to us about its conditions and about the environment'.[8] This small demonstration project is part of a trajectory of work that uses data from the environment, such as sensors that reveal air quality, water quality or noise levels, to have material and spatial impacts.

7 David Benjamin, mock-up of 'Amphibious Architecture' installation, with mussel bio-sensors, 2015

The next iteration of the project will be a larger and more ambitious version, and include the use of mussels as bio-sensors, to monitor how they open and close in response to changing water qualities.

AN ECOSYSTEM OF INFORMATION

The Living has developed a series of physical interventions with associated bespoke digital interfaces to collect unconventional environmental data, visualise it and enable it to be easily communicated. 'Amphibious Architecture' was a dynamic public engagement project, located in New York's East River and produced in collaboration with the artist Natalie Jeremijenko. A series of floating lights glowed in response to the amount of oxygen in the water, and offered an interface for water quality and the presence and movement of fish.[9] There were two layers of lights, and they blinked as well as changed colours in response to measured water quality levels from the previous week. People walking along the water could see a line of bobbing lights, download the custom app to their phone, and text 'Hey Herring' to an automated computer application, which texted them back details of the real-time water quality and details of fish activity underwater at that spot. Benjamin designed the system as a two-way interface that communicated with users, not only reported visualised information.[10] The emphasis on designing a user-friendly environmental interface and on gathering super-local, real-time data is tested in this project and could offer potential for sustainable architecture.[11]

A new version of 'Amphibious Architecture' will be a part of the permanent Pier 35 EcoPark, commissioned by the New York City Economic Development Corporation. This larger and more ambitious version of the installation includes the use of mussels as bio-sensors. Benjamin explains: 'this allows another layer of environmental input, using living organisms as sensors. The first attempt used digital sensors to sense dissolved oxygen and in this case we are using live mussels because it turns out that the rate and amount that mussels open their shells is a very sensitive detector of pollution in the water'.[8] Benjamin proposes attaching a tiny magnet to one side of the mussel shell and a low-cost sensor to the other, so it is possible to detect how the mussels are opening and closing.

BUILDINGS=DATA: UTILISING BEHAVIOUR AS DESIGN INPUT

HARNESSING NEW TECHNOLOGIES

The design of buildings not only *consumes* data, but it also *creates* data. Speaking at the 'Buildings=Data' conference in 2015, Andy Payne of the technology consultancy Case, explained why they had used a variety of indoor positioning tools and custom apps to conduct a series of experiments, including tracking the movement of Case's staff for six weeks. Payne explained that traditionally, designers relied on qualitative metrics, largely from post-occupancy evaluations, to understand how buildings were being used, but at Case they were interested in harnessing new technologies and the benefits of cheap easy-to-use sensors and networks to gather different kinds of empirical data about how people use space. Mani Williams from SIAL collaborated with Payne and others at Case on this project, and her work focused on data collection and analysis to understand how different business units behave differently, for example in

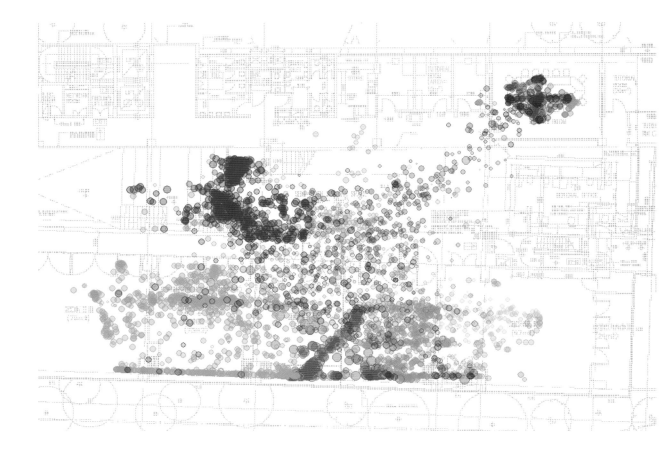

8 Mani Williams, indoor tracking study,
Smartgeometry 2014, Hong Kong, China
The tracking data was collected by using an off-
the-shelf, Zigbee-based indoor tracking system,
which periodically output proximities of the tags
that participants at the event were wearing, to
several static tracking beacons. This graphic
shows the tracking data projected onto the
floor plan of the workshop area, representing
the spatial usage of the eight project groups.

9 Mani Williams, indoor
tracking study, Smartgeometry
2014, Hong Kong, China
This graphic represents the
interaction network that
modelled the behaviour of
the workshop participants
compiled over the data
collection period.

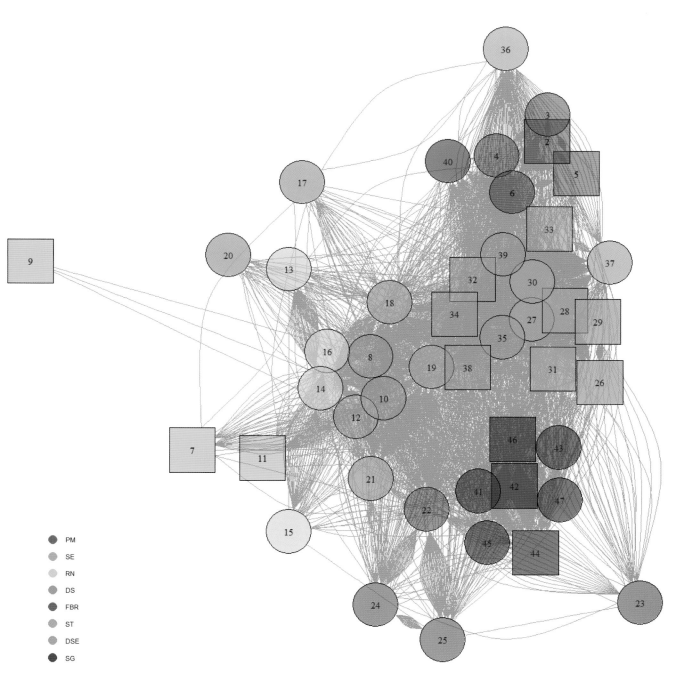

PM
SE
RN
DS
FBR
ST
DSE
SG

6. NEAR FUTURE DEVELOPMENTS 82-83

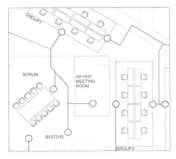

1 Adjacency

2. Desk preference

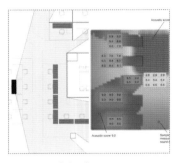

3. Productivity

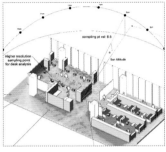

4. Daylight

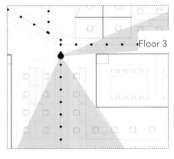

5. Views To outside

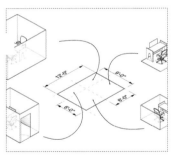

6. Adaptability

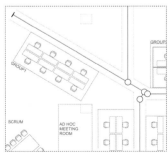

7. Circulation

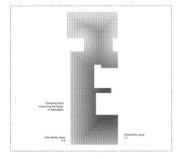

8. Equality

10 David Benjamin, generative design of the interior of Autodesk's new Toronto offices in the MaRS building, Toronto, Canada, 2016
Diagram of the eight defined design goals of the new MaRS building, an important first step in the generative design process.

Floor 3

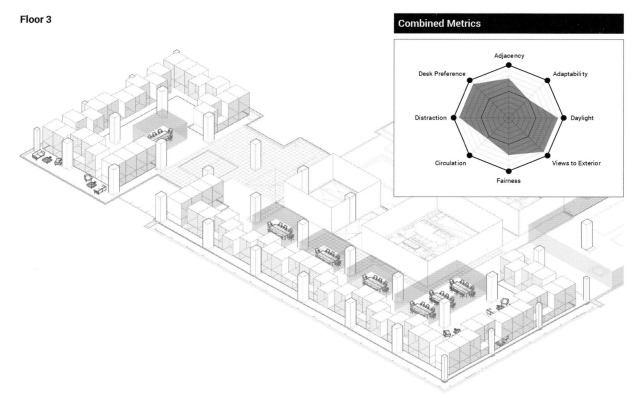

Combined Metrics

Adjacency · Adaptability · Desk Preference · Daylight · Distraction · Views to Exterior · Circulation · Fairness

11 David Benjamin, generative design of the interior of Autodesk's new Toronto offices in the MaRS building, Toronto, Canada, 2016
An automated process runs thousands of possible layout and spatial options to achieve the defined design goals. This option was the best fit and the highest performing one.

their spatial usage pattern, movement pattern and people-people interaction network pattern. In 2015, the consultancy Case joined WeWork (see their profile in Chapter 18).

Williams has carried out other indoor positioning studies, including an experiment at Smartgeometry in 2014. A team from SIAL carried out an analysis of participant behaviour in the workshop areas, using indoor-tracking sensors and time-lapse photography. The aim was to demonstrate the capacity of indoor tracking as a data collection system for the study of socio-spatial interactions that occur in a collaborative work environment.[13] Using the Zigbee data collection tool, which supplies people with movement data, researchers analyse people's behaviour and spatial usage information. For Smartgeometry, SIAL researchers plotted each person's Zigbee data onto the floor plan to analyse how people used the space. [13]

Williams' research is extending from Smartgeometry into real estate and technology applications in industry through collaborations, such as the one with the consultancy Case. In terms of future applications for this kind of simulation, she explains: 'human behaviour is complex, the ways people determine how to behave in a new environment depends on many factors. Yes you can model a simple behaviour model like a random walk, but you'd be more close to reality if you base your simulation on real data collected from the users'. In the future, as it becomes easier

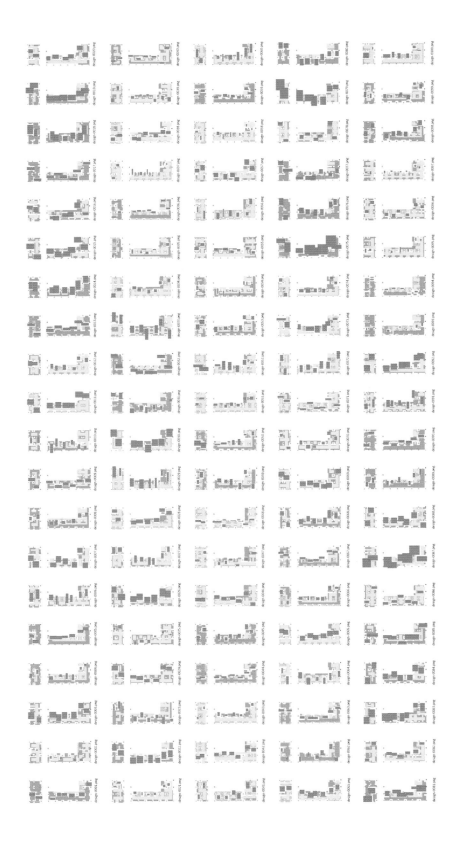

to collect data, designers will have more data than they know how to analyse. As Williams says:

> Data collection is becoming easier, with data supplied from personal devices and other small wearable devices. It may be too easy nowadays, I have experienced projects where people jumped into data collection without much thought on what they want to know, and realised afterwards all the data they collected was rubbish. I see the future to be more data-driven, feedback-based design—ongoing evaluation and iterative/adaptive design to archive the desirable outcome [14].

BUILDING GENERATIVE DESIGN

For Autodesk's new research headquarters in Toronto, Canada, researchers including David Benjamin decided to utilise the project as a way of creating their first built example of performance-driven, generative design for architecture. The primary drivers from the client's perspective were to increase the brand's visibility, to nurture talent and to support maker activities. These were translated into design elements, such as cabin offices and lab spaces. From surveying staff using questionnaires and focus groups, data was gathered about what people wanted from their workspace. In the initial phase of generative design, eight main goals were established: adjacency preferences, desk preferences, productivity goals, access to daylight, views to outside, adaptability of the layout, circulation and equality. There were so many variables to consider for spatial planning that it would be difficult to negotiate by human intuition. At Smartgeometry 2016, Phil Bernstein introduced the generative design concepts and explained that this process allowed the automatic creation, evaluation and evolution of thousands of options to meet the project goals.[15] The aim was to make informed data-driven trade-offs. Generative design paired with performance evaluation was used to develop the brief, the interior concept and layout, the design components and furniture, and to determine how the project could be evaluated. Further feedback came from the construction of full-scale mock-ups. Autodesk moved into its new space in late 2016.

GRADIENTS OF PERFORMANCE

> The design composition principle of the 'Taichung Jade MeteoPark' is based on climatic variations that we have mapped by computational fluid dynamics simulation (CFD) … We have augmented these differences of microclimates in order to increase the coolness, the dryness, the cleanness of the places that are naturally cooler, less humid and less polluted, for creating more comfortable spaces for the visitors.
> —Philippe Rahm 2011[16]

ARCHITECTURE AS METEOROLOGY

Architect Philippe Rahm is known for his experimental architectural proposals that push the boundaries of environmental design.

12 David Benjamin, generative design of the interior of Autodesk's new Toronto offices in the MaRS building, Toronto, Canada, 2016
This illustrates how the automated generation of viable design options can be achieved quickly, accurately and graphically. When the interior was constructed in late 2016, it was Autodesk's first built design using a generative process.

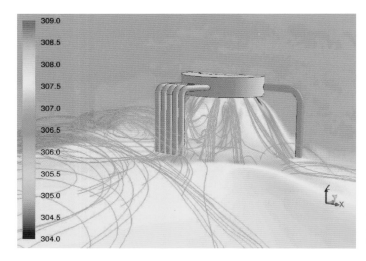

13 Philippe Rahm, computational fluid
dynamics (CFD) simulation, Jade Eco Park,
Taichung, Taiwan, 2012–2016

15 Philippe Rahm,
construction of Jade Eco
Park, Taichung, Taiwan,
photographed in 2014

14 Philippe Rahm, simulation
showing microclimates and
people, Jade Eco Park,
Taichung, Taiwan, 2012–2016

Gradients of performance are heightened and exaggerated in his 'architecture as meteorology', offering a critique of modern contentions. Aspects of heterogeneous comfort, atmosphere, weather, diet, thermal comfort climate and neurology are explored in his 1:1 installations.[17] His provocative proposal for Jade Eco park, by far his largest project to date, is the outcome of his collaboration with Mosbach Paysagistes, and Ricky Liu & Associates. Transsolar KlimaEngineering provided expertise relating to the CFD analysis as the flow of air and microclimate was essential to the design. Rahm explained: 'we began not to create the program, but first to create the climate'.[18] The site is very hot and '200 days per year it is more than 29 degrees celsius on this site'. So the design uses passive cooling strategies, and trees are planted for shading, and the different areas of the design are programmed around the air velocity, air temperature, noise levels and pollution levels. Rahm began by reinforcing cooler areas, diagramming heat maps, and considering seasonal and daily events on the site, and then thinking of the function.

FABPOD: DESIGNING FOR AFFECT
The FabPod is a prototype for a free-standing meeting room, developed by a collaborative and international team of design researchers: Nick Williams, Brady Peters, John Cherrey, Jane Burry, Mark Burry, Alexander Peña de León and Daniel Davis. It was built as an acoustically tuned meeting room within an open-plan office at the RMIT Design Hub. The challenge was not only how to design the meeting room to have optimal acoustic performance, but additionally how to design the structure, so it could positively contribute to the acoustic performance of the open-plan working environment in which it was situated. Meeting rooms are places where decisions are made, creative ideas are constructed, and where listening and communicating are critically important, and

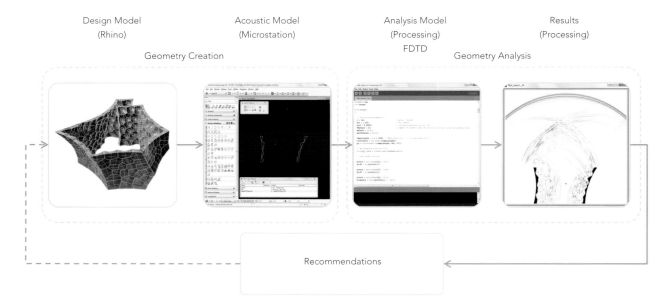

Design Model
(Rhino)

Acoustic Model
(Microstation)

Analysis Model
(Processing)
FDTD

Results
(Processing)

Geometry Creation

Geometry Analysis

Recommendations

16 Workflow diagram for FabPod, 2013, an acoustic installation for a meeting room within a larger space at RMIT University, Melbourne, Australia

The design team of this project included Nick Williams, Brady Peters, John Cherrey, Jane Burry, Mark Burry, Alexander Peña de León and Daniel Davis.

17 An interior photograph of FabPod, an acoustic installation for a meeting room within a larger space at RMIT University, Melbourne, Australia, 2013

so the acoustic performance of meeting rooms is an important design criterion. To predict this performance, four acoustic design workflows were developed. The first two workflows predict the acoustic qualities of the room by using existing simulation software that implements geometric algorithms. The other two workflows predict the acoustic qualities of the surface and the simulations in these workflows use numerical modelling algorithms.[19]

There are several critical performance considerations for meeting rooms: the reduction of room resonances, the removal of acoustic defects such as flutter echoes, the tuning of the room to an appropriate reverberation time, the increase in speech intelligibility through positive early reflections and the reduction in background noise, and the creation of an even and diffuse sound field. These acoustic performance considerations can be dealt with through the manipulation of the overall geometry of the room, the detailed design of the room's surface geometry, and the specification of material. In order to design for sound, designers must be able to get feedback from their digital model on its acoustic performance. As the project's performance criteria and geometric definition become more complicated, these simulation tools need to be customised. In the FabPod project, a customisable series of simulation workflows enabled the designers to predict acoustic effect and, as this was part of a linked series of design workflows, to see how these acoustic effects impacted the material definition, tectonic language and fabrication strategy.

RETHINKING THE ENVIRONMENT

> *Once the technology was developed to control completely the thermal environment, people became curious about what a truly optimal thermal environment might be … According to one report, the British comfort zone lies between 58F and 70F, the comfort zone in the United States lies between 69F and 80F; and in the tropics it is between 74F and 85F.*
> *—Lisa Heschong, 1979*[20]

The trajectories and experiments highlighted in this chapter point to exciting new directions for 'computing the environment'. There is a need for a broader consideration of the 'environment', including not only built space and nature but also atmosphere and human behaviour. The Smartgeometry workshops, perhaps due to their changing themes within digital design, and their ability to curate and peer-review participants and topics, offer important venues for digital design experimentation. The works in this chapter point to more ambitious roles for architects in the simulation process. The increasing ease and speed of gaining feedback from physical and virtual testing enables new ways of designing. Real-time feedback, design for interaction with the environment, not only measuring or simulating its behaviour, and the inclusion of new metrics like sound, are flourishing in experimental projects, and are likely to come to mainstream practice in the near future.

REFERENCES

1. Gregory Bateson, *Mind and Nature. A Necessary Unity*, EP Dutton (New York), 1979, p 91.

2. Terri Peters, 'Billie Faircloth of KieranTimberlake About Research, Which She Defines as "to Search and Search Again"', in *Mark* magazine, no 62, June/July 2017, p 174.

3. Leon van Schaik and Fleur Watson (eds), *Pavilions, Pop-Ups and Parasols: The Impact of Real and Virtual Meeting on Physical Space*, Architectural Design (AD) series (John Wiley & Sons, Chichester), vol 85, no 3, May/June 2015.

4. Brady Peters and Terri Peters (eds), *Inside Smartgeometry: Expanding the Architectural Possibilities of Computational Design*, John Wiley & Sons (Chichester), 2013.

5. Rafael Moya Castro and Daniel Prohasky, 'Mini Airflow Tunnel Project', online at https://miniwindtunnel.wordpress.com/about (accessed 10 May 2016).

6. Mehrnoush Latifi, Daniel Prohasky, Jane Burry, Rafael Moya, Jesse McCarty and Simon Watkins, 'Breathing Skins for Wind Modulation through Morphology', in S Choo, S Chien, MA Schnabel, W Nakapan, MJ Kim, S Roudavski (eds), *Proceedings of the 21st International Conference of the Association for Computer-Aided Architectural Design Research in Asia CAADRIA 2016*, CAADRIA (Hong Kong), 2016.

7. Marc Webb, 'Workshop Summary', Sensory Detectives Cluster, Smartgeometry 2016, online at https://vimeo.com/162747037 (accessed 10 May 2016).

8. A lecture by David Benjamin in The Architectural League's Emerging Voices lecture series, New York, 6 March 2014.

9. Terri Peters, 'Master of Research: David Benjamin Investigates What Computation, Architecture and Biology Have in Common', in *Mark* magazine, vol 55, April/May 2015, pp 114–21.

10. Interview with David Benjamin at Autodesk University, Las Vegas, USA, 3 December 2015.

11. Terri Peters, 'Sustaining the Local: An Alternative Approach to Sustainable Design', in Michael Hensel and Christian Hermansen Cordua (eds), *Constructions: An Experimental Approach to Intensely Local Architectures*, Architectural Design (AD) series (John Wiley & Sons, Chichester), vol 85, no 2, March/April 2015, pp 136–41.

12. A lecture by Andy Payne at the 'Buildings=Data' conference New York, 28 May 2015.

13. Mani Williams, Jane Burry and Asha Rao, 'Understanding Face to Face Interactions in a Collaborative Setting: Methods and Applications', in *The Next City – New Technologies and the Future of the Built Environment [16th International Conference CAAD Futures 2015]*, CAAD Futures (São Paulo, Brasil), 2015, pp 155–74.

14. Email interview with Mani Williams, 29 January 2016.

15. A lecture by Phil Bernstein at Smartgeometry 2016, Gothenburg, Sweden, 4 April 2016.

16. 'Philippe Rahm architectes', online at http://www.philipperahm.com (accessed 10 May 2016).

17. Terri Peters, 'Philippe Rahm's Architecture as Meteorology', in *Onsite*, summer issue, 2009, pp 20–4.

18. A lecture by Philippe Rahm, 'On Atmospheres: Spaces of Embodiment' conference, Harvard Graduate School of Design, USA, 4–5 February 2016.

19. Brady Peters, 'Integrating Acoustic Simulation in Architectural Design Workflows: The FabPod Meeting Room Prototype', in *SIMULATION: Transactions of the Society for Modeling and Simulation International*, vol 91, no 9, 2015, pp 787–808.

20. Lisa Heschong, *Thermal Delight in Architecture*, The MIT Press (Cambridge, MA), 1979, pp 15–16.

IMAGES

7. DESIGNING ENVIRONMENTS AND SIMULATING EXPERIENCE:

FOSTER + PARTNERS SPECIALIST MODELLING GROUP

BRADY PETERS

F+P AND THE SMG

Foster + Partners is one of the world's most well-known architectural practices. Founded in 1967, the office has made a significant impact on both design culture and our collective built environment. The firm maintains a focus on sustainable design, drawing on both vernacular traditions and the latest in building technologies, creating innovative buildings that are sensitive to location and culture. In the late 1990s, Foster + Partners founded the Specialist Modelling Group (SMG) to address the growing need for digital design expertise in geometry, building performance and fabrication integration. The SMG is an in-house consultancy, comprised of about 24 digital design specialists with expertise in geometry and modelling, parametric design, computer programming, building information modelling (BIM), digital fabrication, structural engineering, thermal comfort, lighting, acoustics and wind analysis, and post-occupancy evaluation and real-time sensoring. The group is organised in two units: geometry and building physics. The geometry unit is led by partner Xavier De Kestelier, who is an experienced architect and educator, a director of Smartgeometry and a guest professor at the Bartlett School of Architecture and the University of Ghent. The building physics unit is led by partner Irene Gallou, an expert in sustainable design, environmental simulation and post-occupancy research.

1 Foster + Partners,
Oceanwide Center, San
Francisco, USA
Visualisation of the mixed-use
development.

The SMG is an in-house consultancy within Foster + Partners and this relationship allows them to have a good working relationship, to meet regularly and to develop workflows for integrated design systems. Sometimes members of the SMG will sit with design teams, but equally sometimes designers will come and sit with the SMG to learn new tools, techniques and workflows.[1] The SMG believes that there is a need to integrate architecture and engineering on a digital workflow level. Likening themselves to a mediator or translator, the team at SMG often works between

Average Daily Sun Exposure (June)
Excluding Golden Gate University Tower

Average Hours of Solar Access per Day

| 0 | 5 | 10hrs |

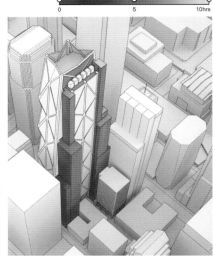

"Sunshine On My Shoulders"

1. Light Collection / Reflection
- Use frequently-exposed "shoulders" as a surface for light collection
- Can take advantage of core facade flexibility (ie. no glazing)

2. Secondary Reflection
- Fixed reflector bounces light collected above into Urban Room
- Could double as a "wind break" to disrupt downdraft flow

multi-axis rotation

fixed reflector

2 Foster + Partners,
Oceanwide Center, San
Francisco, USA
Solar radiation analysis study.

Core Solar Exposure (View from the Sun)

June 21

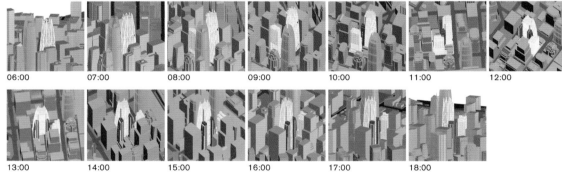

| 06:00 | 07:00 | 08:00 | 09:00 | 10:00 | 11:00 | 12:00 |
| 13:00 | 14:00 | 15:00 | 16:00 | 17:00 | 18:00 | |

December 21

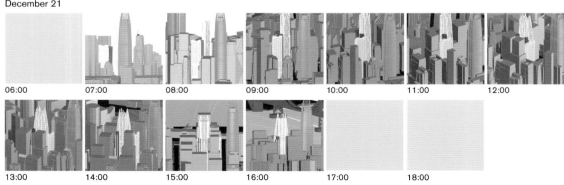

| 06:00 | 07:00 | 08:00 | 09:00 | 10:00 | 11:00 | 12:00 |
| 13:00 | 14:00 | 15:00 | 16:00 | 17:00 | 18:00 | |

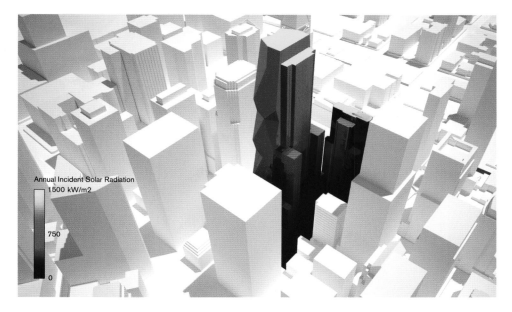

Annual Incident Solar Radiation
1500 kW/m2

750

0

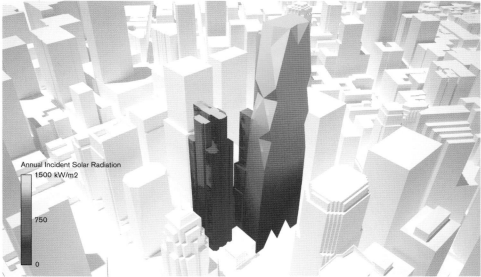

Annual Incident Solar Radiation
1500 kW/m2

750

0

4 Foster + Partners,
Oceanwide Center, San
Francisco, USA
Core solar exposure for the
longest and shortest days of
the year.

3 Foster + Partners,
Oceanwide Center, San
Francisco, USA
Analysis of average daily sun
exposure and the use of fixed
reflectors to collect and reflect
light.

architectural geometry and engineering calculations. Through the development of custom digital tools that integrate engineering calculations within parametric geometry models, the designers can more rapidly produce more relevant analysis—from days to hours or even minutes.[2] De Kestelier observes that 'just like how the software that we customise sits between hard core engineering tools and fluffy architect tools, I think this is where SMG sits as well—we are all designers as well as technical specialists'.[2]

The SMG develops tools, techniques and workflows using commercial software and by developing its own software. Through the customisation of existing software, the use of open-source

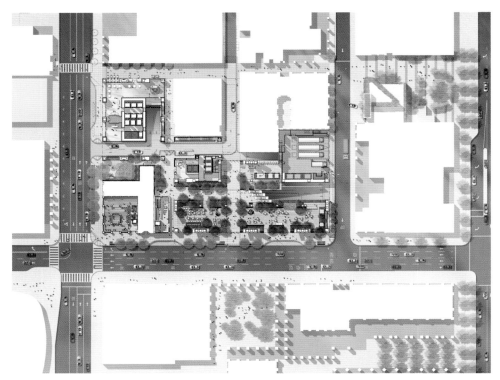

5 Foster + Partners,
Oceanwide Center, San
Francisco, USA
Visualisation of ground floor of
the mixed-use development.

simulation engines and the development of new software, the SMG creates tools for geometry generation; front-end solutions that access existing simulation engines, develop new simulation engines and create customised data visualisation. Interoperability is an important part of the workflows that they develop.

One of the roles of the group is to find better ways of doing standard analysis routines. The group develops workflows using Grasshopper with Honeybee and Ladybug, and then disseminates this knowledge to design teams. In terms of developments in environmental performance, Gallou sees that interoperability is improving, 'designers don't need to export and import into Ecotect as solar analysis tools are available right in Rhino'.[1] The SMG has written a custom tool for MicroStation that implements Radiance, and has created its own wrapper for widely available environmental tools Ladybug and Honeybee called Ladybee. The team is always developing workflows that are more accurate, quicker and more in service of the way the office works architecturally, thereby feeding the Foster + Partners office with better and better tools. For example, solar radiation analysis of a building envelope is an analysis that is done on every project and the SMG helps to give designers the knowledge necessary to do this on their own. The SMG develops tools for design teams to use, and they only get involved themselves in the most complex and more difficult simulation tasks.

DESIGNING THE OCEANWIDE CENTER
The Oceanwide Center is a 215,000 square-metre (2,314,240 square-feet) mixed-use development in San Francisco, USA. Designed in collaboration with Heller Manus Architects, the development comprises two high-rise towers, new public spaces and pedestrian links. The large, urban project takes over seven land parcels between First Street and Mission Street, and consists of a 185-metre (607-foot) tall condominium tower, which will be one of the tallest residential buildings on the West Coast, and a 260-metre (853-foot) tall mixed-use tower, which will include hotel, residential and office space. The residential tower reflects the scale of San Francisco's existing tall buildings, while the taller hotel, residential and office tower rises above it, matching that of the nearby Transamerica Pyramid, which has been the city's tallest structure for many years. The towers have an innovative orthogonal structural system, developed for seismic stability. This structural system enables super-sized office floor plates, which promotes flexibility and the designing of customised spaces.

The SMG was involved extensively in the Oceanwide Center project—from geometry set out to structural design to environmental performance. While Foster + Partners has long used MicroStation as the primary computer-aided design (CAD) software for the office, the SMG and design teams use whatever digital design tools are necessary to best accomplish specific tasks. For the Oceanwide Center, a variety of software packages were used: the main structure and geometry were done using CATIA, the interiors used Revit and the facade was done using

6 Foster + Partners, Oceanwide Center, San Francisco, USA
Visualisation of the spaces and microclimate under the towers.

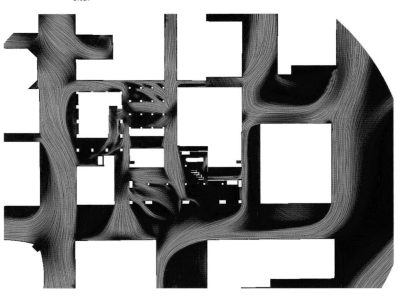

7 Foster + Partners,
Oceanwide Center, San
Francisco, USA
Wind velocity analysis on the
site.

8 Foster + Partners,
Oceanwide Center, San
Francisco, USA
Visualisation of exterior
airflows on the site.

Dynamo. Rhino was the go-to 3D CAD sketching environment.[2] With regard to the industry move to BIM, Gallou notes that 'the industry is pushing for BIM, for Revit, and this is a lot of work for us, you can't draw things that don't exist, and people need to think a little bit harder—you need to use the right tool for the right stage'.[1]

The SMG worked closely with the design team to achieve aspirations in terms of form, detail and performance, but also had to follow the very strict guidelines of the San Francisco planning department. Guidelines stated that new buildings should not block sunlight to any public parks, and so quite early in the design process, the SMG created a software program to rapidly analyse designs. The software discretised the building into a matrix of cells and used a method of tracing rays from the sun to see if the design was blocking sunlight to any parks. This custom tool made use of a commercially available simulation engine but carried out substantial pre-processing of data, which broke down the complex design into something that could be done much more quickly.

EXPERIENCING THE URBAN ROOM

A key part of the design of the Oceanwide Center is at the ground floor, where the building has been 'lifted up' to create a new urban room for the local area that is 'open, accessible and transparent'.[3] This urban room is crossed by pedestrian routes, and through 'bringing together places to live and work with the city's most important transport hub', the project promotes a 'sustainable model of high-density, mixed-use development'.[3] Beyond developing standard digital workflows, the SMG develops customised analysis and design workflows, responding to the specific design aspirations of a project. For the Oceanwide Center project, the idea was to take sunlight incident on the top of the tower and drive it deep down into the city, to the urban room. The design concept was not just about getting enough daylight, but to design a feature that would delight people. Through the use of computational tools, the SMG helps to create interest and delight. Gallou explains that 'for the SMG the analysis is all about the user experience'. The team uses performance simulation to understand the user experience in various ways: light, temperature, the thermal environment, the warming effects of the sun, the light that comes through glass and where it goes, light levels both artificial and natural, glare and acoustics.[1]

DESIGNING HUMAN COMFORT

Over the last 10 years, the SMG has developed expertise in computational fluid dynamics (CFD), which is used to predict wind and airflow, and is therefore useful in the determination of user comfort. For the Oceanwide Center project, a series of CFD simulations were carried out to provide insight into the conditions for users at various places around the tower and also to study the influence of various building shapes on wind distribution. Both CFD and physical wind tunnel testing were done, but CFD offered considerable advantages as it could be completed much faster and

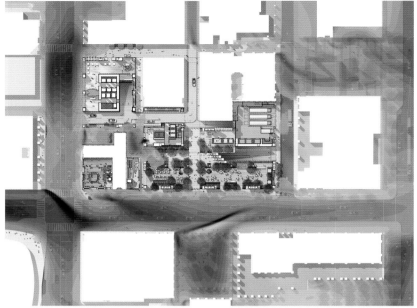

Rain Catch Ratio
200 %

150 %

100 %

50 %

0 %

9 Foster + Partners,
Oceanwide Center, San
Francisco, USA
Study of rain intensity on the
site and wind speed.

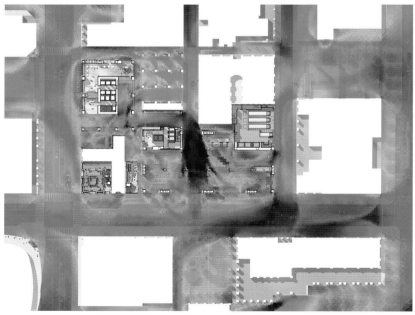

Thermal Comfort
80%

70%

60%

50%

40%

30%

10 Foster + Partners,
Oceanwide Center, San
Francisco, USA
Study of thermal comfort on
the site during occupied hours.

in-house. The SMG ran simulations for 16 wind directions, and this data was combined with weather data to get a statistical analysis of what was going on on the site. The tower was intercepting wind at high level and pushing these winds down to lower levels, causing accelerations in air speed, and so in response the SMG designed a wind canopy, so the wind did not reach the inhabited level.

OPEN-SOURCE SIMULATION

An aspect of human comfort is protection from rain. To simulate this, the SMG used a backbone of open-source CFD code and added rain data. In developing this in-house design tool, the team found relevant research papers, to make sure that they were using the right distribution of droplets for different rain events. To solve the problem, the designers find the right theory and implement it as a digital tool. There is a trend in the work of the SMG towards an increase in the use of open-source software tools, for example Radiance, Daysim and OpenFOAM. De Kestelier has observed that 'in the last five years people are using more open-source code … not just in architecture but also in other industries'.[2] Open-source software enables the team to access the source code, so that they can customise the tool to meet their needs. An in-depth understanding of how the software is working is crucial, so that it can be customised to carry out specific analysis tasks. As Foster + Partners associate partner Stefano Capra explains, 'the number one criterion in software we select is that we are able to get enough information about it, that we can really understand how it works and then we can gain the control we need over it'.[2] Philip Robinson, the SMG team's acoustic specialist, explains that it is substantially about workflows: 'the software may be internally doing what we want but we can't access it and so we have to be able to break it apart to be able to get the information we want out of what the software is doing'.[2] Additionally, the SMG has the in-house computational capacity that enables the team to run any simulation without the need to go to an external company.

MIDDLE GROUND TOOLS

The SMG aims to develop design tools that exist in the middle ground between sketchy architecture tools and robust but inflexible engineering tools. The team has found that the software architects use to compute the radiant environment is generally fairly inaccurate, and because alternatives from other industries such as engineering are very heavy to run, they aim to develop tools that predict performance with a level of confidence that is reasonable and yet still run fairly fast. For the urban room, the design aspiration was to make sure that the space was more comfortable than that offered by the competitors. So, using the Universal Thermal Climate Index (UTCI) metric, the team simulated the public space along with similar spaces in the surrounding area for percentages of the year that are comfortable. De Kestelier explains that 'we find ourselves in a middle ground, creating tools related to design but also with really accurate analysis, and that, from a software perspective, doesn't exist, and this is where we are trying to build our expertise'.[2]

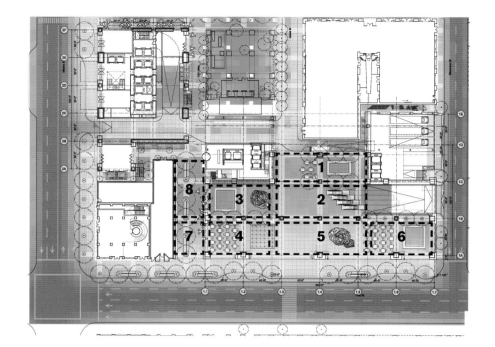

Zone	SPL (dBA)	AVG
1	63	
2	67	
3	65	
4	70	
5	72	
6	68	
7	68	
8	60	

Sound Pressure Level (dBA)
Average

40   50   60   70   80

THE SOUND OF SAN FRANCISCO

For the Oceanwide Center, the SMG conducted studies on how noise would affect the public open-air spaces at the base of the tower, noise incident on the facade, noise transmission through natural ventilation openings and noise from wind passing over facade elements, and also undertook qualitative studies of the urban soundscape. While interior acoustic performance considerations were limited to achieving appropriate noise levels for office uses, further investigations will be undertaken at later stages. The acoustic analysis was largely done with a plug-in to Rhino called Pachyderm, an open-source software tool that computes performance using ray-tracing algorithms. Robinson, the team's acoustic expert, has found importing geometry from CAD to commercially available acoustic simulation software to be onerous. By using Pachyderm in Rhino, he is able to both design and simulate using the same software, and therefore does not have to bother with translation. The SMG also carried out qualitative soundscape analysis, recording sounds all over London in different types of environments that the designers were familiar with, and then presented them in a way that allowed architects to determine what soundscapes they were trying to achieve. At the same time, they took a collection of recordings of the signature elements of San Francisco, birds singing, types of traffic, fountains, street musicians, the elements that make the city unique, and

11 Foster + Partners, Oceanwide Center, San Francisco, USA
Study of sound pressure and noise levels around the tower. The noise propagation across the site was simulated, and the results were used to inform decisions about where to place program elements.

through comparing the different sounds of the city, the design team could better define the soundscape that they aspired to create.

DESIGNING EXPERIENCE

The architects at Foster + Partners SMG see themselves and the tools they are creating as lying in a 'middle ground' between design and engineering. With a focus on both geometry generation and environmental performance, the group works on projects from conceptual design to fabrication and the study of buildings in use. Members of the group have advanced degrees in architecture and engineering, and regularly disseminate their research to communities such as Smartgeometry. The group's work is project-focused and they have little allegiance to any particular software or approach—they will use whatever tools are needed to solve the problem at hand. Commercially available software, open-source code and bespoke software solutions are often combined together in creative new design workflows that enable design teams to realise the office's innovative and sustainable architecture. Things are changing for architects and for the SMG—there is an increased focus on the issue of user experience: simulation tools are being applied more and more to understand how users will feel in buildings. Gallou speculates that 'it is similar to when you first study architecture, you don't have any experience when you design, of what it is like to be in a space. Whereas an experienced architect has an understanding of how things will perform … simulation gives young architects a tool to understand how the environment will work inside the building. These simulation tools let them understand how the light comes in'.[1] As computational tools for environmental design mature, the potentials of what teams like the SMG can do with them becomes much greater. De Kestelier concludes that 'the next step is to design buildings based on the user experience, to design buildings that feel great, that are amazing, and that just work. Because the tools are better, we can do what architects did before by intuition and experience, to determine what it is that you want to feel, design the surfaces around that, and give the user the experience they expect'.[1]

REFERENCES

1. Author interview with Xavier De Kestelier and Irene Gallou, in Foster + Partners Specialist Modelling Group (SMG), December 2015.
2. Author interview with Foster + Partners SMG team: Xavier De Kestelier, Stefano Capra, James Sherman and Philip Robinson, August 2016.
3. 'Foster + Partners website', online at www.fosterandpartners.com (accessed 15 August 2016).

IMAGES

All courtesy of Foster + Partners

8. MAXIMISING IMPACT THROUGH PERFORMANCE SIMULATION:

THE WORK OF TRANSSOLAR KLIMAENGINEERING

TERRI PETERS

Transsolar KlimaEngineering's approach to sustainable buildings is informed by its deep expertise in engineering principles, building physics and thermodynamics. Experience enables it to tune its workflows to simulate, measure and model complex project-specific parameters, using advanced simulation tools. Founded in 1992, the company of about 50 engineers has offices in Stuttgart, Munich, New York and Paris. The office pioneered the concept of 'klimaengineering', which describes its approach to climate-responsive design that takes advantage of the specific local climate and surroundings to maximise user comfort and passive strategies.[1] Transsolar is a world leader in environmental consulting for building design, typically collaborating with a design team from the early stages of a project to help conceptualise the approach to the environment, and identify effective techniques to achieve high performance goals. Transsolar works with award-winning international architects, including Gehry Partners, SANAA, Foster + Partners, MASS Design Group and Herzog & de Meuron.

1 Behnisch Architekten, John and Frances Angelos Law Center, University of Baltimore, USA, 2013
Daylight enters the atrium through the north- and south-facing facades, where it can penetrate into interior spaces at all levels, rather than relying on overhead daylight, which does not reach lower levels.

The office has been part of a research consortium that develops and sells TRaNsient SYstems Simulation program (TRNSYS) energy simulation software since the 1970s.[2] TRNSYS is a completely modular simulation software tool that is more in-depth and detailed than many energy simulation programs. The office has in-house researchers dedicated to updating and programming using TRNSYS. It is flexible and accurate, and Transsolar has been instrumental in its development; in fact, the office's name comes from the tool.[3] Transsolar 'computes the environment' in a variety of ways, with tools and approaches that differ from project to project, working from first principles. The office uses building performance simulation and computation to maximise locally specific site conditions and to enable the adoption of passive strategies, therefore minimising required energy use. Its projects often incorporate on-site energy generation, use ecological approaches and test new technologies with the aim of creating more sustainable architecture.

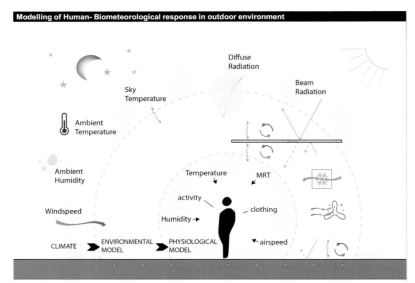

Modelling of Human- Biometeorological response in outdoor environment

2 Breathe.Austria, Austrian Pavilion at Milan Expo in 2015, a collaborative project by team.breathe.austria
This diagram shows the structure of the modelling of human-biometeorological response to the outdoor environment.

COMFORTABLE CLOUDSCAPES

Transsolar has experience in simulating extreme environments at a range of scales. Recent projects include calculating and predicting outdoor comfort and performance at the urban scale, in the Masdar City masterplan and the Al Fayah Park, both in Abu Dhabi.[4] The office also has a portfolio of smaller scale, responsive and dynamic installations for temporary pavilions. For example, it has been experimenting with creating indoor cloud environments from first principles for several years. Transsolar partner Thomas Auer explains, 'for us it is the visualisation of climate engineering'.[5] The 'cloudscapes' involve the specification of particular compositions of air and humidity. These have been installed in various contexts, with iterations at the Venice Biennale in 2010 and at the Museum of Contemporary Art in Tokyo in 2013 with Tetsuo Kondo, both featuring staircases that have encouraged visitors to experience the environment by walking through it. Other related temporary installations have included the 'Augmented Atmospheres' installation at the Venice Biennale in 2014 with Diller Scofidio + Renfro. This project also involved designing an outdoor environment, in this case the design of a small park with concrete benches and surfaces that modified the experience of temperature, humidity, sunlight and sound.

HIGH COMFORT, LOW IMPACT: BREATHE.AUSTRIA

Working from first principles was central to the success of the Breathe.Austria pavilion at Milan Expo in 2015, which aimed to create the feeling of a cool Austrian forest in the hot Milan summer. Transsolar tested the potentials of using elevated air speeds and a bespoke dry mist technology system to achieve outdoor comfort without mechanical cooling. Constructed on an old industrial site, a new environment was planted with well-watered vegetation, designed to reduce ambient air and radiant temperatures. This kept the mean radiant temperatures significantly lower, in comparison to using hard surfaces, thus reducing the urban heat island (UHI) effect using evapotranspiration.[6] Building on its experience of developing this technology in a project in Singapore in 2014, Transsolar was able to optimise the system for this climate, using it to add moisture to the air without making people feel wet, and silencing the fans so as not to distract from the experience.[7]

After reducing the need for energy use on site as much as possible, the photovoltaic system on the roof provided the required electricity on site. During the design process, Transsolar created a dynamic simulation model to predict all relevant environmental parameters, including evapotranspiration, estimated mean radiant temperatures considering the effects of the vegetation, and the impacts of adiabatic cooling to understand the impact on comfort levels. The model was verified against detailed modelling with the energy modelling software tool TRNSYS and compared to on-site measurements carried out by the team.[6] The project won several design awards, including the EXPO Sustainability Award, and had more than 2.2 million visitors.[7]

EXTREME CLIMATE STRATEGIES: MANITOBA HYDRO

Transsolar worked on the Manitoba Hydro building, designed by architects Kuwabara Payne McKenna Blumberg, and located in Winnipeg, which is not only one of the coldest cities in the world, but also one of Canada's sunniest and most humid cities. The completion of this project in 2009 established an international quality benchmark for sustainable cold-climate design. This pioneering building has been widely published due to the 'quantum leap in energy efficiency and carbon emissions reduction'[8] and the successful integrated design process used by the design team that ensured aesthetics, sustainable design and energy performance worked together.[9] As with all of its projects, Transsolar began by maximising the potentials for passive systems and seeing where the potentials on site could offer benefits for the project. The building form has two towers that open up the south side of the building to form the 'lungs'

3 Breathe.Austria, Austrian Pavilion at Milan Expo in 2015, a collaborative project by team.breathe.austria
Transsolar conducted minute-by-minute on-site measurements of the radiant environment temperature to understand how people's experience of the ground-level microclimate changed as they moved through the shaded areas.

4 KPMB Architects, Smith Carter Architects and Prairie Architects, Manitoba Hydro Downtown Office, Winnipeg, Manitoba, Canada, 2009 Located in an extreme climate and featuring many passive and active strategies, such as operable windows as part of a natural ventilation strategy, and high ceilings, the Manitoba Hydro offices feature a glazed double skin facade that allows natural daylighting.

of the building, the stacked atria that act as solar collectors combined with a solar chimney to harness the site's strong southerly winds and maximum daylight. Transsolar used its building simulation tools and computational analyses workflows to evaluate each of these steps, supporting the integrated design process, and as a result this project remains one of the best-performing buildings in Canada, and an architectural landmark. In 2012, it was certified LEED Platinum and the client tracked the energy usage for two years, and found that while conventional office towers use about 300kWh per square metre, this building used under 85kWh per square metre, an estimated energy savings of more than $500,000 annually.[10] Usually, LEED buildings have a low window-to-wall ratio, and this building took an entirely different approach, with high levels of glazing and interior comfort.

INTERIOR COMFORT: BALTIMORE LAW CENTER

The John and Frances Angelos Law Center at the University of Baltimore was designed by Behnisch Architekten in 2013. On a tight urban site, the three main programmatic elements are the classrooms and offices, the legal clinic and the law library. Each one is expressed on the building's facade in the form of a distinct L-shaped, interlocking volume. A narrow atrium rises through the building, connecting all spaces, bringing in daylight and enabling air to circulate through the building. The building achieves generous daylighting in all inhabited spaces, minimal glare and overheating from the facade, and natural airflow through cross ventilation. The offices, teaching areas and atrium all have operable windows, so people can adjust their environment to suit their comfort levels. Transsolar carried out a range of environmental simulations, specifically relating to airflow, daylighting and energy performance, using digital tools to obtain feedback into the building design process, and to predict how the building would perform in all seasons. Transsolar conducted energy simulations using TRNSYS software, performed

5 KPMB Architects, Smith Carter Architects and Prairie Architects, Manitoba Hydro Downtown Office, Winnipeg, Manitoba, Canada, 2009
A drawing of the seasonal climate concept.

6 Behnisch Architekten, John and Frances Angelos Law Center, University of Baltimore, USA, 2013
This analysis of atrium comfort in cooling mode by Transsolar shows a section through the building, illustrating the contours of air temperature and operative temperature.

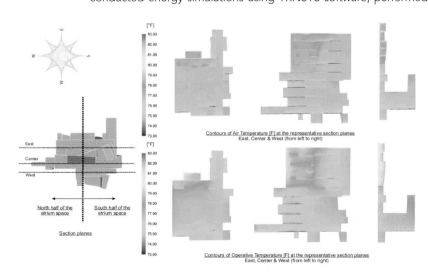

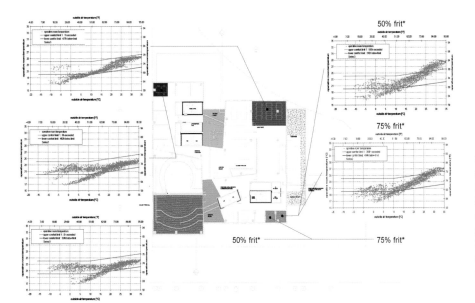

7 Behnisch Architekten, John and Frances Angelos Law Center, University of Baltimore, USA, 2013
Solar-tuning study by Transsolar, showing the impacts of the percentage of frit pattern, filtering light into the spaces relative to the outside air temperature and the operative room temperature.

8 Behnisch Architekten, John and Frances Angelos Law Center, University of Baltimore, USA, 2013
Interior lighting studies at schematic design stage show a diffuse sky for two options of library floor plate. This study explores the impact on the daylight entering the building at various heights.

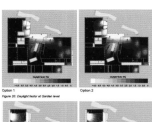

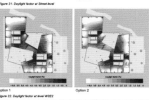
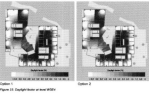
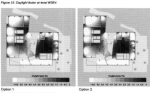

9 Herzog & de Meuron, Ricola Herb Centre, Laufen, Switzerland, 2014
An exterior photograph of the rammed earth building facade.

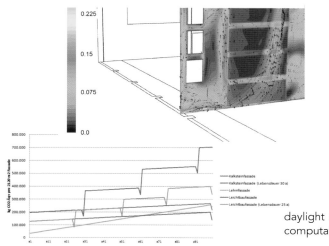

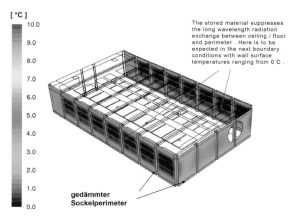

The stored material suppresses the long wavelength radiation exchange between ceiling / floor and perimeter . Here is to be expected in the next boundary conditions with wall surface temperatures ranging from 0 C .

gedämmter
Sockelperimeter

10 Herzog & de Meuron,
Ricola Herb Centre, Laufen,
Switzerland, 2014
Analysis diagrams show the
thermal mass of the facades
and the impact on global
warming potential.

daylight simulations using Radiance, and analysis of airflow and computational fluid dynamics (CFD) using Fluent.

MATERIAL AND LIFE CYCLE: RICOLA HERB CENTRE

An example of Transsolar's approach to material and life-cycle design is the Ricola Herb Centre in Laufen, Switzerland, designed by Herzog & de Meuron in 2014. The building is used to store and process herbs used as food additives, so the interior temperature and humidity need to meet unusually stringent requirements. The building is constructed of rammed earth, with a self-supporting facade, using a damp mixture of compacted sand, gravel and clay from local quarries and mines. The choice of materials allows the building to achieve a high level of insulation and a cool internal environment, lowering the need for mechanical cooling. Transsolar calculated the annual energy demand for heating, cooling and dehumidification, using the dynamic simulation tool TRNSYS and heat and moisture simulation tool WUFI Plus. Those values were included in the life-cycle impact assessment (LCIA) carried out using life-cycle assessment software GaBi, developed by sustainability consultant PE International (now known as thinkstep), which used an assumed building life period of 100 years.[11] The LCIA analysed the typical parameters of global warming potential (GWP), ozone depletion potential (ODP), acidification potential (AP), eutrophication potential (EP), summer smog potential (POCP), abiotic consumption of resources (fossil) and the abiotic consumption of resources (elemental). Three different materials were analysed in the LCIA, including rammed earth, lime sand and brick, and a lightweight sandwich panel. The rammed earth facade was chosen in part because it was showing the lowest global warming potential of the three options.[11]

PASSIVE AND ACTIVE SYSTEMS: SCHOOL DESIGN

Transsolar has collaborated on a number of naturally ventilated school projects that have little or no mechanical systems. The Lycée Français Charles de Gaulle was designed by Ateliers Lion in Damascus, Syria, in 2008. Despite the dry desert climate, the intention was to minimise the need for mechanical cooling, and Transsolar used removable shades, operable windows and the building form to create indoor comfort. The architecture and climatic

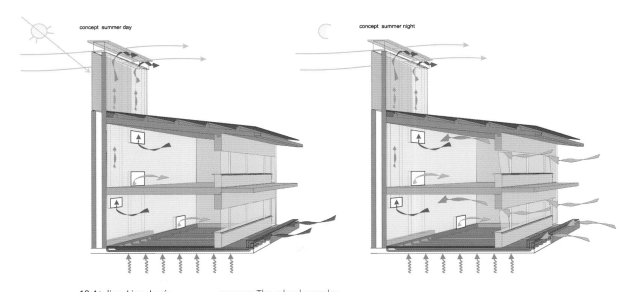

concept summer day

concept summer night

12 Ateliers Lion, Lycée Français Charles de Gaulle in Damascus, Syria, 2008
Diagrams show natural ventilation and cooling during summer. The school complex is a series of small buildings with courtyards, each with two levels of classrooms and a solar chimney.

11 Ateliers Lion, Lycée
Français Charles de Gaulle in
Damascus, Syria, 2008
Attuned to the local dry desert
climate, the school relies on
passive design strategies to
achieve the required comfort
levels. The design optimised
classroom ventilation using
passive strategies and
removable shading devices,
and created a microclimate
in the courtyards that can be
used by students and teachers.

approaches work together, pairing small-scale classrooms with outdoor courtyards and patios that create comfortable microclimates.

Another school project, the Zollverein School of Management and Design designed by SANAA, was completed in 2006 in Essen, Germany. This distinctive building is designed as a simple concrete cube with varied window openings. Transsolar's challenge was to enable the facade to be extremely thin, uninsulated concrete yet to achieve high interior comfort. Transsolar simulated and prototyped a new 'active insulation' approach[12], which involved running thin plastic water pipes within the concrete facade, providing radiant heat. This unique approach came about due to local site resources, namely the discovery that it would be possible to take advantage of the waste water from a local mining facility as a CO_2-free energy source. Even though this system was far from efficient—Transsolar's simulation and modelling took into account the fact that the active insulation system loses about 80 per cent of its heat because the walls are uninsulated—since the energy source was free, they didn't worry about the 'waste' and were able to still meet inner surface temperatures of 18 degrees celsius for a comfortable interior environment. This project illustrates Transsolar's locally specific approach to sustainable architecture, which starts by making the most of the site and its resources, and then endeavours to take advantage of new and untested ways of approaching energy and life cycle.

TECHNOLOGY AS AN ALLY FOR GOOD DESIGN

Transsolar is continuing to work in multiple scales. The office exhibited an installation at the 2016 Venice Biennale with Anja Thierfelder, called 'Lightscapes', which involves manipulating rays of light using humidity, temperature, stratification and air movement. In the catalogue for the Biennale, curator Alejandro Aravena wrote: 'Transsolar has put design and precise engineering at the service of common sense, showing that it is able to solve the most complex problems. In addition, Transsolar has used technology to verify and strengthen local knowledge, turning it into a powerful ally that values the identity of a specific building, neighbourhood, or a city'.[13] Transsolar's work shows a positive new direction for collaborative workflows for environmental design and it is taking a strong leadership role with respect to performance-based design and computing the environment.

The success of Transsolar's benchmark projects is not a result of its proficiency with simulation tools or new digital workflows; in fact, when discussing technical matters, Transsolar's Thomas Auer prefers to talk about the underlying building physics and potentials for impact on people's experience of the building, rather than details of calculation and simulation.[12] Transsolar's first principles approach and the office's open-minded focus on site-specific opportunities gives its architects a competitive advantage, not only in terms of climate engineering but also in terms of getting along with other members of the design team and successfully communicating its environmental philosophy. The office's collaborative, technically rigorous and flexible approach has allowed for gradients in

13 SANAA and Heinrich Böll Architekt,
Zollverein School of Management and
Design, Essen, Germany, 2006
Interior view of facade with closed interior
solar and glare protection curtain, highly
reflective towards the outside and with a
low-e coating towards the space to minimise
heat radiation from the hot curtain but reflect
the cold activated ceiling.

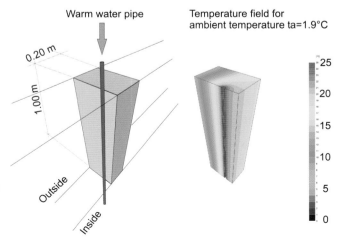

Warm water pipe

Temperature field for
ambient temperature ta=1.9°C

0.20 m

1.00 m

Outside

Inside

25

20

15

10

5

0

14 SANAA and Heinrich Böll
Architekt, Zollverein School
of Management and Design,
Essen, Germany, 2006
A three-dimensional evaluation
of the heat fluxes in the active
insulated wall determined
spacing and position of the
pipes.

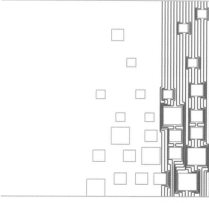

East elevation SI-200

15 SANAA and Heinrich Böll Architekt, Zollverein School of Management and Design, Essen, Germany, 2006
East elevation showing the placement of windows in the concrete facade in relation to the pipe layout. The pipes carry warm water from a depth of 1,000 metres (3,280 feet)

performance and experience, and for extending and reinforcing the architectural intentions of an environment.

REFERENCES
1. Anja Thierfelder (ed), *Transsolar Climate Engineering*, Birkhäuser (Basel), 2004.
2. 'TRNSYS Transient System Simulation Tool', online at http://www.trnsys.com (accessed 20 November 2016).
3. Monika Lauster, Anna Lermer and Joshua Monk Vanwyck (eds), *Connect ideas—Maximize Impact: Transsolar KlimaEngineering*, fmo publishers (Stuttgart), 2014.
4. A lecture by Matthias Schuler, 'On Atmospheres: Spaces of Embodiment' conference, Harvard Graduate School of Design, USA, 5 February 2016.
5. A lecture by Thomas Auer, 'Making Climate Performative Places' conference, Lund University, Sweden, 21 September 2015.
6. Wolfgang Kessling, Martin Engelhardt and Alexander Greising, 'The Expo 2015 Pavilion: Breathe.Austria Outdoor Comfort in the City', a poster presented during the 'International Conference on Passive and Low Energy Architecture (PLEA)' 2015, Bologna, Italy, 9–11 September 2015.
7. 'terrain architects', online at http://terrain.de/awarded-airship-breathe-austria-summer-breathe (accessed 20 November 2016).
8. Matthias Schuler and Anja Thierfelder, 'In Situ: Site Specificity in Sustainable Architecture', in *Harvard Design Magazine*, vol 30, spring–summer 2009, pp 50–59.
9. Kiel Moe, *Integrated Design in Contemporary Architecture*, Princeton Architectural Press (New York), 2008, pp 20–23.
10. Canadian Architect, 'Manitoba Hydro Place Sets New Record with LEED Platinum', *Canadian Architect,* 25 May 2012, online at https://www.canadianarchitect.com/architecture/manitoba-hydro-place-sets-new-record-with-leed-platinum/1001413553 (accessed 20 November 2016).
11. Transsolar, 'Life Cycle Impact Assessment for Transsolar's first rammed earth building', in *Green & Sexy* blog, 15 January 2014, online at http://blog.transsolar.com/post/73398445510/life-cycle-impact-assessment-for-transsolars (accessed 20 November 2016).
12. Author interviews with Thomas Auer, 1 April 2016 and 12 July 2016.
13. Alejandro Aravena, *Reporting from the Front: 15th International Architecture Exhibition*, Marsilio (Venice), 2016, p 232.

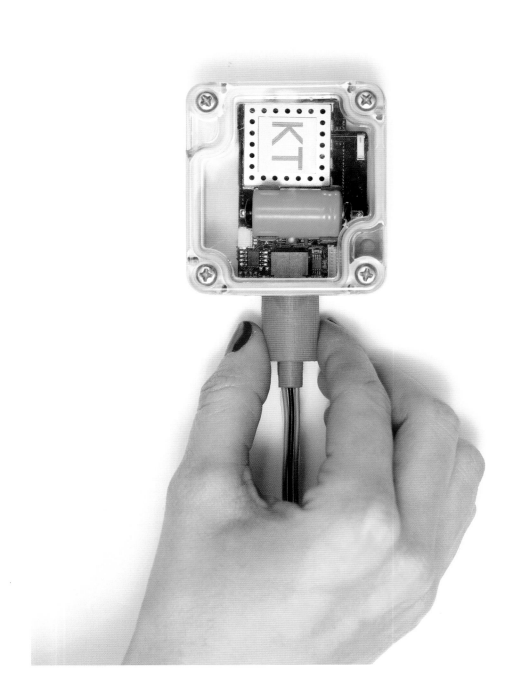

9. DESIGNERS NEED FEEDBACK:

RESEARCH AND PRACTICE BY KIERANTIMBERLAKE

TERRI PETERS

The question mark thrives in the mode 'searching and searching again'.
—Billie Faircloth[1]

KieranTimberlake has a creative problem-solving approach to design and its firm is a leader in practice-based research and construction innovation.[2] The architects are known for their award-winning sustainable buildings, such as the LEED Platinum Keeling Apartments, their transformation of Dilworth Park, and ongoing building research projects including low-cost housing in India. Increasingly, the firm is being recognised for its non–building-specific innovations in technology development, which support sustainable architecture, including digitals tools that provide early-stage design feedback such as Tally, a life-cycle analysis app, developed in collaboration with Autodesk and thinkstep. The architects have also collaborated to develop custom hardware for designers, in particular the Pointelist sensor networks. Research, building construction and design process refinement are all parts of their work as designers, with overlapping approaches and resources simultaneously working to address these challenges to support sustainable architecture. Their research approach is driven by the desire to improve the 'collective intelligence' of the building industry. They pursue this not only through their many planning and architecture projects, but also by redesigning systems of design using computational approaches.

TRANSDISCIPLINARY PRACTICE

Stephen Kieran and James Timberlake founded the 130-person office in 1984 in Philadelphia, USA. Early adopters of building information modelling (BIM), the office has incorporated building simulation and environmental modelling in all areas of their work, at all scales.[2] The office's applied research approach involves digital and physical testing, using predictive digital modelling, as well as full-scale prototyping in its on-site workshop. Research-driven projects such as the pioneering design-for-disassembly Loblolly House (2006) and the fully recyclable Cellophane House (2008) are important architectural reference points in applied research in practice.[3] Over the past decade, KieranTimberlake's in-house research group has expanded into a transdisciplinary team of designers, scientists and other experts, working in diverse fields such as environmental management, chemical physics, materials science and architecture. Transdisciplinary means that the designers not only work together with experts from different disciplines to address a given problem (often called multidisciplinary or interdisciplinary), but that they work in integrated teams to come up with the research questions together and to solve them in a

1 KieranTimberlake, Generation 7 prototype, wireless sensor network, 2012
The office has developed, tested, refined and prototyped wireless sensor networks in an iterative process over the past six years. In 2016, the most recent version was branded as Pointelist and the kits are currently undergoing beta testing.

TIME

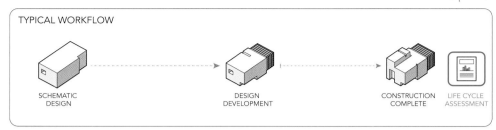

TYPICAL WORKFLOW

SCHEMATIC
DESIGN → DESIGN
DEVELOPMENT → CONSTRUCTION
COMPLETE   LIFE CYCLE
ASSESSMENT

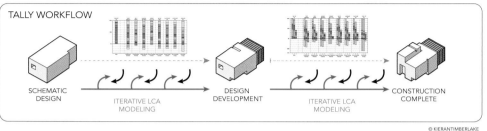

TALLY WORKFLOW

SCHEMATIC
DESIGN → *ITERATIVE LCA
MODELING* → DESIGN
DEVELOPMENT → *ITERATIVE LCA
MODELING* → CONSTRUCTION
COMPLETE

© KIERANTIMBERLAKE

2 KieranTimberlake, iterative life-cycle analysis (LCA) workflows using Tally, 2013 Tally enables early-stage design feedback directly through Autodesk Revit, allowing designers to compare design options and benchmark environmental impacts, based on material selections as part of an iterative design process.

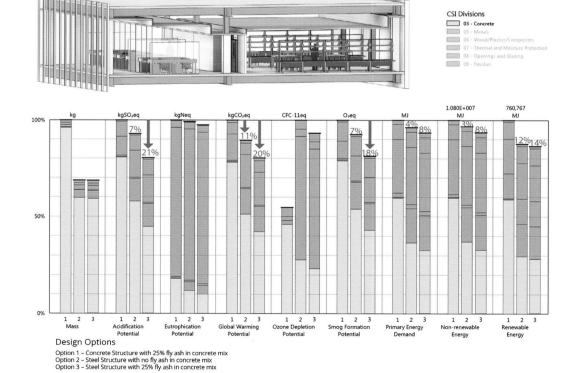

CSI Divisions
- 03 - Concrete
- 05 - Metals
- 06 - Wood/Plastics/Composites
- 07 - Thermal and Moisture Protection
- 08 - Openings and Glazing
- 09 - Finishes

Design Options
Option 1 – Concrete Structure with 25% fly ash in concrete mix
Option 2 – Steel Structure with no fly ash in concrete mix
Option 3 – Steel Structure with 25% fly ash in concrete mix

team. In the current project for the US Embassy in London, they have used a transdisciplinary approach in the facade design, which has involved multiple experts and disciplines. They have developed a custom multi-layered laminate glazed panel system with an ETFE (ethylene tetrafluoroethylene) outer screen. This building envelope gathers solar energy and mitigates wind downdraughts. The team at KieranTimberlake has found that digital tools have aided its design process, and enabled more efficient and effective collaboration during the design process.

DESIGNERS NEED FEEDBACK: INTRODUCING TALLY

The office has been intrigued by the potentials of life-cycle analysis for several years, searching for a tool to gain early-stage feedback about the relative sustainability of material choices and building systems in their designs. This has led to a collaboration with the software company Autodesk and the sustainability software and consulting company thinkstep (formerly PE International), for the production of Tally, a new digital tool that calculates life-cycle and material options during the design process within BIM software Revit.[4] It is now available on the Autodesk website and its unique early-stage applicability and easy-to-use interface make it ideal for architects who want to compare options, using the tool as a compass rather than an answer. It works by using life-cycle inventory (LCI) data, a database that is a mix of custom data developed by thinkstep and KieranTimberlake, and life-cycle assessment data using GaBi. The interface with Revit is key, because it allows architects to use it easily and quickly during the design process, without having to add too much extra input or redraw the building.

In 2016, Tally won one of *Architect* magazine's R+D Awards. One award juror called it 'absolutely necessary for any kind of building design. Finally: a method of life-cycle assessment that is user-friendly'.[5] KieranTimberlake's main concern is that life-cycle analysis should be carried out continuously throughout the design process, not at the end when main choices are already made. The assumption is that an information gap exists in the design process: if designers know more, they will make better and more effective choices. But building performance and its relation to the design process is complex. The 'performance gap' between design use and measured use depends on also knowing more detail about what the building is made of, where the components have come from, the level of workmanship in construction, and detail of the people in the buildings, including their behaviour, expectations and plans to use the building. KieranTimberlake's approach is to gather data in multiple ways, and at various scales, and this 'questioning' and curiosity about the specifics of site and environment has led to experiments with real-time environmental data in its wireless sensor networks research.

SENSORED ENVIRONMENTS

The quest to determine how buildings perform in use and how people behave in buildings is at the heart of sustainable design. KieranTimberlake has pioneered the development and

3 KieranTimberlake, comparison of structural systems using Tally, Brown University School of Engineering, Providence, Rhode Island, USA, 2013 Tally was used in this project to enable the designer to compare options based on embodied environmental impact. Using the material values and quantities from the Revit model, this example shows the impacts of two different design options for structural steel systems.

4 KieranTimberlake, photograph and visualisation of daylight in KieranTimberlake studio, 2015
This visualisation of different environmental data sources shows the daylight in the office interior, taking into account the time of day, glass transparency and furniture.

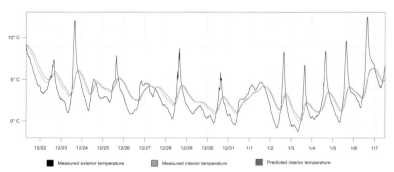

■ Measured exterior temperature   ■ Measured interior temperature   ■ Predicted interior temperature

5 KieranTimberlake, real-time environmental data collection in the KieranTimberlake studio, 2013
Before moving into its new offices, KieranTimberlake embedded a network of sensor prototypes into the walls to collect real-time, local data about temperature and humidity. The digital interface allows this data to be monitored and tracked off site. The sensor data informed its renovation.

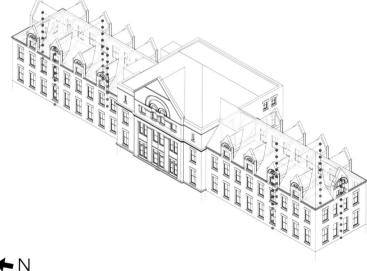

←N

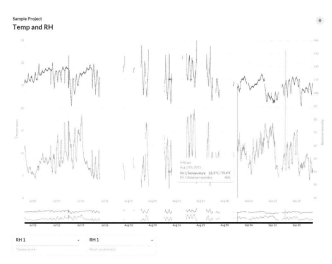

Sample Project
Temp and RH

RH 1   -   RH 1   -

6 KieranTimberlake, Pointelist web interface for displaying sensor network data, 2016
Pointelist has a fully developed application program interface (API) and this allows users to interact with the data in various ways and use other pieces of software for visualisation.

7 KieranTimberlake, location of 150 sensors in Richardson Memorial Hall, Tulane University, Louisiana, USA, 2013
In advance of the renovation of Tulane University's School of Architecture building, KieranTimberlake installed temperature and humidity sensors in the building in a grid, horizontally and vertically, to accurately determine how the building performed over time. This data was used to do specific mean radiant temperature calculations and informed decisions about how to best achieve interior comfort.

deployment of high-density, low-cost sensor networks that offer real-time feedback of environmental conditions on a site. Paired with other environmental standards and data sets, it offers designers the possibility of knowing the particular thermal conditions on their sites. After tests with commercially available, off-the-shelf sensors, beginning in 2007 at Loblolly House, the firm developed its own wireless sensor networks. The designers tested these systems in two major installations in 2013, including the renovation of building 661 at the Consortium for Building Energy Innovation at the Philadelphia Navy Yard.[6] They used their own offices in a former bottling facility in the Northern Liberties district in Philadelphia as a test bed in 2014, installing 300 temperature and humidity sensors in the facades, roof, interiors and floors before they moved in. They aimed to harvest fine-grained environmental data to identify locally specific design solutions for increasing comfort and reducing mechanical systems.

By bringing together multiple sources—their experienced observations on the site, the outputs of the real-time sensor data and the government-issued weather data from the site—they were able to learn about how the building's performance varied around the building and over time. This information informed their renovation of the space, and various studies including interior daylight and airflow analysis. Based on the feedback, they decided not to use mechanical cooling, and rely on using desk fans and operable windows, and to monitor the environment using the sensors. In addition, the team gathered weekly survey data from staff about comfort levels and satisfaction with their work environments, sending emails to staff about options for keeping comfortable in the office in relation to outdoor conditions.[6]
 This qualitative data produced another layer of data about the environment, and it was useful for making decisions about the building and understanding its performance. The environmental performance of the office is continually being tracked and monitored, and this means that it is being updated and adjusted, creating an ongoing model for analysing the environment.

8 KieranTimberlake,
personal weather station at
KieranTimberlake studio, 2015
In 2015–16, KieranTimberlake
installed 10 custom weather
stations on project sites to
create site-specific data to
augment standard weather
files for use in energy and
climate simulations in the
design process.

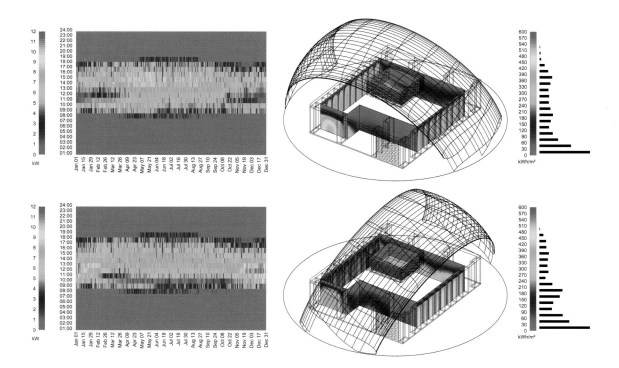

At Tulane University in 2013, they installed a network of 150 sensors in the existing School of Architecture building, to understand mean radiant temperature across the facades. Using this data, they designed a renovation and addition with the goal of achieving maximum comfort using minimal energy. The team was surprised to find that in the winter, there was significant temperature stratification and the mean radiant temperature results were inconsistent throughout the building, whereas in the summer the interiors were relatively comfortable and consistent.[7] This data was plotted in a psychrometric chart, compared with other data, and considered in relation to the existing forced air system, which appeared to adequately achieve required comfort levels in the summer. The sensor data enabled them to predict areas of higher interior comfort and to inform systems sizing and design. Test cases such as this have proven to the team that sensor networks can offer useful data in the design process, and the team is planning further installations in other projects to be able to predict performance and tune the architecture to the local environment.

POINTELIST AND PERSONAL WEATHER STATIONS

In summer 2016, the wireless sensor network research was branded as Pointelist, and it offered free kits to beta testers.[8] The hardware and software can be integrated with a web app, and users can export .csv files to use the data elsewhere. It has an open .api file extension, making it suitable for users to adapt to their own needs and workflows. Pointelist enables the collection of real-time temperature and humidity data, sending environmental data over Wi-Fi in five-minute intervals.

In an article published in the *Journal of Architectural Education*, entitled 'Pardon me—May I Borrow your Umbrella', KieranTimberlake partner Billie Faircloth argued that knowledge of the environment should not be 'solely based on synthesis of data collected by a device—a weather station, temperature sensor or suite of sensors. Nor is it one solely based on a methodology which compresses many years of weather data into one "typical" annual data set'.[9] Instead she argues that we must combine this knowledge, the numerical values collected from the environment of conditions such as 'irradiance, sky cover, temperature, relative humidity, precipitation, wind speed and wind direction—are a proxy for our lived-out bodily experiences of the environment'.[9]

Typically, designers inform their digital models with precise location data of the site but can only offer approximations of weather and climate data. This is because the industry standard is that of government-provided TMY (typical meteorological year) weather files, which are used by EnergyPlus and eQuest for energy modelling. KieranTimberlake uses weather files for many kinds of environmental assessments and it finds that standard TMY files are often not accurate enough. These files are essential for thermal comfort and microclimate assessments, and to understand vegetation types and corroborate certain regional trends, such as fog formation or urban heat islands (UHI) on a site. TMY weather files are derived from 30 years of average data, and are usually

9 KieranTimberlake, proof-of-concept temperature prediction application, 2012
To visualise weather data in a user-friendly way, KieranTimberlake developed a smartphone app to collect and compare historic, site-specific weather data with real-time data to be able to predict what would happen in the future on the site. This proof-of concept research project enabled users to utilise Wi-Fi access to search sortable, accurate, real-time and aggregated weather information.

10 KieranTimberlake, KT Solar Modeler tool, 2013
A Revit plug-in was developed and used by project teams at KieranTimberlake to map cumulative isolation and allow a graphic representation of the greatest heat gains. It was designed to integrate typical meteorological year (TMY) data with modelled building geometry. The tool was designed to aid the design process and analysis steps are intentionally not segregated from the digital design environment.

based on weather stations located at airports. Often a site's environmental conditions will be impacted by unusual topography or microclimatic conditions, but the idea is that the airport data will still have value and offer a guide. For more targeted querying, the firm deploys weather stations or local temperature and humidity sensors to collect information about aspects such as local material types and shading conditions to enable modelling at a higher resolution. This gives more certainty as to the specific microclimate of the site as design input. These locally specific inputs become a part of the model, and a part of the way in which the designers define, and design for, energy, vegetation, outdoor thermal comfort and other environmental parameters.

KieranTimberlake is able to create its own custom weather files, and combine the real-time sensor network data with weather station data. Over the past year, the office has installed 10 low-cost custom weather stations, known as personal weather stations (PWS), on sites for clients, and it has found that there is a growing market in this area.[10] The designers find that the data does vary from site to site, even within a neighbourhood. For example, they often compare the data from their roof and another station, which they have installed for a client two blocks away, and find they are getting subtly different weather readings. They register their weather stations on the online weather service Weather Underground, an online database that makes PWS searchable for the public, and their growing number of sites contribute to the community.[11]

BESPOKE ENVIRONMENTAL TOOLS

The sensor and weather data can have an impact on the building's form to work in synergy with local environmental conditions. The KT Solar Modeler tool, developed by KieranTimberlake in 2009, is one of a palette of digital tools that assists project teams in understanding site-specific environmental considerations in relation to a building's form. The Solar Modeler tool was designed to use typical meteorological year (TMY) data or site-based sensor measurements and to give analysis in a format that would be useful as feedback for the design process. It is designed to integrate with Rhino and it has evolved on the basis of user feedback. It uses the modelled building geometry to enable insolation studies and visualise results. The tool also enables the impacts of vegetation to be quantified and considered as part of the building performance in the design process. Seasonal vegetation data, including leaf-on/leaf-off data, can contribute to design strategies. Faircloth calls the tool 'malleable and question-based' because it can be customised to address the workflows needed by a design team. The Solar Modeler tool was created within KieranTimberlake's research group and then serially adapted by project teams to a range of site-specific questions. It was used during a green-roof post-occupancy evaluation on one of the office's campus green-roof projects to report results in terms of average hours of direct sunlight to understand why certain plants grow in particular environmental conditions. The tool has also been used to study the impacts of tree foliage on sites, and the relationship between greenery and seasonal variations of comfort and solar gain on facades.

11 KieranTimberlake, facade studies using the KT Solar Modeler tool, 2013
The thermal performance of the building can be tested and modelled at different times of the year with different amounts of vegetation to predict seasonal performance variation.

PREDICTIVE MODELLING IN THE FUTURE

KieranTimberlake's first principles approach and mix of expertise and curiosity has developed into a regular routine of finding new approaches to established questions. The office probes the environment for potentially useful data and bringing new areas of inquiry into the domain of the architect, such as building life-cycle or weather data, and this has allowed new workflows and collaborations. KieranTimberlake's approach offers designers more control over the design outcome, and places building performance earlier in the design process. The transdisciplinary approach, development and commercialisation of software and hardware for design feedback, and use of weather stations and real-time climate data, are being integrated into all aspects of the office's work. The firm continually finds new ways of using digital tools and computation to predict how a building will perform in the future, offering potential energy savings, improved comfort and overall environmental effectiveness.

REFERENCES

1. Quoted in Daniel S Friedman (ed), *Goat Rodeo: Practicing Built Environments*, CreateSpace Independent Publishing Platform, 2016, p 31.
2. Stephen Kieran and James Timberlake, *Refabricating Architecture: How Manufacturing Methodologies are Poised To Transform Building Construction*, McGraw-Hill (New York), 2004.
3. Stephen Kieran and James Timberlake, *Cellophane House*, ORO Editions (San Francisco), 2013.
4. 'Tally', online at http://choosetally.com (accessed 20 July 2016).
5. Gideon Fink Shapiro, 'Award: Tally, an App for Assessing Environmental Impact', in *Architect*, 13 July 2016, online at http://www.architectmagazine.com/awards/r-d-awards/award-tally-an-app-for-assessing-environmental-impact_o (accessed 20 July 2016).
6. Author visit to KieranTimberlake and interview with Billie Faircloth, 2 March 2016.
7. KieranTimberlake, 'Creating a Comfort Benchmark at Tulane', 2 March 2015, online at http://www.kierantimberlake.com/posts/view/298 (accessed 20 July 2016).
8. 'Pointelist', online at http://pointelist.com (accessed 20 July 2016).
9. Billie Faircloth, 'Pardon Me—May I Borrow Your Umbrella', in *Journal of Architectural Education*, vol 67, no 2, pp 270–73.
10. Author interview with Billie Faircloth, 7 July 2016.
11. 'Weather Underground Personal Weather Station Network', online at https://www.wunderground.com/weatherstation (accessed 20 July 2016).

IMAGES

All © KieranTimberlake

10. ARCHITECTURE SHAPES PERFORMANCE:
GXN ADVANCES SOLAR MODELLING AND SENSING

TERRI PETERS

GXN is a green design and innovation group based in Copenhagen, Denmark. Founded in 2007, GXN focuses on the integration of 'green' research into design practice, utilising digital tools and workflows; material innovation and adaptation of new materials; and collaborations with industry and research networks. Led by 3XN senior partner and architect Kasper Guldager Jensen, the research group was initially a part of the internationally renowned architecture office 3XN. Since 2012, it has been an independent entity, seeking external collaborators and projects, as well as research funding.[1]

1 3XN, Swedbank Headquarters, Stockholm, Sweden, 2014
The design process included early-stage daylighting simulations and analyses carried out by GXN to create the day-lit interior.

The team at GXN draws together people with a diverse range of backgrounds and expertise, including architecture, engineering, landscape design, computational design and environmental psychology. They perform environmental calculations, simulations, modelling and visualisations to support early-stage design decisions. The international group of about 10 full-time researchers work in their recently renovated historic boat-shed studio in Copenhagen alongside the designers at 3XN. Recent GXN projects include the interior for Noma restaurant in Copenhagen, which has 500 unique CNC-milled shelves; the Green Solution House in Rønne, designed with cradle-to-cradle principles; and the Ballerup Recycling Center in Denmark, which uses recycled and recyclable materials.

SWEDBANK—DESIGNING FOR DAYLIGHT

The team uses a range of digital tools and workflows, and adapts and customises tools and plug-ins to suit the requirements of each project. For the Swedbank Headquarters in Stockholm, Sweden, by 3XN, GXN used and customised parametric software to analyse site orientation, climate, daylight and thermal comfort. The team analysed the amount of daylight in interior spaces, using daylight simulation plug-in DIVA and the Velux Daylight Visualizer simulation tool. The Velux tool was used for calculating sun exposure and identifying potential areas which needed shading from overheating, and for reducing energy use early in the design process. GXN used Ladybug for Rhino, which utilised climate data. This allowed designers to understand and design for specific local site conditions. Ladybug provides visualisation tools for wind, rain, sun-path, solar isolation and cloud cover. Jensen has stated that '90 per cent of a building's form is

2 GXN, daylight factor
calculation for Swedbank
Headquarters, Stockholm,
Sweden, 2014
Using the Velux Daylight
Visualizer simulation tool,
GXN calculated the daylight
factor for interior spaces while
considering the relationship
between the building's
geometry and uses, and the
neighbouring buildings.

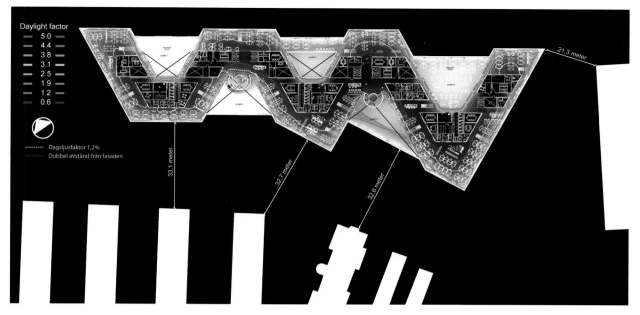

Daylight factor
- 5.0
- 4.4
- 3.8
- 3.1
- 2.5
- 1.9
- 1.2
- 0.6

-------- Dagsljusfaktor 1,2%
-------- Dubbel avstånd från fasaden

33,1 meter

32,7 meter

32,6 meter

21,3 meter

3 3XN, competition entry for Quay Quarter Tower in Sydney, Australia, 2014 Exterior visualisation of the building's elevation, which shows the floor plate shifting in orientation and size as it moves up the tower, responding to site-specific climatic conditions and views.

decided in the first 10 per cent of our design process. To inform our architecture we use software that provides live feedback on daylight quality and environmental impact, right from the first early sketches'.[2]

Daylight was a driving architectural design concept for the Swedbank Headquarters. The design for the office building developed into a singular building with naturally lit workspaces and a floor plan that promoted communication, interactivity and productivity. The zigzag floor plan breaks up the form into a triple-V shape to create internal courtyards and to make a variety of spaces. The densely arranged workspaces, support spaces and meeting areas are organised in a long linear arrangement, and connect to five open, full-height atria. In section, generous staircases and bridges come into and around the atria to ensure an active variation among the scheme's eight levels. GXN's environmental analyses, especially daylight factor analysis, were critical in the sizing and placement of these atria, and for calculating and refining the qualities of these spaces.

TOWER DESIGNS—PERFORMANCE IMPACTS FORM
Three recent 3XN towers have benefited from GXN's building performance analyses, which offered important feedback for advancing the design process. The competition winning design for Quay Quarter Tower in Sydney, Australia (2014), involved the reuse of a large part of an existing building on the site and the addition of more than 45,000 square metres (484,376 square feet) of new construction. GXN analysed the site with particular regard to solar envelope, wind and weather data to inform the building design. The resulting design is a 49-storey tower that is broken up into five stacked glazed volumes, each with a slightly different orientation. GXN worked to connect environmental performance to conceptual

FACADE Solar Radiation Analysis

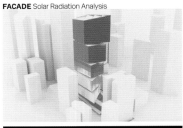

30.4%

Reduction

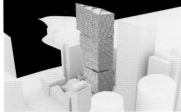

Total annual radiation:

Without frames:
24,714 kWh

With frames:
17,205 kWh

Reduction:
30.4%

annual radiation

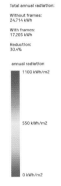

1100 kWh/m2

550 kWh/m2

0 kWh/m2

No Frame

Frame

4 3XN, solar radiation analysis of Quay Quarter
Tower in Sydney, Australia, 2014
GXN carried out building-scale analysis of
annual solar radiation in order to create options
for the design team.

5 3XN, visualisation of the
facade of the design of
Grove Towers, Mumbai, India,
2013–14
Every louvre has a unique
geometry to provide optimised
shading.

ideas and client aspirations. The northern facade of the tower is shifted towards the street-level community at lower levels, but as it gets taller the building shifts towards the east, for higher level views of the Opera House and also for self-shading. The design takes advantage of daylight for natural light yet reduces overheating through louvres and a twisted form.

The competition entry for Grove Towers in Mumbai, India, by 3XN in 2013, features a single mixed-use podium building with two towers and climbing vertical gardens. Inspired by clusters of mangrove stalks, seemingly braided together at the base, the tower forms emerge from the interconnected base and extend upwards in tall thin straws. The towers are sculpted to be self-shading and to provide lower energy demands than typical interiors. The facades were detailed as highly varied, mass-customised concrete components. An important ambition for the project was that it could be built in cast concrete, using local labour and expertise. Environmental performance of the buildings was analysed at multiple scales. At the large scale, the building forms were optimised, using data from the sunlight shading analyses. Facade studies for the individual windows considered different dimensions and angles for sunshades to block sun, but providing views to outside. The designers' parametric and simulation workflow enabled GXN to offer a range of design options in section and in three dimensions with different levels of radiation reduction.[2]

6 GXN, solar shading studies for Grove Towers, Mumbai, India, 2013–14

Each facade option has been designed according to its location and solar orientation to enable protection from overheating while allowing in daylight.

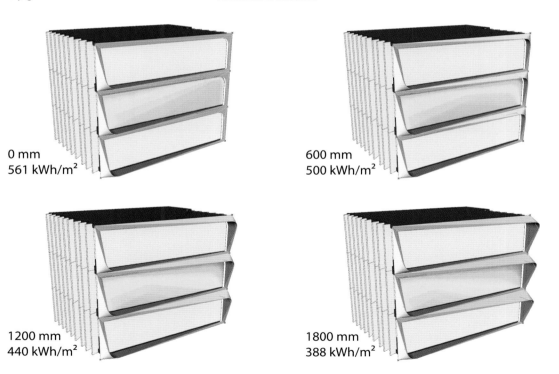

0 mm
561 kWh/m^2

600 mm
500 kWh/m^2

1200 mm
440 kWh/m^2

1800 mm
388 kWh/m^2

7 3XN, Clover Tower, Mumbai, India, 2014
The twisting building that forms the design of Clover Tower in Mumbai, India, by 3XN, was advanced by environmental analysis by GXN.

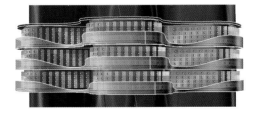

234 kWh/m²
Average anual solar radiation
for facade level 17-19

49 % Reduction

Obstructions:
Building geometry
Floor slabs
Railings

8 3XN, facade studies of Clover Tower, Mumbai, India
GXN calculated the solar radiation for the facades of the Clover Tower project to create design options for building massing and railings that responded to solar radiation in order to minimise overheating.

280 kWh/m²
Average anual solar radiation
for facade level 17-19

39 % Reduction

Obstructions:
Building geometry
Floor slabs

In a follow-up study relating to Grove Towers, funded by the Danish National Advanced Technology Foundation, GXN developed optimisation strategies for the 1,800 bespoke concrete moulds. The architects designed each of the 1,800 windows to be uniquely sized and oriented so that the environmental shading and orientation benefits could be maximised. The research study explored how robotic component production could maximise the variability of components but minimise the number of moulds. In a collaborative industry and academic partnership, called 'Bladerunner', GXN helped to develop a new workflow for the rapid production of inexpensive, unique, non-standard concrete moulds in expanded polystyrene.

The Clover Tower project is a proposal for a mixed-use building in Mumbai, India, by 3XN. The tower footprints began as circles and then indents were made in order to improve natural ventilation, thereby creating the clover form. The forms are twisted, providing cantilevered gardens that shade the floors below. By refining the twist and orientation of the towers during the design process, an 11.4 per cent reduction in solar radiation was achieved. Like Grove Towers, Clover Tower sits on a podium base. Through a combined strategy of parametric modelling and performance simulation, GXN produced many different options for the facades, minimising solar radiation by adding barriers such as balconies and louvres. The best-performing option offered an energy reduction of 49 per cent over the initial design sketches.

SENSORING ENVIRONMENTS

A central theme in much of 3XN's work is the idea that architecture shapes behaviour.[3] The work of GXN has been supportive in advancing this idea by using computational design tools and digital workflows. GXN tracks and monitors people's behaviour in buildings to understand how social spaces such as staircases and corridors are used. 3XN is known for its sculptural grand staircases that encourage people to walk through the building, to see into different spaces and meet people, and to facilitate communication by design. The group aims to develop this research into computational approaches, using real-time data and interactive technologies.

A project that implements sensoring and real-time interaction is the Green Solution House in Rønne, designed by 3XN in 2012. GXN provided overall green consultancy on this project, which was certified by the German Sustainable Building Council (DGNB), used cradle-to-cradle guidelines of 'zero waste' and was based on active house principles.[4] The building generated renewable energy on site with a pyrolysis plant, solar thermal plant and integrated photovoltaics. In the hotel, there are two Smart Rooms, designed with Autodesk Research. Using sensors, energy modelling and an indoor environmental quality app, guests can track the impacts of their stay, monitoring water and energy consumption, daylight levels, air quality, temperature and humidity levels. The app, which is still under development, was designed to monitor real-time energy sources, so that guests

9 3XN, Green Solution House,
Rønne, Denmark, 2012
The Smart Room collective
monitoring of the Green
Solution House by GXN
with Autodesk Research is
designed to allow guests to
visualise the impacts of their
use of the building and to see
real-time building performance
data relating to energy, light,
air and water use.

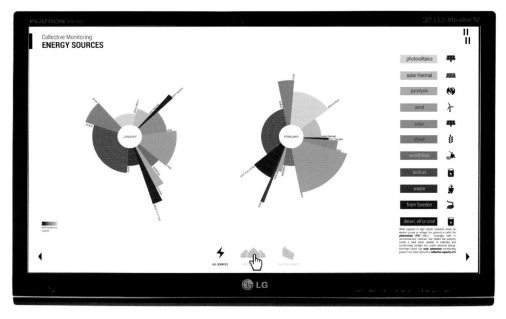

10 GXN and Autodesk Research, collective
monitoring at the Green Solution House,
Rønne, Denmark, ongoing research
The visualisation dashboard application was
designed to show guests the sources of their
energy use in real time, for example what
proportion of their energy use came from
renewable sources.

could see which proportion of the energy they use is from renewable sources.

FORM ENVIRONMENT BEHAVIOUR

GXN's approach of project-driven research, parametric modelling and performance simulation demonstrates how environmental performance can be used to modify building form, as in the Swedbank Headquarters, and how these parameters impact user behaviour, as in the Green Solution House. GXN has a broad focus, seeking to support design processes and advance multiple streams of green research. The daylight simulation and early-stage design optioning are central to the architects' work, but in the future they aim to focus more on real-time energy monitoring, building on the success of their Green Solution House. It is imagined that this stream of inquiry will lead to new workflows for architects and more interactivity with people in their design environments. GXN's work illustrates not only how a variety of environmental computation approaches can shape building form, but also how this can shape users' behaviour.

REFERENCES

1. Terri Peters and Kasper Guldager Jensen, 'GXN: A New Model for Green Collaboration Through Research in Practice', in Michael U Hensel and Fredrik Nilsson (eds), *The Changing Shape of Practice: Integrating Research and Design in Architecture*, Routledge (New York), 2016, pp 85–95.
2. Author interview with Kasper Guldager Jensen, 27 January 2016.
3. 3XN, *Mind Your Behaviour: How Architecture Shapes Behaviour*, Danish Architectural Centre (Copenhagen), 2010.
4. Kasper Guldager Jensen and John Sommer (eds), *Building A Circular Future*, Danish Architectural Press (Copenhagen), 2016.

IMAGES

All © GXN and 3XN

1

11. BESPOKE TOOLS FOR A BETTER WORLD:

THE ART OF SUSTAINABLE DESIGN AT BUROHAPPOLD ENGINEERING

BRADY PETERS

BuroHappold Engineering is a leading international engineering practice, known for its creative design solutions. Sir Edmund Happold founded the practice in 1976, when he left Arup and took up a position as Professor of Architecture and Engineering Design at the University of Bath. Happold had previously been the head of the Structures 3 group at Arup, where he worked on notable projects such the Sydney Opera House and the Pompidou Centre. Happold collaborated extensively with the Pritzker-prizewinning architect Frei Otto, and helped to set up a laboratory to study lightweight tensile structures with him and several other notable engineers. Although BuroHappold started as a small firm in a small town in the UK, the firm has grown tremendously over the last 40 years.[1] The office has a strong focus on sustainable building design and it explores how the construction of new buildings and the renovation of old buildings offer tremendous opportunities for designers.[2] BuroHappold's in-house sustainability specialists model environmental, technical and economic forces, and seek to quantify a project's performance to remove risk and improve sustainability at all stages of the design process. In the sustainability group, there are between 15 and 20 people in London and around 50 worldwide.

1 Foster + Partners, Samba Bank New Head Office, Riyadh, Saudi Arabia, under construction
Architectural rendering. The diamond-shaped 40-storey tower has an innovative three-dimensional facade that reduces energy demands while giving a distinctive presence.

CUSTOM TOOLS FOR SUSTAINABLE DESIGN

Daniel Knott is an award-winning building physics engineer in BuroHappold's London office. An associate with the practice and a member of the sustainability group, he has a broad range of environmental design and simulation experience, relating to energy performance, thermal comfort and daylighting. He specialises in facade design and the physics of buildings, and utilises parametric design and optimisation. Knott is responsible for developing both customised and standardised digital design tools for the sustainability group and throughout the office. In his 10 years with the practice, he has been pivotal in the practice in developing new digital design workflows for sustainable building that integrate parametric design, performance simulation and optimisation. Knott's projects include the Shimoga Processing

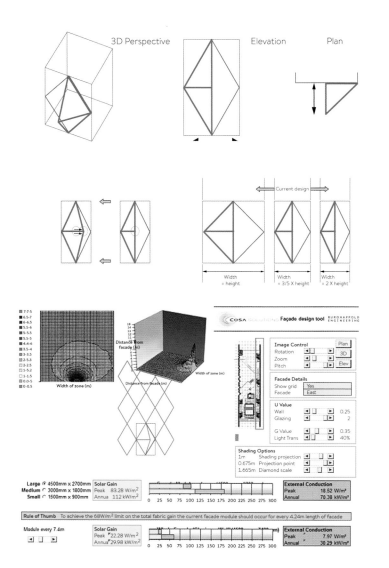

3D Perspective · Elevation · Plan

2 Foster + Partners, Samba Bank New Head Office, Riyadh, Saudi Arabia, under construction
Parametric facade design tool by BuroHappold for glazing optimisation to maximise daylight factor, and to limit solar and conduction gains

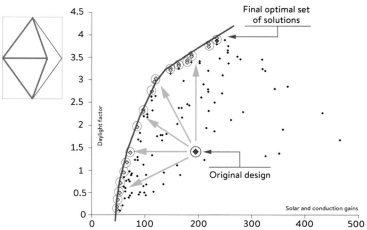

Centre project with Chadwick International, which was the winner of the BEI Outstanding International Design Project Award 2016 for its bioclimatic optimisation. Furthermore, he has worked on many high-profile projects with Foster + Partners, including the Haramain High Speed Rail project, the Samba Bank New Head Office and the National Bank of Kuwait tower; and many projects with Zaha Hadid Architects, such as the Nanjing International Youth Cultural Centre.

Knott develops standardised digital tools, which are the computational tools designed for more general use by design teams, and these tend to focus on building performance issues, such as glazing area, external shading and facade orientation. With a Maths degree from Oxford University and a master's degree in Aeronautical Engineering from Imperial College, he builds his design tools from first principles. These digital design tools are then used and tested by the sustainability group to design passive and low energy strategies for energy-efficient and low-carbon solutions at a scale ranging from individual buildings up to masterplans. One example is a digital climate tool. For environmental performance, Knott states that the output results are only as good as the input weather data, so it is crucial to take time to select the right data files.[3] He studied how different digital tools were being used in the office and observed that while the now defunct Ecotect software was being well used, about 95 per cent of the time engineers used it just to get the weather data. To replace this functionality, he initiated a process of custom tool writing the computer code in VBA in Excel. The tool accesses raw data from weather files to create wind roses and a variety of other visualisations. Engineers are able to use this tool to quickly access weather data, to use the graphics for reports and to compare options. Knott has similarly created solar facade and daylighting parametric tools for design teams.

Beyond developing tools for common building physics applications, Knott also develops bespoke digital design tools for form generation, performance prediction and multi-parameter optimisation. He was one of the first engineers to develop a digital tool that utilised the Universal Thermal Climate Index (UTCI). The digital tools and workflows are developed in a rapid and creative manner for projects at an early stage of design, and his work is a mixture of technical maths and graphical communication of complex results. He argues that it is when 'geometry and data are on the same page' that design works well, and he feels that most of his environmental design work is a balancing act between form and performance.[3]

COMPUTING ENERGY USE
When thinking about what aspects of sustainability can be computed, Knott believes that the current state of the art is still in the realm of energy and carbon. He explains that 'hard metrics', such as solar gain, air temperature and relative humidity, can be estimated to quite a high degree of certainty.[3] BuroHappold frequently carries out parametric analysis and

3 Foster + Partners, Samba Bank New Head Office, Riyadh, Saudi Arabia, under construction
Graph of optimised solutions by BuroHappold.

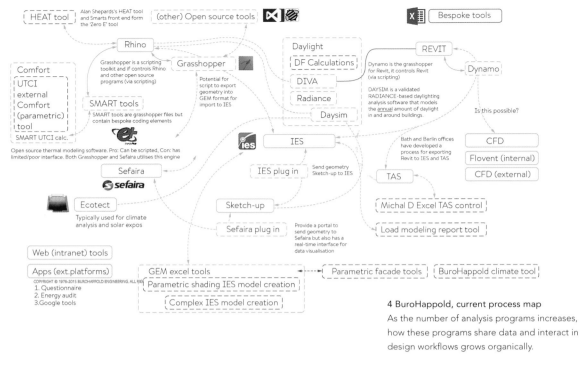

4 BuroHappold, current process map
As the number of analysis programs increases, how these programs share data and interact in design workflows grows organically.

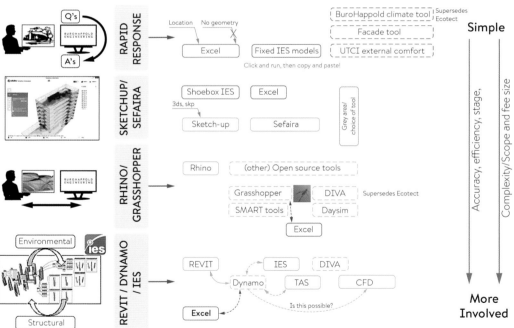

5 BuroHappold, proposed process map
BuroHappold has created a variety of design workflows, depending on the stage and complexity of the project, and accuracy and efficiency of the results needed.

optimisation of building elements to reduce energy consumption. The office uses a variety of tools, such as IES and EnergyPlus. However, for building geometry, Knott explains that he writes these computer scripts in Excel. These scripts combine to create multiple performance analysis models, using IES software, which he can then analyse in a single run in IES simulation. This parametric design strategy generates all of the applicable options within a solution space in Excel, runs the analysis in IES and then brings the data back to Excel for visualisation. Knott stresses that it is important to design from first principles, to understand the mathematical principles behind these simulations in order to be able to ask the right questions and to design the workflows. An example of this computational approach to energy modelling can be seen in the National Bank of Kuwait by Foster + Partners. The design of the office tower has a complex form that curves in two directions, and deep shading elements to protect the interior from the solar gains. A digital model was built, but the architects built their digital model using CAD software MicroStation, which is incompatible with energy-performance modelling software IES. Therefore, BuroHappold needed to rebuild the model, which required a huge amount of time. Knott wrote a script for a parametric floor plate that generated the correct partitioning and energy model for every floor of the tower. In this script, the geometric principles were applied in Excel. With this computational approach, a task that previously took four weeks, now took minutes. While it did take a week to write the computer script, once the parametric model was developed, the design could be modified and alternative design options could be tested.

6 Batley Partners with BuroHappold, Jeddah Corniche Towers, Saudi Arabia
Parametric optimised shading devices to reduce annual solar gain and reduce peak loads.

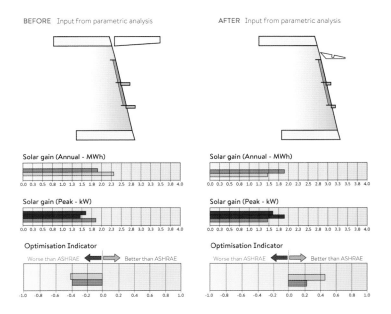

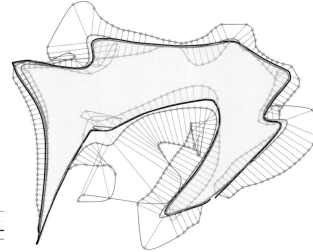

Solar gain value
Daylighting penitration
Roof edge
Glazing form

Original design

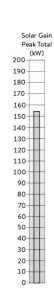

Solar Gain
Peak Total
(kW)

200
190
180
170
160
150
140
130
120
110
100
90
80
70
60
50
40
30
20
10
0

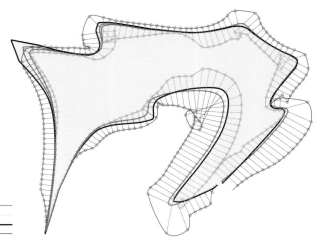

Solar gain value
Daylighting penitration
Roof edge
Glazing form

Optimised dsign

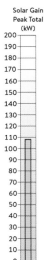

Solar Gain
Peak Total
(kW)

200
190
180
170
160
150
140
130
120
110
100
90
80
70
60
50
40
30
20
10
0

SOLAR GAIN AND DAYLIGHT

Many of the solar tools that BuroHappold uses relate to climate data, solar gain and daylight. These tools were available in the (now retired) Ecotect software, and so many of the new tools for environmental performance replicate the functionality that the engineers used to have with Ecotect. Knott explains that in creating new tools to compensate for not having the Ecotect software, he has found that he can improve upon them, and he has discovered ways to more efficiently handle the data, add efficiency and therefore create more nimble tools that work much faster.[3] The long-term goal is to publish a full suite of environmental tools that are super-efficient and highly compatible with word processing, image manipulation, design software and simulation engines. This will enable engineers to investigate complex and interesting problems without spending time worrying about software.

OPTIMISING DESIGN SOLUTIONS

Typically, when confronted with a complex performance issue on a project, BuroHappold will implement a parametric design approach, to generate and analyse a range of building designs. The geometry and performance of these options can be visualised, which gives the architects and engineers knowledge of what works and what does not, and the relationship between form and performance. However, as the computer is generating and analysing the geometry, this computational process can be iteratively looped, so that the design 'evolves' to find a better performing building system. This optimisation strategy is called a 'genetic algorithm' as it imitates the process of evolution to optimise buildings and/or parts of buildings. The technique can involve hundreds of loops and result in the generation of thousands of different options. However, this technique can yield new and better performing geometries than could be found otherwise. This technique is powerful, but as Knott explains, the most important questions are still, 'what is the goal of the optimisation?' and 'what is being optimised?'.[3]

Knott utilises a range of tools: IES, EnergyPlus, Ansys, FloVENT, Matlab and Excel are used to model and simulate for environmental performance. While some aspects of performance cannot easily be computed and included in optimisation routines, many can: solar gain, daylight, conduction, internal loads, energy and views are all quantities that can be calculated. As designs progress, more variables can be included in the performance evaluation. Performance issues involve multiple parameters, and the selection of parameters, and how the parameters are weighted, are key questions being investigated, which are always project specific. While optimisation is often talked about, Knott says that often it is best not to optimise at all—better results can be found more efficiently just by using parametric modelling, analysing all different options, and then visualising the trade-off curves.[3] Knott explains that 'there are benefits to keeping the computational processes relatively simple as it is a balance of speed and graphic sophistication'. He has

7 Project by Zaha Hadid Architects
BuroHappold used a computer script to generate and analyse different form options, producing an optimal roof edge and glazing form that reduced solar gain.

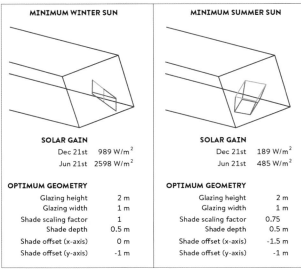

MINIMUM WINTER SUN		MINIMUM SUMMER SUN	
SOLAR GAIN		**SOLAR GAIN**	
Dec 21st	989 W/m^2	Dec 21st	189 W/m^2
Jun 21st	2598 W/m^2	Jun 21st	485 W/m^2
OPTIMUM GEOMETRY		**OPTIMUM GEOMETRY**	
Glazing height	2 m	Glazing height	2 m
Glazing width	1 m	Glazing width	1 m
Shade scaling factor	1	Shade scaling factor	0.75
Shade depth	0.5 m	Shade depth	0.5 m
Shade offset (x-axis)	0 m	Shade offset (x-axis)	-1.5 m
Shade offset (y-axis)	-1 m	Shade offset (y-axis)	-1 m

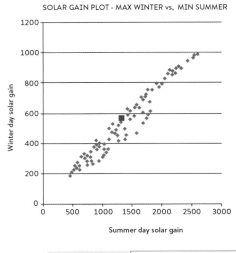

SOLAR GAIN PLOT - MAX WINTER vs. MIN SUMMER

Select analysis peroid | June 21st and December 21st

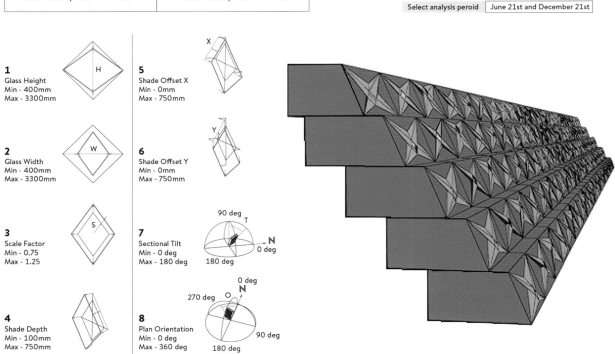

1
Glass Height
Min - 400mm
Max - 3300mm

2
Glass Width
Min - 400mm
Max - 3300mm

3
Scale Factor
Min - 0.75
Max - 1.25

4
Shade Depth
Min - 100mm
Max - 750mm

5
Shade Offset X
Min - 0mm
Max - 750mm

6
Shade Offset Y
Min - 0mm
Max - 750mm

7
Sectional Tilt
Min - 0 deg
Max - 180 deg

8
Plan Orientation
Min - 0 deg
Max - 360 deg

8 Zaha Hadid Architects,
Nanjing International Youth
Cultural Centre, China, 2014
Parametric facade design tool
by BuroHappold.

developed a library of digital tools in Excel, many of which now have user interfaces that enable other designers and engineers to use them. Additionally, he has developed an in-house database so that the methods and results from previous projects can be easily referenced.[3]

RESEARCHING TECHNOLOGY FOR SUSTAINABILITY

BuroHappold has a history of data- and technology-driven design. The firm has an in-house computational design consultancy, the SMART Solutions group, and it has expertise in areas including finite element analysis and form-finding, geometry and panellisation studies (form to fabrication), form and grid optimisation, fabrication and economic analysis. More recently, it has developed expertise in the design of real-time design engineering optioneering tools. Shrikant Sharma, the leader of BuroHappold's SMART Solutions group, believes that the team's goal is not only to design innovative buildings, but also to discover what it is that makes a building great. Sharma explains that his primary focus is the design of the built environment, using technology that is data-driven and people-centred.[4] While previous work of the group has revolvd more around questions of the relation of form to structural performance, recent research has indicated that there are many factors worth considering, and many of these relate to environmental performance such as: temperature, ventilation, humidity, light, air quality and wind. The SMART Solutions group develops computational tools to model, analyse and map performance.[4] Many of these design tools have been implemented in Rhino and Grasshopper, such as SmartForm, SmartMove and SmartSpaceAnalyzer.

Environmental conditions can also be discussed in terms of efficiency, accessibility, comfort, flexibility, safety, inspiration, security and experience. BuroHappold is developing an understanding of how people move through space as they find that their clients are interested in creating excellent experiences for their buildings' visitors through efficient, comfortable and safe journeys.[4] The SmartMove software began with a desire to understand how crowds move through buildings, but has developed into an interest in people (activities), processes (timetables) and space (layout).[5] Sharma explains that all new designs for airports, stadiums, theatres, schools and hospitals should design for aspects, such as layout, wayfinding, visibility, processes and management. Therefore, there is a need to incorporate user characteristics, including culture, age, gender, disability and group size. To better simulate for human movement and behaviour, new projects are incorporating real-world and real-time data. The SMART Solutions group is now using sensors to map existing conditions and map movement in buildings and neighbourhoods, using visitation data, survey reports, geographic information systems (GIS), satellite imagery and 3D street maps. To design and optimise buildings and cities requires the ability to measure current situations, visualise the data, model and optioneer new design proposals, and realise a calculated response.

9 Zaha Hadid Architects,
Nanjing International Youth
Cultural Centre, China, 2014
Exterior photograph of the
building.

THE FUTURE: COMFORT, HEALTH AND WELLBEING

The environments that are computed by BuroHappold's sustainability team are both the larger environment of the Earth and the personal environment that is experienced through humidity, temperature, wind and daylight. Knott's investigations into analysing comfort in buildings led him to be among the first to use the UTCI as a way to compute comfort. This environmental comfort equation incorporated four parameters: air temperature, relative humidity, wind speed and mean radiant temperature. His work involves calculating what the conditions will be inside and outside future buildings, and he figures out what design decisions can be made to improve comfort conditions. The engineers have established computational design tools for metrics relating to energy, solar gain and air movement, and Knott's goal is to develop computational techniques to predict 'soft metrics', such as productivity, health and wellbeing.[3] These metrics are sometimes considered harder to understand and have more parameters that influence them. Currently, Knott, together with the SMART Solutions group, is developing a Rhino Grasshopper digital tool that outputs both categories of metrics. Looking to the future, Knott argues that these soft metrics will become increasingly important and that the focus will shift away from energy and carbon. To design for sustainability is to design all aspects of the experienced environment, considering air, humidity, and temperature and people's wellbeing.

REFERENCES

1. 'BuroHappold Engineering', online at www.burohappold. com (accessed 13 October 2016).
2. Peter Davey, *Engineering for a Finite Planet: Sustainable Solutions by Buro Happold*, Birkhäuser (Basel and Boston), 2009.
3. Author interview with Daniel Knott, BuroHappold Sustainability, December 2015.
4. Shrikant Sharma, BuroHappold SMART Solutions group, presentation at 'Digital Reveal' conference, Bogotá, August 2016.
5. Shrikant Sharma and Al Fisher, 'Simulating the User Experience: Design Optimisation for Visitor Comfort', in Brady Peters and Xavier de Kestelier (eds), *Computation Works: The Building of Algorithmic Thought*, Architectural Design (AD) series (John Wiley & Sons, Chichester), vol 83, no 2, March/April 2013, pp 62–5.

IMAGES

1, © Foster + Partners; 2 to 6, © BuroHappold Engineering; 7, Courtesy of Zaha Hadid Architects; 8, © BuroHappold Engineering; 9, Courtesy of Zaha Hadid Architects

12. BIG IDEAS:
INFORMATION DRIVEN DESIGN   BRADY PETERS

Bjarke Ingels, the founding partner of his eponymous architecture firm, Bjarke Ingels Group (BIG), writes that 'architecture is more than designing pretty facades or expressive sculptures, it is creating man-made eco-systems'.[1] Architecture does not happen in a vacuum, it is created on this planet with its climates and landscapes, biomass and minerals. From those conditions, we add and subtract, adapt and evolve, modify and manipulate matter, to achieve conditions even more conducive to human life. Similar to British architectural critic Reyner Banham before him, Ingels feels that one of architecture's primary roles is to make existing environmental conditions more hospitable to human life.[2] BIG's architecture reminds us that buildings are not just informed by the culture but also by the climate. The environment and the social conditions are two inescapable components to any work of architecture.

1 BIG, The Spiral, New York, USA

Wind simulation of tower building. As the wind hits the building, high pressure areas are created, which cause the wind speed to decrease. As the wind is forced around the building, the speed increases and creates an area behind the building with low wind velocities.

BIG presents its architecture in the context of three frameworks: 'Engineering without Engines', 'Information Driven Design' and 'Hedonistic Sustainability'. 'Engineering with Engines' refers to how a building's form and material can impact its environmental performance. Ingels envisions ways in which architects can play much more active roles in the passive conditioning of the environment through design, rather than relying on accepted technological solutions. In BIG's work, this design approach is enabled through the use of new digital design tools that allow architects to simulate and calculate the performance of the building before it is built. In this way, rather than being driven by arbitrary aesthetic or stylistic prejudice, all decisions are based on project-specific information. The reasoning that underlies the concept of 'Information Driven Design' is that design decisions are always informed by specific information. Ingels argues that the quality of an architectural design is dependent on the quality of the information that designers have to work with.[3] The concept of 'Hedonistic Sustainability' extends beyond certification systems, and aims to develop a positive and additive approach to sustainable design that not only meets or exceeds expectations and local standards, but through architecture, proposes new design solutions that bring additional benefit to users, the community and the environment.[4]

BIG Ideas is the office's internal, semi-independent, technology-driven special projects unit that was created to 'expand the

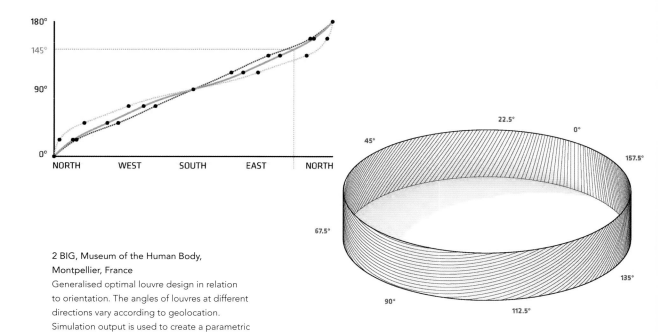

2 BIG, Museum of the Human Body,
Montpellier, France
Generalised optimal louvre design in relation
to orientation. The angles of louvres at different
directions vary according to geolocation.
Simulation output is used to create a parametric
graph.

View from east

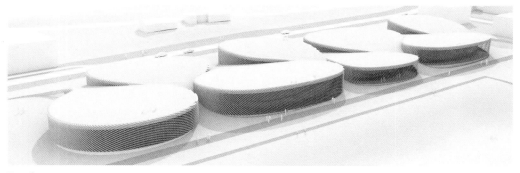

View from west

3 BIG, Museum of the Human Body,
Montpellier, France
View of louvres on east (top image) and west
(bottom image) facades.

traditional scope of the architect into *Information Driven Design*'[3], The design process at BIG starts with the identification of key criteria for a project. What are the biggest problems? What are the greatest potentials? Given the local environment, programme and communities involved, what bits of information can inform our design decisions? And, finally, what design constraints can be used to drive the design? The BIG Ideas group is based in the Copenhagen office and is led by partner Jakob Lange. The team includes Tore Banke, an architect specialising in computational design and simulation, and Kristoffer Negendahl, an engineer specialising in the computer simulation of energy, indoor climate and fluid dynamics. Their mandate is 'to test ideas and explore new intellectual territory in both the digital and built realms'. The group studies performance concepts such as energy, indoor climate, daylight, direct sunlight, shadow, radiation, acoustics, rain, water flow and wind.

MUSEUM OF THE HUMAN BODY, MONTPELLIER, FRANCE

BIG won the competition to build the Museum of the Human Body in Montpellier, France, in 2014. The building is located on the boundary between a large park and the urban condition. The programme was organised linearly, in an interlocking fashion like a zipper. The form of the building, combined with the inhabited roofscape, allowed for the urban pavement and park turf to interweave and to flow together. The organic shapes emerged from the programmatic needs of the project and desired views and connections with the neighbouring park and buildings.[1]

In response to the hot climate, the interior needed to be protected from the intense heat gain coming from direct sunlight. Exterior louvres were designed along each facade to

4 BIG, Museum of the Human Body, Montpellier, France
Simulation of the annual radiation incident on facades without louvres.

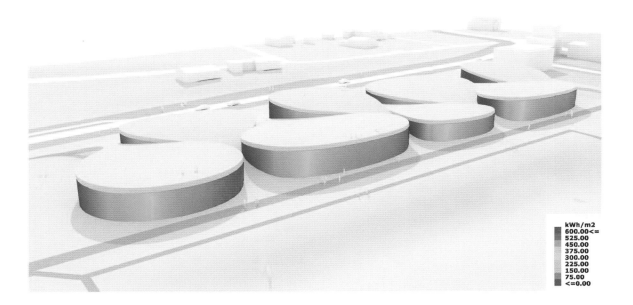

kWh/m2
600.00<=
525.00
450.00
375.00
300.00
225.00
150.00
75.00
<=0.00

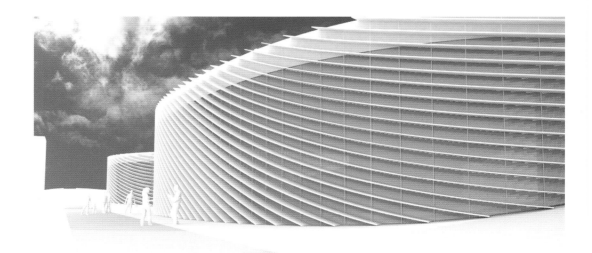

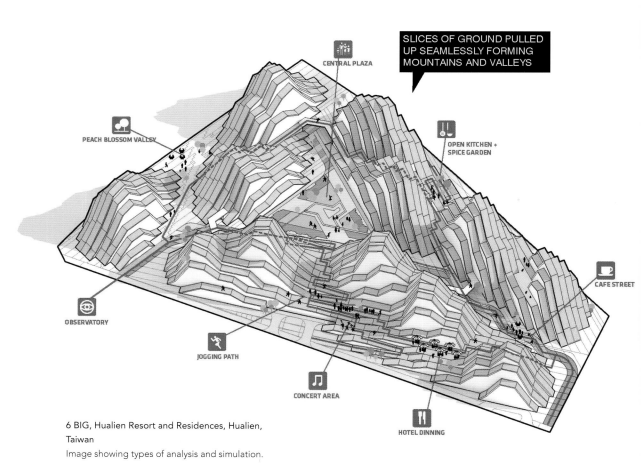

SLICES OF GROUND PULLED UP SEAMLESSLY FORMING MOUNTAINS AND VALLEYS

CENTRAL PLAZA

PEACH BLOSSOM VALLEY

OPEN KITCHEN + SPICE GARDEN

CAFE STREET

OBSERVATORY

JOGGING PATH

CONCERT AREA

HOTEL DINNING

6 BIG, Hualien Resort and Residences, Hualien, Taiwan
Image showing types of analysis and simulation.

block incoming sunrays. However, studies done by the group demonstrated that facades that faced in different directions required louvres with different orientations. In the northern hemisphere—for shading purposes—the northern facade requires vertical louvres, the south-facing facade requires horizontal louvres, and facades to the east and west should be somewhere in between. This simple relationship between form and geometry, when applied to the organic shapes, generates louvres that gently blend between horizontal and vertical.[5]

RESORT AND RESIDENCES, HUALIEN, TAIWAN
Hualien is situated on the west coast of Taiwan. The region is currently rural; however, tourism is becoming an important industry, and so future development appears inevitable. This proposal was for a dense development of a resort with a hotel and housing. It was designed to preserve and enhance the natural beauty and dramatic landscape while increasing the regional population. Formally, this large project took cues from the character of the local mountainous landscape.[1]

Several different types of analysis were used on this project, which is located on a triangular site surrounded by mountainous buildings that form a courtyard space in the middle. Sunlight access, circulation, views, solar heat gain and the creation of pleasant microclimates were important considerations in this project. The design called for a man-made stream to flow through the site and central courtyard space. However, because of the twists and turns of the stream and its limited elevational drop, it was unclear how well this stream would work.[5]

The BIG design team came up with an innovative simulation strategy to answer the question of how water would flow through

5 BIG, Museum of the Human Body, Montpellier, France
Simulation of the annual radiation on glazing with an optimal louvre design. Louvres decrease the amount of radiation on the facade surface.

7 BIG, Hualien Resort and Residences, Hualien, Taiwan
River flow design tool.

$$Q = 0.743 \cdot \sqrt{S} \cdot Zl \cdot d^2 \cdot \frac{\left(\frac{A}{(Zl^2+1)^{\frac{1}{2}} \cdot d + (Zr^2+1)^{\frac{1}{2}} \cdot d + B}\right)^{\frac{2}{3}}}{n} \cdot i + 0.743 \cdot \sqrt{S} \cdot Zr \cdot d^2 \cdot \frac{\left(\frac{A}{(Zl^2+1)^{\frac{1}{2}} \cdot d + (Zr^2+1)^{\frac{1}{2}} \cdot d + B}\right)^{\frac{2}{3}}}{n} \cdot i + 1.486 \cdot B \cdot \sqrt{S} \cdot d \cdot \frac{\left(\frac{A}{(Zl^2+1)^{0.5} \cdot d + (Zr^2+1)^{\frac{1}{2}} \cdot d + B}\right)^{\frac{2}{3}}}{n} \cdot i$$

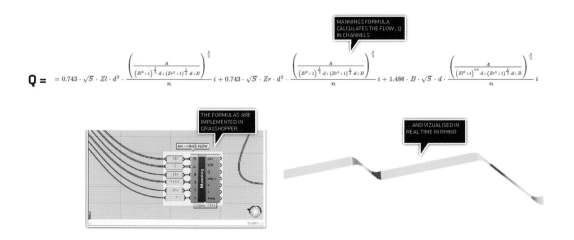

MANNINGS FORMULA CALCULATES THE FLOW, Q IN CHANNELS

THE FORMULAS ARE IMPLEMENTED IN GRASSHOPPER

...AND VIZUALISED IN REAL TIME IN RHINO

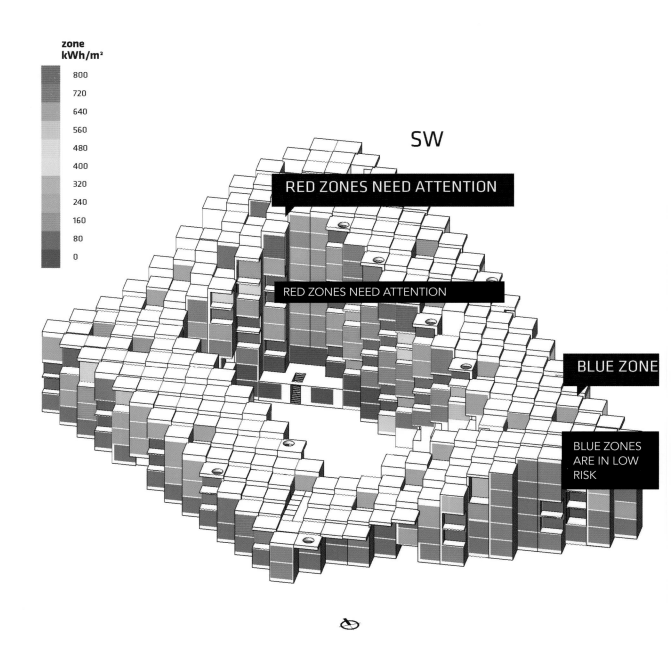

zone
kWh/m²

800
720
640
560
480
400
320
240
160
80
0

SW

RED ZONES NEED ATTENTION

RED ZONES NEED ATTENTION

BLUE ZONE

BLUE ZONES
ARE IN LOW
RISK

8 BIG, Stettin Residences,
Stockholm, Sweden
Annual solar radiation on
facade.

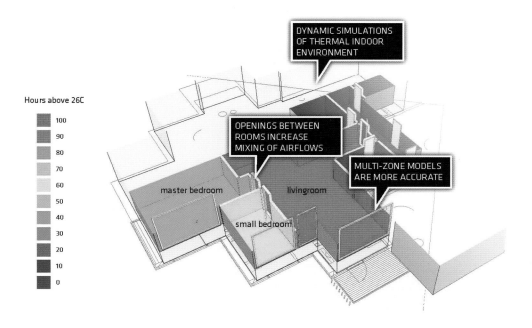

Hours above 26C

■	100
■	90
■	80
■	70
■	60
■	50
■	40
■	30
■	20
■	10
■	0

DYNAMIC SIMULATIONS OF THERMAL INDOOR ENVIRONMENT

OPENINGS BETWEEN ROOMS INCREASE MIXING OF AIRFLOWS

MULTI-ZONE MODELS ARE MORE ACCURATE

master bedroom

livingroom

small bedroom

9 BIG, Stettin Residences, Stockholm, Sweden
Room-level thermal indoor climate simulation. The team is now able to handle more complex simulations of indoor climate. It is currently testing different simulation tools to better support the design process.

the site. To answer this question, the BIG team developed a custom-made parametric digital tool. This tool implemented the Manning equation in the Rhino Grasshopper architectural design environment. The design tool enabled the team to draw different sections through the river, to experiment with different plan arrangements, to change material and to see how these impacted the amount of water flowing through the river.

STETTIN 7 RESIDENCES, STOCKHOLM, SWEDEN
Stettin 7 is a 20,000 square-metre (215,279 square-foot) sustainable luxury residential building, currently under construction in Stockholm, Sweden. The building is located at the edge of a treasured national park. Formally, the building is akin to another BIG project, the well-known W57 project, a residential building on West 57th Street in New York City, which was completed in 2016. The Stettin 7 Residences were designed to be sensitive to neighbouring buildings, and the height matched the height of neighbouring buildings on two corners, with the other two corners varying, one lower, facing the park, and the other higher. On the corner nearest to the park, the lower height not only created a humane edge between the building and nature, but also allowed more apartments across the courtyard to gain park views. This forming strategy also meant that the courtyard received more sunlight. As in many BIG projects, the apparent size of the building was reduced through a language of smaller units. The use of smaller units not only enabled a more organic expression, but also worked with the use of prefabricated units and standardised elements. Digital simulation tools enabled the study of consequences of these formal moves.[3]

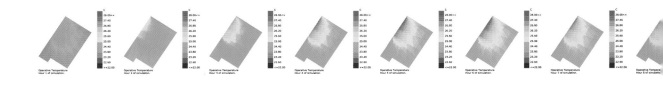

10 BIG, Stettin Residences, Stockholm, Sweden
Hourly thermal indoor climate simulation.

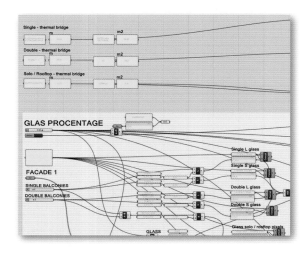

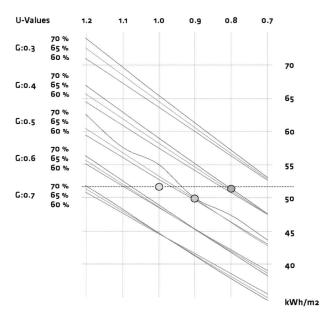

11 BIG, Stettin Residences, Stockholm, Sweden
Energy calculation matrix using the program Termite in Rhino
Grasshopper and Be10.

12 BIG, King Street
Residences, Toronto, Canada
Pixellated mountain shaped
by environmental and
architectural forces.

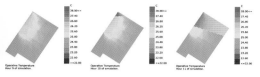

Operative Temperature Hour 9 of simulation. Operative Temperature Hour 10 of simulation. Operative Temperature Hour 11 of simulation.

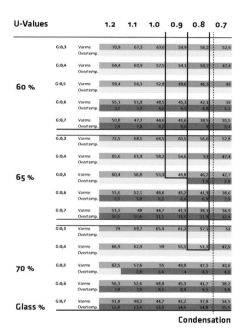

U-Values			1.2	1.1	1.0	0.9	0.8	0.7
60 %	G:0,3	Varme	70,9	67,3	63,6	59,9	56,2	52,6
		Overtemp.						
	G:0,4	Varme	64,4	60,9	57,5	54,1	50,7	47,4
		Overtemp.						
	G:0,5	Varme	59,4	56,1	52,8	49,6	46,3	43
		Overtemp.						
	G:0,6	Varme	55,1	51,8	48,5	45,3	42,1	39
		Overtemp.	3,5	3,9	4,2	4,5	4,8	5,1
	G:0,7	Varme	50,8	47,7	44,6	41,6	38,5	35,5
		Overtemp.	7,4	7,8	8,2	8,5	9	9,4
65 %	G:0,3	Varme	72,5	68,5	64,5	60,5	56,6	52,8
		Overtemp.						
	G:0,4	Varme	65,6	61,9	58,2	54,6	51	47,4
		Overtemp.						
	G:0,5	Varme	60,4	56,8	53,3	49,8	46,2	42,7
		Overtemp.					1,9	2,8
	G:0,6	Varme	55,6	52,1	48,6	45,2	41,9	38,6
		Overtemp.	5,5	5,8	6,2	6,6	6,9	7,3
	G:0,7	Varme	51,3	48	44,7	41,3	38,1	34,9
		Overtemp.	10,1	10,6	11,1	11,5	11,9	12,4
70 %	G:0,3	Varme	74	69,7	65,4	61,2	57,1	53
		Overtemp.						
	G:0,4	Varme	66,5	62,9	59	55,1	51,3	47,5
		Overtemp.						
	G:0,5	Varme	62,5	57,6	55	49,9	47,3	43,6
		Overtemp.		2,8	3,4	4	4,3	4,6
	G:0,6	Varme	56,3	52,6	48,9	45,3	41,7	38,2
		Overtemp.	2,4	7,9	8,3	8,8	9,3	9,8
Glass %	G:0,7	Varme	51,8	48,3	44,7	41,2	37,8	34,5
		Overtemp.	12,8	13,4	13,9	14,4	14,9	15,5

Condensation

While issues of view and sunlight access were very important and were studied by the design team, using specialised digital design tools, in this project energy use and thermal comfort were two driving performance considerations. Working closely with engineers in Sweden, BIG created a three-dimensional model of the building. The engineering team analysed the model and found that there were opportunities to improve indoor climate because certain areas were not performing well. The engineer's solution was to look at only a few problematic units and study these in detail— they did not have the capabilities in terms of modelling and setting up a parametric or automated process. To address thermal comfort issues, the engineers proposed a universal strategy of shading elements, automatic opening windows and high performance coatings on the glazing. However, the BIG Ideas team wanted to develop a more customised solution, so they developed their own simulation tools to enable customised parameters, to carry out more studies, and to do these analyses much earlier in the design process.[5]

The whole building was studied in relation to thermal comfort, and so were individual units and rooms within each unit. These analyses demonstrated that while the whole building on average might be performing well, or even that units as a whole performed well, there were finer grain issues. There were problems in the performance of individual rooms and areas within rooms. This led the BIG Ideas team to suggest a different approach where various facade panels could have different specifications of glazing, so that each face could have its own u-value and g-value. The team developed a new design tool, Termite, which connected Rhino Grasshopper and Be10 (a Danish software tool for energy-demand calculations). These dynamic simulations were multi-zone models and were more accurate. They included the provision for openings between rooms to allow for the mixing of air. This workflow has enabled the team to handle more complex situations of indoor climate. The development of new simulation tools has proven to support the office's design processes. The set-up in Rhino Grasshopper is very fast, which means that a lot of simulations can be done, offering more design options.[5]

KING STREET WEST, TORONTO, CANADA
Similar to the Stettin 7 Residences project, the King Street West proposal in Toronto, Canada, looks like a pixellated mountain. The design has the pixels oriented at an angle to the grid of the perimeter block. Like many BIG projects, it relates to the typical Danish courtyard building. King Street West is organised as a traditional perimeter block with an open plaza in the middle. Here, the facade seems to be pulled up to allow public access to the plaza; and it also works to avoid the existing heritage buildings, to allow sunlight to penetrate into the entire building and to create green open terraces for each unit.[3]

To assist in the forming of this pixellated mountain, and to make sure that the different design considerations were accommodated, the BIG Ideas team developed a new digital design tool. A key

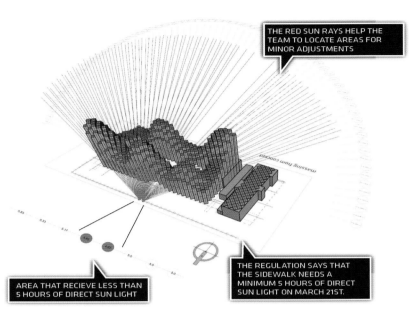
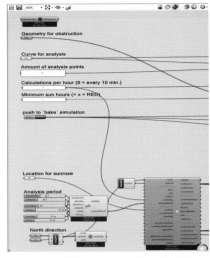

13 BIG, King Street Residences, Toronto, Canada
Direct sunlight simulation. Local city regulations state that the pavement needs a minimum of five hours of direct sunlight on 21 March of each year.

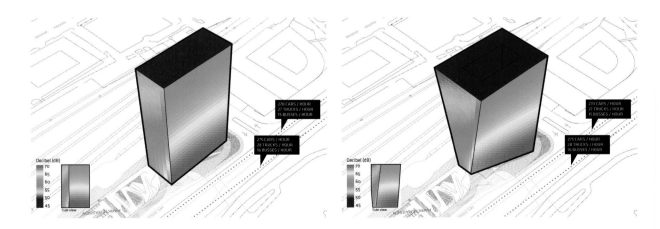

14 BIG, VTC Tower, Copenhagen, Denmark
Acoustic noise simulation.

design consideration in this case was a local planning regulation that stated that the pavement across the street must get at least five hours of direct sunlight on 21 March of each year. By customising the environmental design plug-in Ladybug, the design team came up with a workflow that simulated the sunlight hours from a particular building form. This simple tool saved the designers time, made it easy for the team to produce workable concepts and identified areas where the design should be modified.[5]

VTC TOWER, COPENHAGEN, DENMARK

The VTC Tower project is located in Copenhagen, Denmark, in an area near highways and railway lines—all of which generate high levels of noise. In this project, the BIG design team investigated the question of how the building form can affect the noise incident on the facade. The team turned to the expertise of Arthur van der Harten, an architect, engineer and software developer who developed Pachyderm, a plug-in for Rhino and Grasshopper that simulates acoustic performance. The important innovation of Pachyderm is not its simulation algorithms, but that it is a customisable open-source simulation engine that runs natively within computer-aided design (CAD) software.[6] Working with van der Harten, the BIG Ideas team created a custom workflow where the geometry from Grasshopper could be sent to Pachyderm and the results from Pachyderm were then re-mapped onto the 3D model of the building. In this way, the design team developed new architectural forms that reduced noise and created new visualisation techniques for better understanding sound within the visual domain of CAD software.

BIG IDEAS

BIG is now a global design practice and its projects embody a Scandinavian sensibility, great concern for the environment and a desire to create incredible architecture. Although it has projects all over the world, BIG adjusts its designs to the locally specific social and environmental conditions of each project. The practice has developed a philosophical position on design for sustainability that responds to contemporary challenges and opportunities. The office has developed its own internal consultancy, BIG Ideas, which combines expertise in design, computation and performance simulation. The studio develops its own parametric tools to generate geometry, and it has the expertise to develop bespoke simulation tools as its members have advanced degrees in architecture and engineering fields relating to building simulation. Importantly, for BIG's design process, they link the generative digital models to performance prediction. Rhino and Grasshopper are the environments in which the team develops most of their tools. While BIG Ideas often uses simulation tools that are free and widely available, such as Ladybug and Honeybee, DIVA and Pachyderm, the team is very capable of developing its own tools if needed. In the Stettin 7 project, a new digital tool, Termite, was created. Termite is an energy-modelling tool that links Grasshopper to established Danish energy modelling methods. In the Montpellier project, a louvre generation tool was developed,

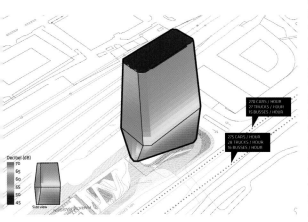

Decibel (dB)
70
65
60
55
50
45
Side view

270 CARS / HOUR
27 TRUCKS / HOUR
15 BUSSES / HOUR

275 CARS / HOUR
28 TRUCKS / HOUR
16 BUSSES / HOUR

which was linked to simulation software. Throughout the design process, the tool was modified and ultimately a continually varying geometry was developed that responded to the site, orientation and performance requirements.

Ingels argues that a building's geometry can passively influence its environment, thereby reducing the need for modern mechanical intervention; that feedback from digital tools is necessary to make the design decisions that will shape and inform architecture; and that through an optimistic approach to sustainable design, a better environment can be created.[1] The design philosophy of BIG sees that buildings are shaped by various forces, including daylight, thermal exposure, airflow, turbulence, wind, space syntax and traffic flow. While still very much design-focused, the architects find that they are increasingly using performance simulations that would normally be part of a more technical engineering workflow. The magnitude of many of these forces can be calculated, and these calculation routines can be combined with parametric and generative design procedures to enable the exploration of a range of different building forms. The exploration of these shaping forces in an architectural design process requires a more immediate feedback loop. In an architectural design process, many options are proposed, considered and discarded daily, and so rapid modelling and analysis are essential. With the work of the BIG Ideas group, the office has the capability to translate these environmental form-finding concepts into architecture. The group combines a deep knowledge of environmental design, a flexibility and expertise in new digital design technologies, with a curiosity and ability to ask the right questions.

REFERENCES
1. Bjarke Ingels, *Hot to Cold. An Odyssey of Architectural Adaptation*, Taschen (Cologne, Germany), 2015.
2. Reyner Banham, *The Architecture of the Well-Tempered Environment*, second edition, University of Chicago Press (Chicago), 1984.
3. 'BIG Bjarke Ingels Group', online at http://www.big.dk (accessed 11 May 2016).
4. Bjarke Ingels, 'The Joys of Economy: How to Make Sustainability a Haven of Hedonism', in Ilka Ruby and Andreas Ruby (eds), *Re-Inventing Construction*, Ruby Press (Berlin, Germany), 2010.
5. Author interview with Tore Banke, 2016.
6. Arthur van der Harten, 'Pachyderm Acoustical Simulation: Towards Open-Source Sound Analysis', in Brady Peters and Xavier de Kestelier (eds), *Computation Works: The Building of Algorithmic Thought*, Architectural Design (AD) series (John Wiley & Sons, Chichester), vol 83, issue 2, March/April 2013, pp 138–9.

IMAGES
All courtesy BIG – Bjarke Ingels Group

13. SIMULATING THE INVISIBLE:
MAX FORDHAM DESIGNS LIGHT, AIR AND SOUND

TERRI PETERS

Max Fordham is a group of leading environmental engineers, known for its creative problem-solving and first principles approach.[1] They customise their workflows to suit each design challenge. Founded in 1966, the firm has about 220 engineers and staff in five offices around the UK. Their portfolio includes high-profile projects, such as the RIBA Stirling Prize-winner, the MAXXI Museum of 21st Century Arts in Rome, the RIBA Stirling Prize-winning, Damien Hirst-owned Newport Street Gallery in London, and renovations to national treasures, such as the Royal Festival Hall at the Southbank Centre, St Martin-in-the-Fields and Westminster Abbey.

The office is arranged in five thematic engineering groups, Mechanical Engineering, Electrical Engineering, Acoustics, Sustainability and Light + Air, and the office has found that creating teams enables in-depth specialisation and focus on particular issues. Designing the performance of the invisible aspects of the environment, such as light, air and sound, is at the heart of Max Fordham's work, and the firm's approach to computing the environment incorporates digital simulation, physical testing and multiple overlapping analyses, using digital tools to visualise and realise experiential aspects of architecture.

DESIGNING LIGHT AND AIR
The Light + Air group focuses on environmental physics, lighting design, facades and envelope analysis. Led by Max Fordham senior partner and engineer Nick Cramp, the group begins a project by considering it from a building physics standpoint and then develops models and simulations using a variety of methods and tools.[2] The group of engineers, physicists and designers constructs detailed 3D digital models but also uses analogue physical modelling methods. It builds and tests 1:1 prototypes and scale models for parameters, such as wind, daylight and airflow, with the support of research facilities at partnering universities. The group checks and calibrates digital tools with on-site conditions where possible, as many of the projects are renovations and additions to existing buildings, adding a further layer of complexity.

For example, in engineering the Tate Britain renovation by architects Caruso St John, scale physical models provided an additional design discussion point and communication tool.

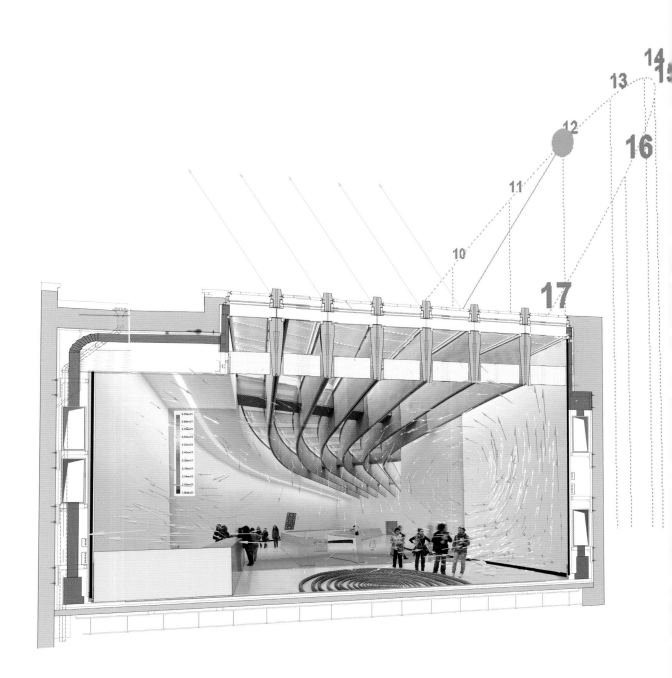

1 Zaha Hadid Architects, MAXXI Museum of
21st Century Arts, Rome, Italy, 2009
Airflow analysis by Max Fordham, which used
Fluent CFD software to study airflow in the
complex gallery spaces, in order to ensure
optimal conditions were met.

The physical models illustrated different options for the shading system, and proved useful for explaining engineering concepts. Some scale models showed form, some spatial arrangement and some were used for analyses. For example, at University College London, various physical models were tested in a simulated sky dome and then the results were used as input into the digital model, in order to predict dynamic, time-dependent behaviour.

Max Fordham's approach and workflow illustrates a shift in recent years, in relation to how engineers use digital tools. Not only has there been a rise in the number of digital tools and computer programs used, due to the desire for overlapping analyses, to make sure that the complexities of the site are included in multiple ways, but also there has been an increase in how the engineers trust the accuracy of the tools. Digital tools offer certain types of analysis and accuracy that physical testing cannot accomplish. In particular, they allow the team to analyse the cumulative environment over a long period of time, which is more useful than studying it at any one moment in time. However, cumulative environmental data can be difficult to conceptualise and translate into useful concepts and options during the design process.

PARAMETRIC AND CLIMATE-LINKED DAYLIGHT MODELLING: THE HAYWARD GALLERY RENOVATION

The Hayward Gallery renovation by architects Feilden Clegg Bradley Studios challenged Max Fordham to improve the internal daylight qualities provided through the gallery's existing roof lights while ensuring that no direct sunlight reached the artworks. They used numerical analysis for daylighting calculations. Cramp explains: 'We used a program created in Grasshopper for Rhino to

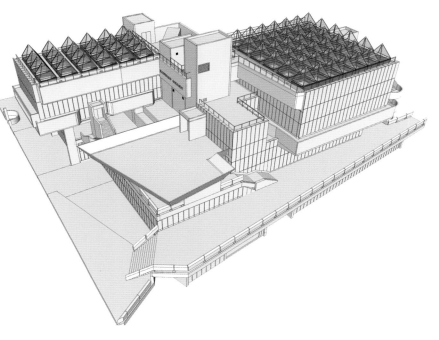

2 Feilden Clegg Bradley Studios, Hayward Gallery, London, UK, 2015: architectural model
Max Fordham analysed the SketchUp model, using a custom daylight plug-in, developed for this project, to test if and where direct sunlight strikes any gallery walls and to calculate daylight transmission values.

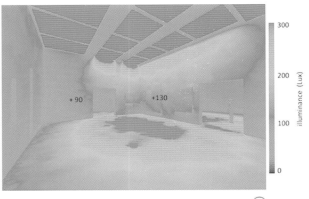

3 Max Fordham, Hayward Gallery, London, UK,
2015: roof light refurbishment
This image analysis is based on a Radiance plot
using Rhino and DIVA.

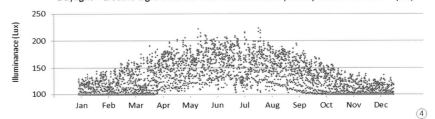

4 Max Fordham, Hayward Gallery, London, UK,
2015: daylight and electric light internal wall
illuminance study
The team modelled the optimised daylight
shading and then linked these findings to
historic climate data of solar radiation and
cloud cover, to be able to predict the daylight
received inside the gallery for every hour of
a sample year. The data is produced using
DIVA and automated and collected with
Grasshopper.

5 Max Fordham, Hayward Gallery, London, UK,
2015: beam tracer plug-in for Rhino 3D
Max Fordham developed a custom digital tool,
to enable the team to simulate and draw paths
taken by beams of light passing through spaces
with multiple specular reflections. The office
was able to create an annual map of the areas
where sunlight lands, including contribution
from multiple transmissions and reflections from
glazed surfaces.

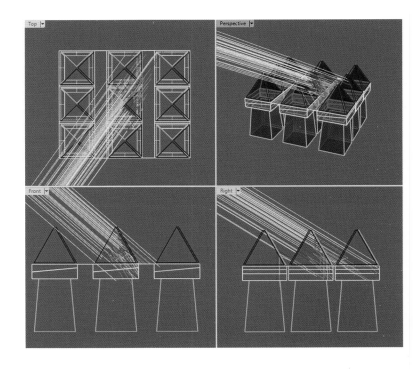

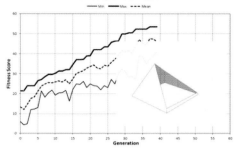

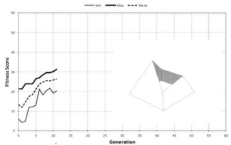

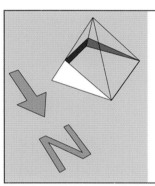

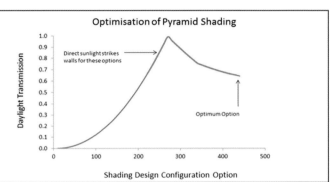

6 Max Fordham, Hayward Gallery, London, UK, 2015: optimisation studies

Max Fordham used a genetic algorithm to optimise the shapes for shading elements, providing the most diffuse daylight while adhering to conservation requirements that dictate no direct sunlight on the artwork. The genetic algorithm used SketchUp to shape the pyramids to keep out the sun. This tool allowed the generation of thousands of possible shade patterns that were calculated using an optimisation algorithm to find the best solution for maximising diffuse daylight while ensuring that no direct sunlight reached the gallery walls.

run a genetic algorithm to size the pyramidal roof lights to keep out direct sun year round, and a second program to check for the transfer of specular reflections between panes of glass into the gallery below'.[2] Parametric modelling was an important part of the design process, and the team developed and programmed algorithms to simulate diffuse daylight and direct sunlight into the gallery spaces. Max Fordham partner Hareth Pochee adds: 'Rather than directly designing objects, we design algorithms (sets of rules) that in turn design the objects. Thousands of design options were tested by rapid, virtual prototyping to find one or more solutions that were the best fit'.[2]

TOOLS FOR COMPLEXITY
Increasing environmental performance specifications means that multiple scales and modes of analyses are required. There is a rapidly growing number of digital tools for environmental analysis, and on a given project, Max Fordham employs a variety of tools. Cramp says that the team regularly uses Ecotect, DIVA, Ladybug and Grasshopper, as well as writing custom scripts and plug-ins for software like Radiance as needed. Depending on the project, the designers also use open-source codes such as OpenFOAM for complex fluid dynamics (CFD). He explains: 'We also use commercial tools like 3ds Max software by Autodesk, which we use for some daylight work, CFX or Fluent for fluid dynamic analysis, or tools like IES for dynamic thermal analysis and energy modelling. We also have a smaller number of proprietary tools either from manufacturers or made in-house that we use for

13. SIMULATING THE INVISIBLE 166-167

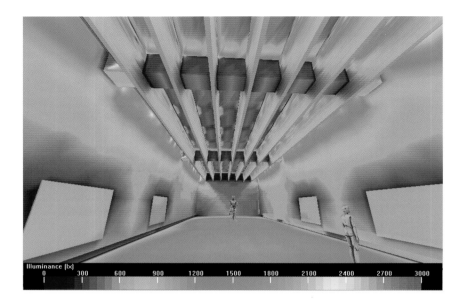

Illuminance (lx)										
0	300	600	900	1200	1500	1800	2100	2400	2700	3000

aspects like facade analysis.' The complexity of the environmental design challenges has led to these workflows. Cramp reveals, 'Any one study will use probably all of these, possibly because not all results are trustworthy, so we can't rely on one tool. We tend to be asked to do quite complex analyses, because if an environmental engineering problem is not very complex I suppose it is unlikely to fall into our lap'.[2]

DESIGN FOR DAYLIGHT: MAXXI MUSEUM OF 21ST CENTURY ARTS, ROME, ITALY

The MAXXI Museum of 21st Century Arts in Rome, Italy, was designed by Zaha Hadid Architects as an architectural landmark in the city, offering a striking expression of 'flowing' and 'streaming' structures in the urban setting.[3] Inside, it is just as dramatic and the procession through the spaces, the qualities of daylight, and integrated shading devices in the complex and highly glazed roof and facades afford the visitor a unique experience. The building won the prestigious Royal Institute of British Architects (RIBA) Stirling Prize in 2010. Much of the jury's citation remarks on the environmental design: 'The building is bravely day-lit with a sinuous roof of controllable skylights, louvres and beams, whilst at the same time conforming to very strict climate control requirements of modern galleries; the skylights both orientate and excite the visitor, but also turn them into uplifting spaces'.[4]
Max Fordham encountered environmental challenges in relation to the 2,600 square metres (27,986 square feet) of glass on the roof and walls, and the firm aimed to discreetly integrate the required environmental services that were critical to the comfort and concept of the gallery. To finely tune the amount of heat and light that could come into the gallery, Max Fordham digitally simulated the airflow and heat that entered gallery spaces. The specialist team used a variety of tools in an iterative process of simulating and modelling to improve the building's performance

7 Zaha Hadid Architects, MAXXI Museum of 21st Century Arts, Rome, Italy, 2009
Max Fordham used several digital tools, including Lightscape, Ecotect and Radiance, to analyse daylight and design a complex shading system, in order to keep out hot sun and limit light exposure in the gallery spaces.

throughout the design process. Engineers were able to model and measure the interior in all seasons, to maximise natural light. Max Fordham designed a system of operable louvres, which were both sculptural elements and light filtering components, necessary for environmental performance. Using solar tools Lightscape, Ecotect and Radiance, they analysed the solar gains and designed the shading system to optimise the interior environment for each orientation around the building.[2] The high-efficiency heating, ventilation and air-conditioning systems were concealed from view and, when visible, they were camouflaged as design elements, with vents and ducts following the geometric and minimal expressions of floor plates and staircases.

EXPERIENCE AND COMMUNICATING SOUND: BRITISH AIRWAYS LOUNGE FUTURES

'Neuroscientists have found that only about 10 per cent of the visual world that we perceive is the data our eyes collect, about 90 per cent is neural interpretation from the brain,' says Cramp. 'The 90 per cent has to be incorporated into our simulations in some way to give a real impression of what you are going to get'.[2] Computing sound as an environmental design parameter is challenging as no commercial computed-aided design (CAD) software includes sound as a parameter. Unless a building is an opera house or a performance space, which has special acoustic needs, its acoustic character is often overlooked. In the Lounge Futures project for British Airways (BA), Max Fordham measured and simulated sound in a variety of ways. The office developed geometric models to predict the acoustic environment inside each space, with particular attention to the surface finishes and location. The designers used the auralisation suite in the office (auralisation is the acoustic equivalent of visualisation) and invited the clients to experience the sound of the space. Cramp notes that earlier in the project, they had built 'a biodynamically adapted environment for them to sample, though it included light, heat, smell and air movement rather than sound'.[2] The suite translates the results from the computer model into acoustic simulations of the spaces, so a person can enter a virtual reality world, which has sound as well as video. The design team was able to make decisions based on the sound environment, created by the geometry and materials, and consider options that would have otherwise been hard to describe. Another technique that Max Fordham used was to create acoustic walkthroughs of the model. This enabled them to show the changes in between the rooms or areas with different performance levels. The walkthrough simulations were used to describe options and discuss requirements for acoustic buffering between spaces.

APPROACHES FOR SIMULATING DAYLIGHT: WESTMINSTER ABBEY

Another project with precise environmental requirements is the renovation and development of the historic Westminster Abbey triforium level in London, UK. The designers at Max Fordham were appointed specialist daylight consultants and conservation analysts for the project. This work is part of the renovation led by architect Ptolemy Dean, the 19th Surveyor of the Fabric at

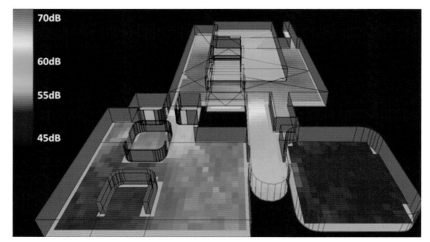

8 Max Fordham, acoustic analysis and design for British Airways First Class Lounge, Heathrow Airport Terminal 5, London, UK
Max Fordham built an acoustic model using vestibules for sound separation. The model took input from existing noise measurements at Heathrow Airport Terminal 5, to simulate these different environments.

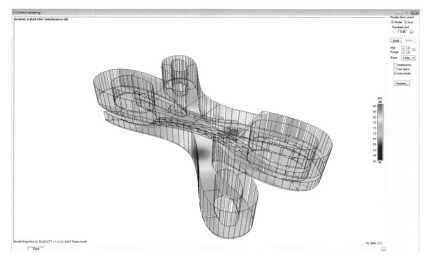

9 Max Fordham, acoustic analysis and design for British Airways First Class Lounge, Heathrow Airport Terminal 5, London, UK
Max Fordham used acoustic simulation modelling to ensure the design meets the performance aspirations.

10 Max Fordham, acoustic analysis and design for British Airways First Class Lounge, Heathrow Airport Terminal 5, London, UK
Max Fordham built and used a virtual-reality auralisation suite to invite the user groups to the office to experience the different acoustic environments.

Westminster Abbey. The renovation will include a transformation of the upper deck, above the side aisles of the cathedral, which is currently underused as a storage space with poor environmental quality and access. The triforium will reopen in 2018 as a public exhibition space and requires safe public access and appropriate conservation design.

One of the main challenges for Max Fordham was to figure out how to engineer this space so that it benefited from thermal comfort and daylight while still protecting the historic artefacts to be exhibited in this space. The team carried out a variety of daylight and UV studies to analyse cumulative exposure to the light in this space, using digital tools such as Radiance with Gensky, 3D Studio Max with EPW weather data files, and 3ds Max with image-based lighting. Multiple tools enabled the team to gain a range of data and to ensure accuracy. The team worked with different presentation methods, including architectural plans, 3D false colour visualisations and a virtual reality model.

Architecture and design critic Hugh Pearman visited the site during the renovation and noted that the complexity of the historic structure offered unique challenges in engineering the visitor experience:

> This has to be a seemingly light-touch conversion in which the character of the spaces is as important a part of the experience as the objects on display. Those will be taken from the treasures and collections of the Abbey's thousand-year history, ranging from the Liber Regalis, a 14th century illuminated manuscript which is a how-to-do-a-coronation manual, through glass and silverware and funeral effigies to sumptuous vestments.[5]

11 Max Fordham, triforium renovation, Westminster Abbey, London, UK, 2014–17
Max Fordham's team of designers were appointed as specialist daylight consultants and conservation analysts, and they carried out a variety of daylight and UV studies to analyse cumulative exposure to the light and UV of the existing historic triforium level.

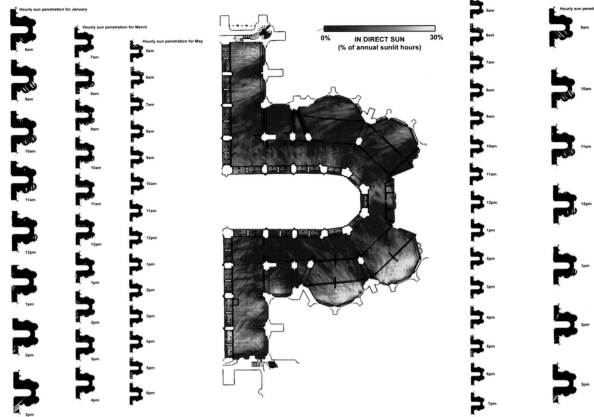

Hourly sun penetration for January

8am
9am
10am
11am
12pm
1pm
2pm
3pm

Hourly sun penetration for March

7am
8am
9am
10am
11am
12pm
1pm
2pm
3pm
4pm

Hourly sun penetration for May

5am
6am
7am
8am
9am
10am
11am
12pm
1pm
2pm
3pm
4pm
5pm
6pm

Hourly sun penetration for July

5am
6am
7am
8am
9am
10am
11am
12pm
1pm
2pm
3pm
4pm
5pm
6pm
7pm

Hourly sun penetratic

9am
10am
11am
12pm
1pm
2pm
3pm

0%   IN DIRECT SUN   30%
(% of annual sunlit hours)

12 Max Fordham, direct sun penetration study
This analysis used 3ds Max software and measured EPW solar data to plot the paths of every hour of sunshine in a year, in order to position important museum objects out of the direct light.

13 Max Fordham, study of cumulative solar exposure
This study used 3ds Max software with image-based lighting to plot annual solar exposure, to determine whether delicate objects were being sufficiently protected from direct sun. The study was validated by on-site measurements and sky recordings.

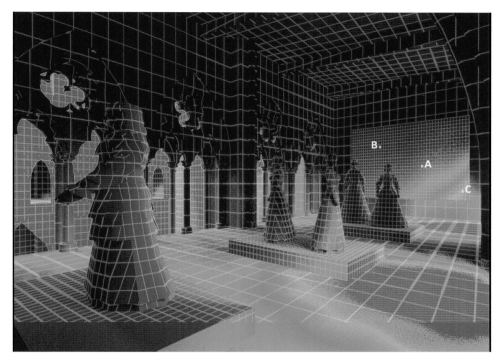

14 Max Fordham, solar exposure simulation
This is an analysis of solar exposure using Radiance and the Gensky cumulative sky module. Its purpose is similar to the 3ds Max study with image-based lighting, but the team used two codes, as well as on-site measurements, to ensure accuracy.

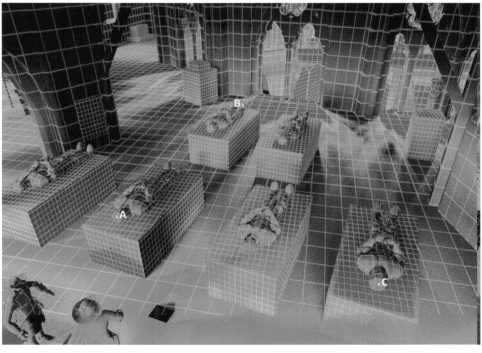

far end solid Lt = 0%

far end obscured Lt = 45%

totally clear case Lt =90%

15 Max Fordham, solar exposure simulation
Solar exposure was mapped onto a 3D model
to enable the analysis of different parts of
Westminster Abbey. The varied techniques
for solar exposure simulations ensure greater
accuracy and the different presentation
methods—architectural plans, 3D false colour
visualisations and a virtual reality model—allow
different aspects to be evaluated.

The data collection and analyses carried out by Max Fordham provided feedback for the exhibition planners to design the layout and placement of the treasures on show, enabling them to be confident that the artefacts would not be damaged in any way by exposure to heat and light.

SIMULATING TO UNDERSTAND AND CONVINCE

Nick Cramp believes that the future of computing the environment will connect computation and simulation even more to real-time data. Feedback from computer models can be even more integrated into the design process in an iterative workflow. Cramp explains:

> a lot of energy has to go into convincing our clients that what we've done is trustworthy and safe and so we have to invest a great deal into simulation or evidence and approximation of what is really going to happen. We do this to show that the design is not, for example, going to damage Monet's finest works or deteriorate the fabric of the building. Visualisation is part of the act of convincing someone. We convince ourselves and we convince our clients. The first step of the process is to analyse, the second is to validate, and then the third step is to create that tool of persuasion.[2]

The right workflows and tools support the process of accurately simulating and predicting what happens on the site over time.

REFERENCES

1. Randall Thomas, *Environmental Design: An Introduction for Architects and Engineers*, Taylor and Francis (London), 1999.
2. Author interview with Nick Cramp, 26 April 2016.
3. Patrik Schumacher, 'The Meaning of MAXXI – Concepts, Ambitions, Achievements', in Joseph Giovannini and Zaha Hadid Architects (eds), *MAXXI: Zaha Hadid Architects: Museum of XXI Century Arts*, Skira Rizzoli (New York), 2010.
4. Royal Institute of British Architects (RIBA) Press Office, 'MAXXI Museum in Rome by Zaha Hadid Architects Wins the RIBA Stirling Prize 2010', online at https://www.architecture.com/StirlingPrize/RIBAStirlingPrize.aspx (accessed 30 May 2016).
5. Hugh Pearman, 'Secrets of the Abbey, in *RIBA Journal*, 30 April 2015, online at https://www.ribaj.com/buildings/traipsing-the-triforium-in-westminster-abbey (accessed 30 May 2016).

IMAGES

1 White Arkitekter, Kiruna 4-ever, Kiruna,
Sweden: winning competition entry
As part of the design process, the team carried
out wind simulation analysis of wind speed on
the site. This 2D view shows the scale of wind
speed on the site: green indicates the highest
wind speed and dark blue shows the lowest
wind speed.

14. WHITE ARCHITECTS:

BUILD THE FUTURE

TERRI PETERS

How do you move an entire city in an extreme climate? In 2013, White Arkitekter won the international competition to redesign Kiruna, a small Swedish city north of the Arctic Circle, which needs to be relocated over the next 20 years. Sweden's largest iron ore producer founded the town in 1900 and is now funding its relocation in order to continue mining the deposits under the city until the year 2033. White's winning 'Kiruna 4-ever' proposal is a phased 20-year masterplan with a €415.5 million budget for the development of the new town centre, which shifts the city eastwards by two kilometres (1.2 miles).

KIRUNA 4-EVER

White's vision for the city is to create a 100-year plan for Kiruna as a benchmark for sustainable regeneration. Using a variety of digital tools for simulation and calculation, the design team studied the wind speeds on this extreme northern site to develop climate-specific interventions. The office designed strategies for the city to 'crawl', or to move bit by bit, along a new 'urban belt' by using the existing main street, Malmvägen, as a reference point. Buildings will either be moved, such as the local church, or demolished and rebuilt using the same materials. New buildings are part of the revitalisation including a library, a cultural centre and 3,000 new homes. Climatic and environmental simulations helped the designers to analyse options for positioning and orienting buildings and public spaces.

WHITE'S SPECIALIST TEAMS

White has several specialist teams of designers and researchers, focused on developing and utilising digital design tools for environmental simulation and computation. For example, the Dsearch group, which is led by Jonas Runberger, focuses on digital design tools and parametric design. A collective of about 12 designers has formed a working group focused on building performance simulations (BPS), specifically relating to daylight and energy modelling to explore the ways in which building performance simulation tools are used in the office.[1] The BPS group's role is to define processes and methods, to assess building performance tools, and to facilitate knowledge transfer to the larger audience, as well as to enable the continuous development of new skills within the team of specialists. The designers are spread between different offices, and specialise in using digital tools for daylight studies, energy modelling, thermal comfort

2 White Arkitekter, Kiruna
4-ever, Kiruna, Sweden, 2013–
This is an aerial view rendering
of the masterplan, showing
the large size of the site and
the 'urban belt', which is the
organisational element for the
scheme. Currently in design
development, the project is
due to be completed in 2040.

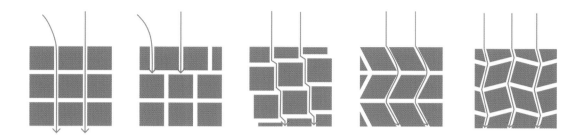

3 White Arkitekter, Kiruna
4-ever, Kiruna, Sweden, 2013–
Various street network
concepts were designed
and simulated by using
computational fluid dynamics
(CFD) to visualise results,
and then compared for wind
flows, wind penetration and air
speeds.

calculations, wind simulations and life-cycle-based analysis.[2] This group is part of Sweden's largest architectural practice with more than 900 staff in Sweden, Denmark, Norway and the UK. The office has traditionally focused on sustainability and has specialists in different areas of sustainability, such as social sustainability, materials, energy and daylight. Within project teams, an increasing number of non-specialised architects are using daylight simulation tools as required.

STOCKHOLM'S SEB BANK HEADQUARTERS

White's design for the SEB bank headquarters in Stockholm is designed to be a bright, open building that communicates transparency and connection to the site. The building is composed of two main volumes: a main 'triangle', which has bridges to a smaller 'shard' volume. The street level features a public plaza and a welcoming 'living room' space for the offices. White developed an environmental strategy based around maximising the daylight benefits of a glazed facade and optimising solar gains to reduce glare and benefit from passive heating. White's digital design and environmental simulation specialists experimented with different types of calculations to determine the solar potential of the facade and to inform the

4 White Arkitekter, SEB bank
headquarters, Stockholm,
2012–14
With varied materials, massing
and facade detailing, the
building offers different
experiences and levels of
public engagement. The
building steps down to the
north, connecting to an area of
planned future dwellings.

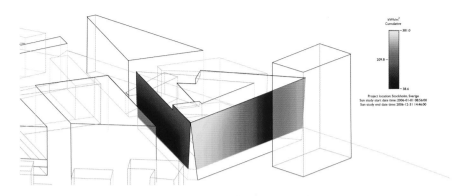

kWh/m^2
Cumulative

381.0

209.8

38.6

Project location: Stockholm, Sverige
Sun study start date time: 2006-01-01 08:56:00
Sun study end date time: 2006-12-31 14:46:00

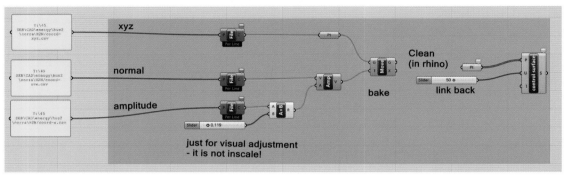

xyz

normal

amplitude

Clean
(in rhino)

bake

link back

just for visual adjustment
- it is not inscale!

5a and b, White Arkitekter, SEB bank
headquarters, Stockholm, Sweden
White calculated cumulative solar gains on each
facade by using Vasari solar radiation analyses.
These produced coordinates that were input
into Revit and then into a custom plug-in, which
was scripted in Visual Studio to test module
orientations and window sizes in an iterative
process of refining design options.

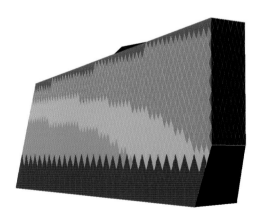

6 White Arkitekter, SEB bank
headquarters, Stockholm, Sweden
Calculations using IES VE to measure the
insolation levels on the exposed
facades were carried out in order to
design effective solar shading devices.
The colours correspond to the scale of
levels of solar radiation on the facade:
dark blue is the lowest level and red is the
highest.

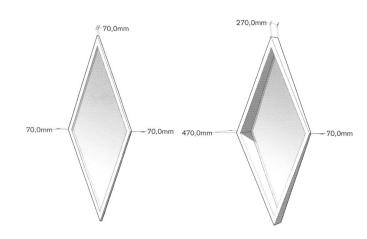

7 White Arkitekter, SEB bank headquarters, Stockholm, Sweden
Options for facade modules were tested to optimise the solar gains, depending on the depth and the location on the facade. On the left, the shallow profile offers less shading and more solar radiation can enter the building, on the right a deeper window frame allows less radiation into the building.

design of bespoke solar shading elements.[3] Shading studies undertaken at early stages offered a guide, although were less accurate than engineering studies, but proved useful in the project's early stages. The depth of the frame of the glazed modules is adapted, depending on the solar insolation level, in order to protect the glass area more effectively from the solar gains. The iterative workflow of designing and simulating options, and then taking the feedback and designing again, allowed the designers to tune the designs to a more optimal solution.[2] The final proposal balanced low solar gains in the summer but still allowed generous access to daylight.

WHITE DESIGNING DAYLIGHT

In 2013, researchers carried out studies on the daylight qualities of White's own Stockholm office, considering comfort and productivity. Constructed in 2003, the building suits its industrial neighbours with its minimal detailing and exposed concrete structure, in the form of a long, narrow, rectangular glass box. Using a cooling system that takes water from a nearby canal to reduce the need for mechanical cooling, the building was designed to offer optimal daylighting conditions for the 200 employees. Exterior sun-awnings respond to sensors, and are only deployed as needed to shade the

8 White Arkitekter, workflow diagram of digital tools
The office uses an iterative design process to carry out preliminary building performance analyses to develop and evaluate options and improve the design.

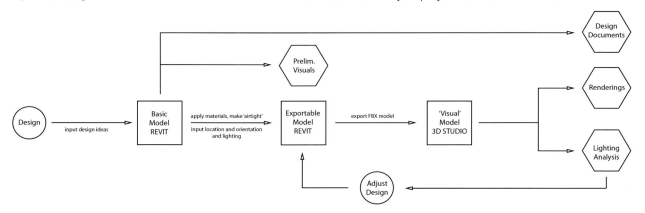

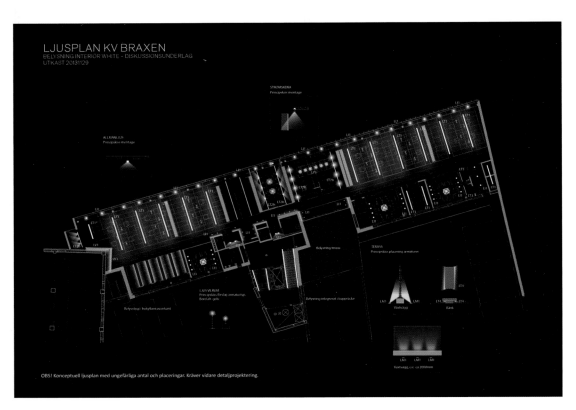

LJUSPLAN KV BRAXEN
BELYSNING INTERIÖR WHITE - DISKUSSIONSUNDERLAG
UTKAST 20131129

STRÖMSKENA
Principskiss montage

ALLMÄNLJUS
Principskiss montage

TERASS
Principskiss placering armaturer

Belysning terass

LJUS VILRUM
Principskiss förslag armatur typ.
Bord alt. golv.

Belysning integrerat i trappräcke

Belysning i bokyllan/avconkant

Vastvägg   Bänk

Vastvägg, c/c ca 2000mm

OBS! Konceptuell ljusplan med ungefärliga antal och placeringar. Kräver vidare detaljprojektering.

9 White Arkitekter, office daylight analyses,
Stockholm, Sweden, 2013
The firm studied its own work environment to
evaluate how the building was performing in
terms of daylight and employee comfort.

10 White Arkitekter, office daylight factor
analysis, Stockholm, Sweden, 2013
Researchers compared measured values with
simulations of the daylight factor in various
office spaces.

facades. The studies conducted a decade later by White were carried out to see if the building was performing as expected. The researchers compared observation studies of conditions and digital simulations of the spaces. Measuring daylight factor in the spaces, in order to calibrate the digital model of the building, allowed designers to gain feedback about how the spaces were performing when in use.

DESIGN TOOLS FOR THE FUTURE

In order to design strategies for sustainable environments over time, such as the Kiruna project where the objectives include performance criteria for a 100-year masterplan, and even to devise smaller research studies, such as the continual observation and improvement of their own Stockholm office, White utilises digital tools to gain feedback about environmental performance and local conditions. The office's goal to push each project to engage with sustainable and innovative design parameters is being advanced through experimentation with digital and parametric design, and making better use of building information modelling (BIM). The office continues to grow its research and development projects, both internally and with academics and other professionals of the building industry, by testing new digital workflows and collaborative approaches.

REFERENCES

1. Dermot Farrelly and Sarah Dahman Meyersson, 'Integration of Building Performance Simulation Tools in an Interdisciplinary Architectural Practice', in proceedings of the 'Sustainable Built Environment Conference 2016' in Hamburg: Strategies, Stakeholders, Success Factors, ZEBAU, Hamburg, Germany, 7–11 March 2016, pp 756–65.
2. Author interview with Dermot Farrelly and Sarah Dahman Meyersson, 9 March 2016.
3. Marja Lundgren, Max Zinnecker, Jonas Runberger, Sara Grahn and Marie-Claude Dubois, 'Daylight Autonomy and Facade Design: From Research to Practice for the Stockholm SEB Bank Head Office', in proceedings of 9th Energy Forum 2014 on Advanced Building Skins, Bressanone, Italy, pp 1301–7.

ARCHITECT

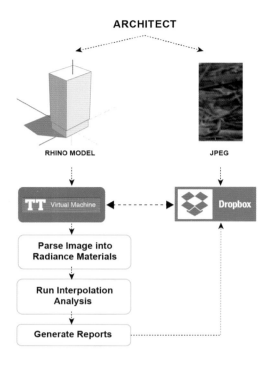

RHINO MODEL

JPEG

TT Virtual Machine

Dropbox

Parse Image into
Radiance Materials

Run Interpolation
Analysis

Generate Reports

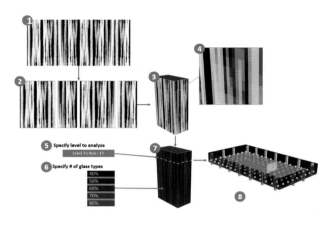

Specify level to analyze
Level To Run : 17

Specify # of glass types
40%
50%
60%
70%
80%

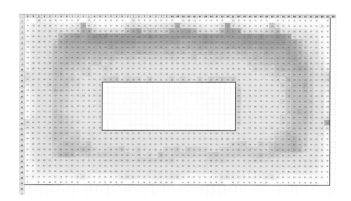

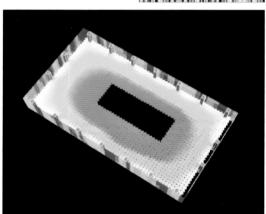

Glazing Transmittance Percentage
40%   80%

Useful Daylight Illuminance 100-2000 lux
5%   95%

1–4 Jahn Architects, Qiantan
Enterprise World Phase II
project: design, workflows
and analysis studies by CORE,
2016
This is an example of CORE's
Remote Solving design
workflow

15. CORE:
INTEGRATED COMPUTATION AND RESEARCH

TERRI PETERS

Engineering firm Thornton Tomasetti's in-house research group, CORE studio, is focused not only on developing innovative and highly customised design solutions, but also on training the firm's project teams to use the new tools and workflows. CORE's leader Jonatan Schumacher explains: 'we want to be as integrated with the office and as transparent and open as possible'.[1] The 15-person team contributes research expertise on a range of unconventional engineering and design projects, of which about 50 per cent is project-based research and about 50 per cent is other research.[1] They sometimes use their unique role in the company to experiment with smaller, more research-oriented projects that the firm would not otherwise be involved with. In 2014, they worked on the design and programming of an interactive Arduino-controlled, carbon-fibre ceiling sculpture for their San Francisco office, which used sensors to respond to people's movements. In 2015, they collaborated with the interdisciplinary design studio Diller Scofidio + Renfro on the facade engineering and optimisation of 'Commonground', an outdoor trellis roof structure where the rods, perimeter beams and cables function as structural supports and growing substrate for vines and plants.

TOOL DEVELOPMENT AND COLLABORATIVE PLATFORMS

Thornton Tomasetti is a 1,200-person engineering firm with 39 offices worldwide. The firm's research and development group was first established in 2011. CORE takes its name from its goal to combine *CO*mputational Modelling and *RE*search on a range of projects. The group focuses on custom tool development for parametric modelling and integrating building information modelling (BIM) workflows. The team is a mix of architects, designers and engineers, and they are distributed around several offices across the world. In addition to doing research-oriented work, CORE becomes involved in many of the firm's most high-profile and complex projects. The studio has been working on the development of new tools and workflows to support the firm's role as a structural engineer for the Bjarke Ingels-designed, sloped 'courtscraper' apartments in New York, and creating new digital tools for the design of 'The Shed', a telescopic retractable cultural centre by Diller Scofidio + Renfro.[2]

For the larger office and also for use within project teams, CORE develops custom tools and collaborative platforms to make sure

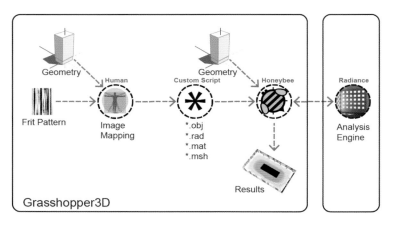

5 CORE, design workflow, 2016
This is an example of CORE's iterative design workflow in a simulation of fritting size, using various digital tools including the Honeybee plug-in for Grasshopper and the Radiance analysis engine.

6 CORE, design workflow, 2016
Grasshopper is one of the tools used for analysis studies in this case, involving daylight levels and frit patterns.

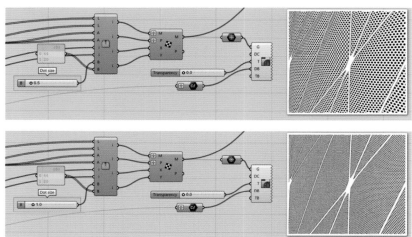

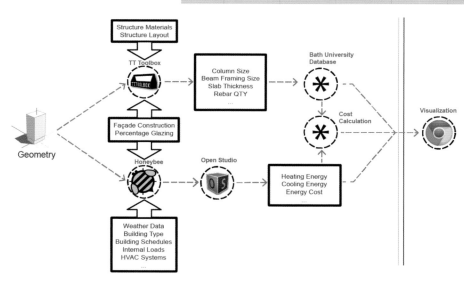

7 CORE, iterative design workflow, 2016
This example of a design workflow for a project incorporates various parameters and inputs, including environmental data and energy use and cost, and structural materials and layout.

that design work can progress smoothly. 'Our role as engineers is often to give useful feedback to designers as they are in the conceptual design phase,' says Schumacher.[1] For example, with the Bjarke Ingels Group (BIG) project in New York, they developed tools and workflows, so that the architects' massing studies could be evaluated quickly. 'There were many options considered rapidly, from 15 storeys, to 20 storeys to 34 storeys, often with only two weeks in between. We would be given a drawing so turn it into a 3D model, find out total cost of structural components and get back to them as soon as possible,'.[2]

At CORE, the problems of practice drive innovation. This chapter explores a few recent examples of their work, including their new tool development for the integration of daylight and structural performance, their advancement of workflows for cross-disciplinary practice using digital automation, and their development of the Design Explorer platform for the visualisation of possible solutions to complex problems to inform the early stages of the design process.

MODELLING FRIT PATTERNS

On a current project, The Shed, a cultural centre designed by Diller Scofidio + Renfro, CORE responded to the need for an integrated design solution, relating to frit pattern design options for the ethylene tetrafluoroethylene (ETFE) pillows that make up the building's facade. The building has a unique telescopic form, and the building can be extended across the site, creating larger interior spaces to suit programming needs. CORE's challenge was to design a frit pattern that would allow appropriate levels of daylight into the interior, while also mitigating overheating and excessive illuminance. CORE developed a custom workflow using Grasshopper3D, which enabled structural, environmental and experiential considerations to be analysed, and that provided a single model for design and analysis. In a recent paper, Mostapha Sadeghipour Roudsari and Anne Waelkens described their process as first mapping frit patterns onto the doubly curved ETFE pillow facade geometries and visualising them in Grasshopper.[3] They used Honeybee to export Grasshopper geometries and assigned material properties to Radiance. They explain: 'the main challenge of the project was to apply several types of frit patterns to ETFE

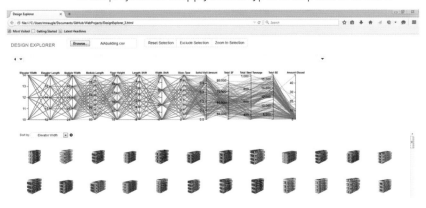

8 CORE, Design Explorer, 2016
Design Explorer is an open-source interface, developed by Thornton Thomasetti's CORE studio, which enables a designer to visualise and filter groups of iterations. Rather than singular answers, this interactive tool finds sets of design solutions that are intimately related and potentially scattered across a vast, high-dimensional possibility space. In this case, parameters include daylighting, relationship between window size, room size and options for light shelves.

9 CORE, photogrammetry study of a damaged
pier, 2015
Drone images were used to construct a 3D
model of the damaged pier for analysis.

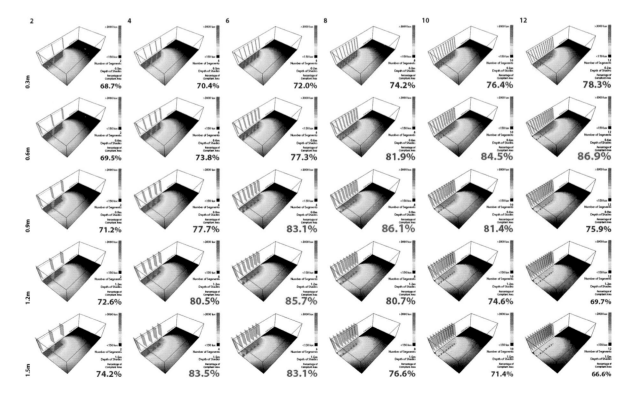

10 CORE, photogrammetry techniques to analyse a car park, 2016
CORE used photogrammetry techniques to inform its analysis by creating a 3D model of the collapsed car park from a series of overlapping drone images and digital photographs. The red flags show where the team was able to take a photograph.

11 CORE, multi-dimensional solver, 2016
CORE developed a custom digital tool to examine multiple parameters at a time in order to effectively evaluate options relating to louvre placement and daylight in a recent project.

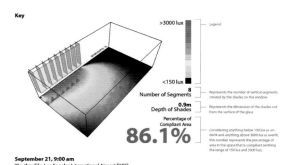

Key

>3000 lux — Legend

<150 lux

8
Number of Segments — Represents the number of vertical segments created by the shades on the window

0.9m
Depth of Shades — Represents the dimension of the shades out from the surface of the glass

Percentage of Compliant Area

86.1% — Considering anything below 150 lux as underlit and anything above 3000 lux as overlit, this number represents the percentage of area in the space that is compliant (within the range of 150 lux and 3000 lux).

September 21, 9:00 am
Weather File: Los Angeles International Airport TMY3

pillows with complex geometries'. They analysed how the different frit patterns would affect daylight distribution inside the building. CORE carried out a number of parametric studies to evaluate different densities and radii for the frit patterns for interior and exterior spaces for the two different placements of the shed due to the unique movable form that can be extended across the site. Their workflows utilised parametric modelling and physically accurate rendering engines to provide an integrated, flexible approach to streamlining the modelling and the analysis of frit patterns in qualitative and quantitative terms. The workflow allowed the team to explore a wide range of solutions in a short time to facilitate early-stage decision-making based on daylighting analyses. This method enables the process of studying frit patterns, which was previously fairly accessible to designers, to be integrated early in the design.

REMOTE SOLVING WORKFLOW
CORE has developed a cross-disciplinary design workflow called 'Remote Solving', which utilises automated computation as a means for enabling rapid design and engineering collaboration between multidisciplinary project teams. Remote Solving connects digital design models to remotely hosted, bespoke engineering analysis engines to provide near real-time engineering feedback.[4] In a recent paper, Matthew Naugle and Mostapha Sadeghipour Roudsari explain that CORE developed the Remote Solving framework as a set of abstract principles and protocols, not as a specific software platform in itself, in order to ensure the workflow could accommodate a wide range of design criteria, software platforms, and design and engineering communication methods.[4] Challenges faced by the team included designing for interoperability between the various computer-aided design (CAD) and simulation systems of the designers and engineers, and the desire to efficiently share only the most relevant data with each member of the project team to maximise effectiveness.

Remote Solving was used in a series of studies on the effects of frit patterns on daylight distribution within the office spaces of two 100-metre (328-foot) tall office towers, designed by Jahn Architects. In the towers, all facade surfaces were glazed with a vertical pattern inspired by bamboo forests. The pattern design was to be created by printing reflective white frit directly onto the glass. Naugle and Roudsari explain: 'The analysis engine was a script created in Grasshopper3D that was linked to a Dropbox folder shared between the design and engineering teams. The Grasshopper3D script used geometry provided by the design team at the beginning of the project as a basis for creating a parametric analysis model'.[4] CORE used a number of Grasshopper3D plug-ins, such as Honeybee, an open-source plug-in for Grasshopper3D. Honeybee connected the Grasshopper script to different validated analysis engines including Daysim and Radiance, which was applied as the analysis engine to run the daylight studies. Honeybee was selected because it uses Radiance material libraries, allowing the designer to execute the analysis from Grasshopper's environment. Naugle and Roudsari report that Remote Solving was a success in this project: 'Having access to the parameters allowed the engineering team the ability to adjust the parameters of the analysis during the process to balance the workflow for accuracy of the results versus speed of analysis'.[4]

DESIGN EXPLORER, HONEYBEE AND LADYBUG

Roudsari's goal is to 'make better designers rather than better tools', and he builds tools such as Design Explorer and Ladybug to support early-stage decision-making in a project-driven environment.[6] He developed the Design Explorer web interface while he was working at Thornton Tomasetti. It is an open-source tool to enable designers and engineers to visually explore the results of multi-dimensional analysis by testing, sorting and filtering options graphically. Rather than finding a singular answer, Design Explorer allows the designer to explore solution spaces and consider trade-offs, and that can meet specific requirements.[5]

Roudsari developed Ladybug and Honeybee in response to the fact that existing tools for environmental design were not designed to run iteratively. He aimed to create a simulation tool linked to parametric design software, which could analyse design iterations and therefore explore solution spaces quickly. While Ecotect was the most popular environmental design software, it was not designed for iterative design, as it lacked the ability to go through iterations very fast. Speed is key. Roudsari says: 'When you have a big software—it is like an elephant, moves in its own way. Trying to put wings on an elephant—it can't fly! Trying to develop a software [is] like creating an elephant. Plug-ins are like birds, they can fly'.[6]

CORE has also built many tools that are used within its own office. The TTX tool (Thornton Tomasetti Exchange) was developed to facilitate the communication of design iterations. The TTX tool is an internal interoperability framework that works off a single model database that can read and write to multiple architecture and engineering 3D modelling platforms. CORE developed this tool in 2010–13 and promotes the workflow to project teams, educating users about how it works through user group meetings, monthly project architect updates and newsletters. Three times a year, CORE offers a company-wide lecture on their newest work.[2] Another custom piece of software that CORE has developed is the TT Toolbox, which is a freely available Grasshopper library of commonly used tools, including automated CAD export and advanced unrolling. It is widely used both within the office and within the Grasshopper community.

SENSING THE ENVIRONMENT

Recently, CORE has been experimenting with new sensor technologies and visualisation techniques to collect and utilise environmental data that would be difficult to collect otherwise. The team has been using photogrammetry, a computationally heavy process that enables accurate measurement from digital photographs, often taken from drone flights. CORE's Matthew Naugle explains that this technique is useful for the team to capture building details for use in determining possibilities for building repair and structural failure analysis. It can also be used to monitor the construction process as a new building gets built.[2] In an early case of using the technology, CORE applied photogrammetry to a damaged area of a pier and it was able to create image maps and models by using the many overlapping photographs of particular areas for analysis. Normally, gathering this data would be almost impossible to draw or 3D scan because it would be difficult to get a 3D scanner in the right spot. Another use of the technology was in the study of a collapsed parking structure. Naugle explains: 'This is an instance where doing a laser scan would be pretty difficult, it is seven levels and the 3D representation is something that you could never experience. Taking these point clouds and mesh models, we are able to overlay it with a Revit model and to understand where and why things failed'.[3]

PROJECT-DRIVEN RESEARCH

At CORE, project-driven research drives innovation. There is a demonstrated need to develop iterative approaches and CORE is responding with new tools and workflows to explore trade-offs and options. Interoperability and lightweight data formats are important to facilitate sharing and collaboration during the design process. The team aims to use an iterative process to enable the generation of a large number of options, but then these need to be efficiently simulated and visualised, so that designers can explore these solution spaces. Customisation and the creation of bespoke software has been key to CORE's continued success at the forefront of computational design research.

REFERENCES

1. Interview with Jonatan Schumacher, in Designalyze, 9 May 2015, online at http://designalyze.com/blog/podcast/episode-002-jonatan-schumacher (accessed 20 March 2016).
2. Author interview with Matthew Naugle, 23 February 2016.
3. Mostapha Sadeghipour Roudsari and Anne Waelkens, 'A New Approach to Modeling Frit Patterns for Daylight Simulation', in proceedings of the Symposium on Simulation for Architecture and Urban Design (SimAUD), Alexandria, Virginia, USA, 12–15 April 2015, pp 22–7.
4. Matthew Naugle and Mostapha Sadeghipour Roudsari, 'Remote Solving: A Methodological Shift in Collaborative Building Design and Analysis', in proceedings of the Symposium on Simulation for Architecture and Urban Design (SimAUD), Alexandria, Virginia, USA, 12–15 April 2015, pp 28–34.
5. Thornton Tomasetti's CORE studio, 'Design Explorer', online at http://tt-acm.github.io/DesignExplorer (accessed 20 March 2016).
6. Author interview with Mostapha Sadeghipour Roudsari, 5 February 2016 .

IMAGES

All courtesy Thornton Tomasetti

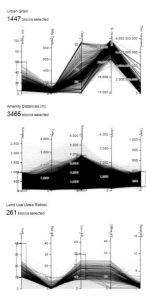

Urban Grain
1447 blocks selected

Amenity Distances (m)
3465 blocks selected

Land Use (Area Ratios)
261 blocks selected

Profile Matches
180 blocks match

- Urban Grain
- Amenity Distances
- Land Use
- All achieved

16. SUPERSPACE:
COMPUTING HUMAN-CENTRIC ARCHITECTURE

BRADY PETERS

For more than 15 years, Christian Derix has been pursuing a rigorous research agenda in computational design, focusing on creating a human-centric architecture. Currently the leader of SuperSpace, a computational research group within the global design and consulting studio Woods Bagot, he is experienced in utilising algorithms and embedding design computation in practice. Prior to his recent appointment at SuperSpace, Derix helped to set up the Centre for Evolutionary Computing in Architecture (CECA) at the University of East London with Paul Coates, and founded the Computational Design Research group (CDR) at Aedas (now AHR).

1 Woods Bagot SuperSpace, CIVITAS urban flow analysis for New York, USA, 2016
CIVITAS is a research study that quantifies the civic aspect of urban and community spaces via computational models. This image shows an analysis correlating urban flows to land-use data in Manhattan and Brooklyn.

2 Woods Bagot SuperSpace, CIVITAS urban systems engine, 2016
This shows the interface of the CIVITAS urban systems engine, allowing users to intuitively reveal conditions in the city. The model comprises investigations at three scales, four computer applications, and accesses about 200 maps of data analysis and visualisation as input for larger analysis and operations processes.

SuperSpace is a multidisciplinary team that champions the use of bottom-up algorithms and has pioneered many models of artificial intelligence (AI), artificial life (AL), spatial analysis, data visualisation, and spatialisation in architectural and urban design. The team's algorithmic models undergo development in-house via stand-alone programming environments, which gives enhanced processing speed, and control over compatibility and adaptability. Within the workflows of the office, SuperSpace creates software and designs that are backed by both pre-occupancy and post-occupancy data.[1] The group has about a dozen members in its main development hubs in Sydney, London and San Francisco; and, it has smaller implementation satellites in New York, Shanghai and Dubai. SuperSpace does more than provide innovative technology, as its work encompasses both design philosophy and underlying models. The group operates across many scales, sectors and phases, spanning conceptual design, spatial consultancy and design delivery.[2]

COMPUTATIONAL METHODOLOGIES
The development of computational tools tends to be tailored to a specific brief and for the automation of tasks. Derix says that computation has been used largely as a 'problem-solving tool' for 'structural, geometric, climatic or statistical' aspects of design[3]; that computing has been used 'to erase differences with engineers, not enhance (architects') own knowledge of the key aspects of architecture: occupation and space'.[3] Both building information modelling (BIM) and parametricism serve the purposes of automating professional deliverables where computation is seen as design tool. For Derix and SuperSpace, computation is a methodology. Derix explains: 'Computation doesn't serve a specific function but as a universal machine that could simulate any mental

tool if its function is abstracted adequately through a computable representation'.[3] The work of SuperSpace is about developing new modes of design thinking and how algorithmic models can align with these to give them more depth, not just speed them up.[2] The approach of SuperSpace is to encourage the development of broader and deeper tools. As opposed to the current trend with visual programming where fewer people are required to learn to program, designers at SuperSpace are finding they have to become even more technical and to increase their development skillset.

COMPUTATIONAL TOOLS

In the last 12 years, Derix has seen that he and his team have gone through four phases of computational tool development.[2] While Java programming has been used since the early 2000s, they have created programs in a broad spectrum of languages, including C++, Java and Python. In 2003, the common approach was to program individual plug-ins for computer-aided design (CAD) software as there was no commercial, generative scripting software. The development of individual tools led to a second phase in which tools were bundled into dashboards. However, as Derix explains, dashboards required too much generalisation and stepped too far away from design discourse and implementation. In the third phase, stand-alone software applications were developed. To inform design decisions, team members were often embedded in design teams and so the deliverables changed as a result. These software applications often became projects in their own right and began to define particular ways of working. By the fourth phase, the team had gone from supporting design roles to being leaders of projects. As design methods are embedded in the digital tools, the software can now take a project from concept to design delivery. The emphasis now is on the creation of whole frameworks that include generative tools, analytical tools, benchmarking tools and different output options, such as reports, studies and analyses. While these frameworks can be used by SuperSpace team members, other design teams can use these tools. As members of the team build and use the library, the framework changes. Derix clarifies that by

framework, he means the design framework as a methodology instead of a development framework.[2]

TOP-DOWN OR BOTTOM-UP

Derix argues that while explicit parametric models will eventually automate the definition of metrically efficient spaces, it is a bottom-up approach that will enable architects and urban designers to focus on designing the experience of users and qualitative spatial correlations.[4] Paul Coates, a pioneer in computational design, was interested in the descriptive form in terms of processes; his work pursued 'the particle physics of architecture': the idea that there were geometric rules that constrain and inform both the unplanned and planned human occupation of space. Coates saw 'boredom and banality' with the top-down approaches of modern housing, particularly when compared with the unplanned vernacular village. He felt that the functionalist tradition was an oversimplification, and that through the complex emergent systems, sought to determine the structure of the pre-industrial architecture and cities. In the systems developed, the designer 'became a "systems designer" and the ultimate design was the emergent outcome of the complex interactions taking place under the software's control on the aggregating system'. Coates explains: 'If architects are systems designers they will need to think algorithmically'.[5]

DATA-INTEGRATED DESIGN

SuperSpace employs data-integrated techniques—generative models associate data to express morphologies and analytical models are used to learn patterns in data. The group applies computational design methods to predict human behaviour and map social and physical trends within organisations and cities: they 'unlock the creative potential within big data'.[1] The group sees that there are vast potentials in the gathering and mapping of data, at a variety of scales for cities, economies, clients, buildings or inhabitants. The group gets data from public sources, observation studies, behavioural mapping, and from client data.[1] Through working with big data, urban data sets, and working at different scales, SuperSpace hopes to expand notions of what is meant by 'environment' and how we can compute it. Designers in the group investigate conditions beyond just how a building might respond to its neighbourhood—they look at qualities of space and place, and many of these analyses are about the interfaces between interior and urban design. SuperSpace develops its own software in line with its agenda to build an experience-based, human-centric, spatial architecture. This approach allows for an even deeper dive into human comfort and wellbeing. Through a holistic analysis of environments, interior programmes and material assembly, SuperSpace simulates and optimises building performance to achieve dynamic experiential goals.

URBAN ECOLOGIES

The team aims to find latent potentials within cities and to deliver projects related to the end-user experience. Derix believes that the key to understanding sustainable environments is a focus

3 Woods Bagot SuperSpace, CIVITAS input maps, 2016
Input maps show different conditions, using open-source data and in-house spatial analysis.

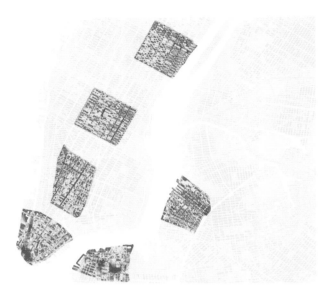

4 Woods Bagot SuperSpace, CIVITAS neighbourhood analysis maps, 2016
The computational routines produce: exact floor specifications for an end-user definition, which starts at the whole city scale, crosses the street scale and arrives at the building and floor scale; profiling of the entire city into exact classes of buildings, according to end-user types; and, design specifications for organisations.

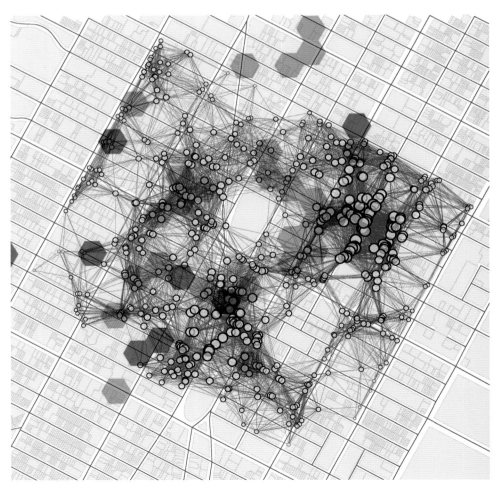

5 Woods Bagot SuperSpace
At the neighbourhood scale a series of densities, such as land-uses, are computed and visualised in relation to certain user groups.

on the interpretation and creation of design processes through algorithmic logic, regarding properties of spatial morphologies and their formation from a user-inhabitant perspective.[6] Design computation for urban design points towards design objectives that describe intentions for spatial configuration—its morphological ecology—and refers to properties of public space, perception of space and the effect of spatial structure on occupation. The team develops computational methods that generate urban structures that synthesise designers' heuristics. For urban design, the team of designers creates flexible tools, divided into components, with compatible inputs and outputs, where applications can be replaced by their manual input and output, thus many different workflows can be assembled. This 'agile principle' has been successful.[2] Their sustainability strategy is aimed at morphological or structural sustainability, and they have found that access-related aspects of spatial configurations are of key importance for designing sustainable places.[7] SuperSpace's urban design framework consists of a matrix of applications including: building scale, walking distance, transport flow patterns, land-use mix, noise and air pollution, visual impact, orientation and passive surveillance.[6] Walking distances can be computed, connectivity ratings calculated, and visibility and circulation mapped. In terms of block and building definition, optimisation includes: unit depths, unit ratios, solar exposure, plot density and perimeter continuity.

THE SPACE OF PEOPLE IN COMPUTATION

According to Derix, designing for spatial experience will require a computational approach with 'new models that recognise spatial domains autonomously through data associations', and this way of designing will not be 'aligned with key performance and compliance indicators identified by building regulations'.[4] Derix argues that three strands provide the basis for a human-centred design methodology: first, space as heuristic generation—generative algorithms and mathematical representations; second, interactions in the field—distributed computing through agent modelling; and third, cognitive conditions—spatial cognition theories and phenomenology. He explains: 'associations between spatiality and experience lead to design methodology'.[8] In Derix's and Åsmund Izaki's views, the organisation of space should be approached from the occupant's perspective—a 'new organic architecture'.[9] They have found that there are five components to developing this method. First, algorithmic transparency develops a productive dialogue between designer and model. Second, the model is a design conversation partner, and its behaviour needs to stem from internal mechanisms that are independent from a designer's intentions—the model's autonomy does not come from material or physical properties but from algorithmic models that will create meaningful spaces for occupants. Third, just as form can be malleable, organisation and programme can be elastic—adjacencies, distributions and connections can be modified to create new spatial behaviours. Fourth, workflows are based on modular assemblies—computational models should be constructed from a minimum number of components. Finally, fifth, by approximating spatial phenomena in algorithmic planning,

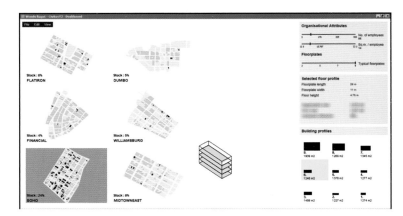

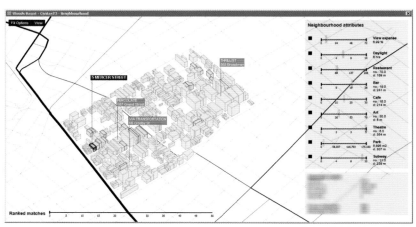

7 Woods Bagot SuperSpace, CIVITAS
neighbourhood analysis maps, 2016
At a medium scale, CIVITAS provides
information on how floors within buildings can
be identified, which derive their performance
from contextual relations and qualities.

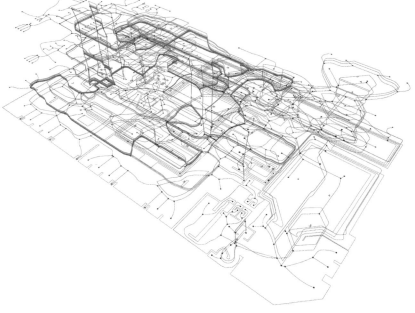

8 Woods Bagot SuperSpace, CIVITAS
neighbourhood analysis maps, 2016
At a detailed scale, buildings can be
analysed for many criteria, among them a
continuation of their spatial logic. For the
Resilient Infrastructure and Building Security
(RIBS) project (an EU FP7 research project),
a series of methods were developed that
allow the X-raying of buildings for movement
performances and spatial structure—developed
at Aedas's (now AHR) Computational Design
Research group (CDR).

spatial typologies are understood through occupant behaviours, and spatial phenomena are no longer clearly defined by geometric thresholds.[9]

VISUALISATION AND SPATIALISATION
SuperSpace uses visualisation, the process of representing abstract data as images, with the goal of understanding and gaining meaning from the data, for upfront strategic analysis. At SuperSpace, the designers additionally use what they call 'spatialisation'. Derix explains that if you want to locally understand how a metric differentiates aspects within a context, one needs to spatialise it.[2] A new representation with a higher schema is needed, than what is happening in maps or diagrams, and spatialisation bundles quantities, data, features so these can be reinterpreted. Visualisation presents a more global view and is not necessarily in the environment. In spatialisation, data is mapped into space and represented in a coherent way—it doesn't just show quantities but how quantities change from one location to the next. Derix explains that spatialisation then becomes a recipe for simulation as simulation operates on these maps. He states that visualisation, spatialisation, and simulation are the three phases in the design process—the ultimate thing is a design cycle, otherwise you need to find a new way to go forward. With its human-centric approach, SuperSpace strives to understand the invisible qualities of space from the user's point of view. However, in this case it is even more critical how these conditions are made visible.

COMPUTING ENVIRONMENT AND GENERATING DESIGN
SuperSpace develops design software that combines advanced algorithmic techniques, with data analysis, visualisation and spatialisation, with simulation to design architecture from an occupant's perspective. Derix explains that once the environmental conditions are computed and understood, then

6 Woods Bagot SuperSpace, CIVITAS neighbourhood analysis maps, 2016
At the lowest scale, CIVITAS first provides the search for buildings according to some organisational constraints.

9 Woods Bagot SuperSpace, CIVITAS neighbourhood analysis maps, 2016
As part of the RIBS project, novel algorithms for visualising visual occlusion and exposure of floors and cross-floor spaces were developed to help identify opportunities for usage—developed at Aedas's (now AHR) Computational Design Research group (CDR).

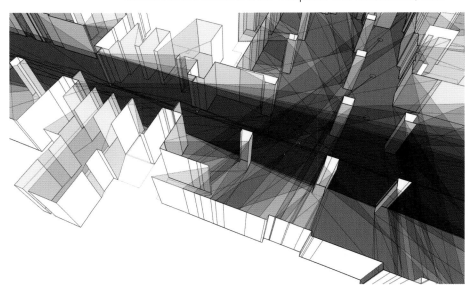

you need to operate on these patterns, and this requires a generative approach.[2] First, compute the environment, then generate the architecture—or the computational models can be used to design space and create place. To compute the environment, the designer must question how to compute the qualities of an environment and its rules rather than computing design processes. The question must be not only how to generate form, but what am I generating and why? A deep understanding of the environment is necessary, and this needs to be encoded, before 'generating' architecture.

REFERENCES

1. 'Woods Bagot SuperSpace', online at http://superspace.woodsbagot.com (accessed 25 August 2016).

2. Author interview with Christian Derix, June 2016.

3. Christian Derix, 'Mediating Spatial Phenomena through Computational Heuristics', in proceedings of the Association for Computer-Aided Design In Architecture (ACADIA) conference, New York, USA, 2010, pp 61–6.

4. Christian Derix and Prarthana Jagannath, 'Near Futures: Associative Archetypes', in Christian Derix and Åsmund Izaki (eds), *Empathic Space: The Computation of Human-Centric Architecture,* Architectural Design (AD) series (John Wiley & Sons, Chichester), vol 84, no 5, September/October 2014, pp 130–35.

5. Paul Coates and Christian Derix, 'The Deep Structure of the Picturesque', in Christian Derix and Åsmund Izaki (eds), *Empathic Space: The Computation of Human-Centric Architecture,* Architectural Design (AD) series (John Wiley & Sons, Chichester), vol 84, no 5, September/October 2014, pp 32–7

6. Christian Derix, Judit Kimpian, Abdulmajid Karanouh and Josh Mason, 'Feedback Architecture', in Terri Peters (ed), *Experimental Green Strategies: Redefining Ecological Design*, Architectural Design (AD) series (John Wiley & Sons, Chichester), vol 81, no 6, November/December 2011, pp 36–43.

7. Christian Derix, 'In-Between Architecture Computation', in *International Journal of Architectural Computing*, vol 7, no 4, 2009, pp 565–85.

8. Christian Derix, 'The Space of People in Computation', in Christian Derix and Åsmund Izaki (eds), *Empathic Space: The Computation of Human-Centric Architecture,* Architectural Design (AD) series (John Wiley & Sons, Chichester), vol 84, no 5, September/October 2014, pp 14–23.

9. Christian Derix and Åsmund Izaki, 'Spatial Computing for the New Organic', in Brady Peters and Xavier de Kestelier (eds), *Computation Works: The Building of Algorithmic Thought*, Architectural Design (AD) series (John Wiley & Sons, Chichester), vol 83, no 2, March/April 2013, pp 42–7.

IMAGES
All courtesy Woods Bagot SUPERSPACE

17. ZHACODE:
SKETCHING WITH PERFORMANCE

TERRI PETERS

Architecture is en route to deliver habitats that parallel those of nature.
—Shajay Bhooshan[1]

ZHACODE, the research group at Zaha Hadid Architects (ZHA), uses bespoke design tools to 'sketch with performance'—that is to say, through the creation of custom design tools, the architects can immediately interact with a model to make informed decisions on customisable aspects of building performance. Both the ZHACODE group, and the wider office, consider aspects of performance at a variety of scales in their projects. The office is known for the concept of parametricism, whereby all elements of a design can be seen as interlinked constraints in a computational design process. Developed by ZHA director Patrik Schumacher, parametricism exists because of sophisticated techniques such as scripting and parametric modelling, that he sees are becoming the new normal in contemporary practice. Schumacher writes that 'one of the most pervasive current techniques involves populating modulated surfaces with adaptive components … components might be constructed from multiple elements constrained/cohered by associative relations so that the overall component might sensibly adapt to various local conditions'. In parametricism, through computational techniques 'forms are the result of lawfully interacting forces'.[2]

ZHA is famous for its complex and sculptural forms; however, the practice maintains a focus on performance-based approaches and on sustainable design. The office was recently awarded the Aga Khan 2016 Award for Architecture for the Issam Fares Institute for Public Policy and International Affairs building at the American University in Beirut, Lebanon—a 'floating building' with a 21-metre (69-foot) cantilever. Recent competition wins include the Urban Heritage Administration Centre in Diriyah, Saudi Arabia, which has a perforated metal facade that allows certain views while reducing solar insolation, and is designed to be geometrically and aesthetically integrated into the natural environment and to support the activities of the UNESCO World Heritage Site. In addition, the office has designed innovations at the scale of furniture, objects and pavilions, creating site-specific and sculptural designs by using new fabrication technologies and digital workflows, to produce designs at a range of scales. Natural forms often inspire the studio's projects and ZHACODE develops new tools and workflows to realise its ambitions.

This chapter explores some recent projects where the ZHACODE group has created innovative site-specific responses, involving a range of environmental parameters. Led by Shajay Bhooshan, the

1 Zaha Hadid Architects, competition proposal for Samba Bank Head Office, Riyadh, Saudi Arabia, 2009
The team simulated the sunlight penetration at various times of day at different times of year and proposed layers of fixed and movable overlapping louvres to allow light into the building and prevent overheating.

2 Zaha Hadid Architects, proposal for a university complex in Morocco, 2012
Solar analysis was used extensively in this project to allow designers to consider how a glazed form could provide a comfortable interior in this extreme climate. Through changing the form of the double-curved thin shell roof and the curved plan, designers tested options to achieve the desired interior qualities.

group works to integrate concepts for daylight, solar shading, wind studies and visibility analyses into projects of many scales. Some projects that have provided great breakthroughs in workflows and tools development remain unrealised, and the design teams learn from these and apply lessons in future projects. Ambitious and unbuilt projects are explored here as showing trajectories of environmentally ambitious parametric design.

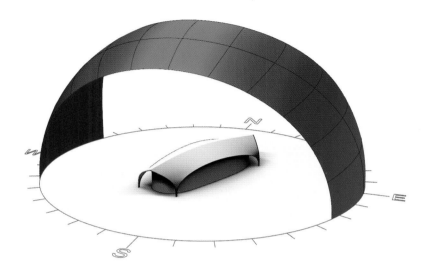

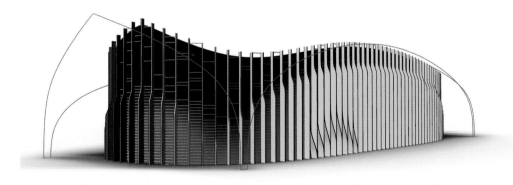

3 Zaha Hadid Architects, proposal for a
university complex in Morocco, 2012
The team modelled the geometry of the
distinctive and varied roof forms and carried out
environmental analyses at early stages of the
design to inform their design decisions.

4 Zaha Hadid Architects, proposal for a
university complex in Morocco, 2012
Solar optimisation studies for the roof apertures
were incorporated into the early-stage design
process.

UNIVERSITY COMPLEX—SOLAR SHADING

To study solar exposure and shading on building facades, ZHACODE utilises existing tools and develops its own custom workflows. The group has many projects in extreme climates where reducing the amount of solar insolation is an important performance strategy. For its competition entry for a university building in Morocco, designed to maximise daylight as well as shield inhabitants from the harsh climate, the group carried out extensive solar analysis and designed a series of louvres and roof forms as shading devices. The team analysed the experience of daylight inside and views outside. The alignment and location of louvres were part of a strategy to reduce solar gains inside the building. The environmental simulation software tool, Ecotect, was used to analyse the overall environmental concepts. The advanced rendering engine in Maya was utilised to test the effectiveness of various aperture strategies.[3] Nils Fischer of ZHACODE explains that tools are customised or developed by the team 'to enable conceptual design, to develop and make possible better early stage design decisions'. He argues that 'it is not about post-rationalising a certain design, because that is where we have fantastic consultants doing an excellent job and we would not try to compete with that'.[3] He adds that it is 'not always about getting super-precise simulations but rather about the super-fast feedback'.[3]

STUDIES FOR WIND AND VISIBILITY ANALYSIS

For the design of optimal forms to achieve comfortable urban spaces, wind and airflow analyses are carried out at various stages

5 Zaha Hadid Architects, early wind simulation studies using Maya, 2007
ZHACODE adapts and develops tools for analysing a site's specific environmental conditions, in this case wind speed and direction on the site at various heights.

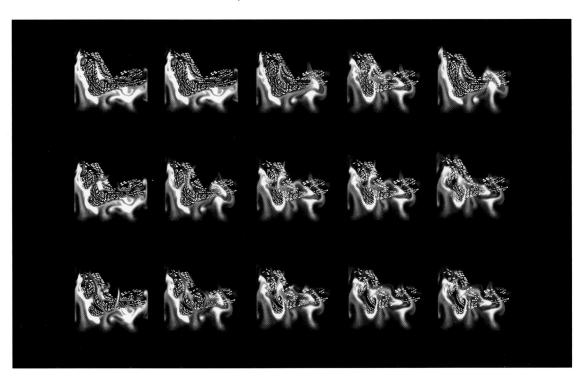

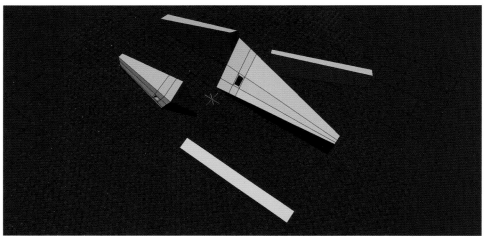

6 Zaha Hadid Architects, computational
visibility analysis
This custom tool was developed by using the
computer animation software Maya to carry out
studies of visibility analysis at the early stages
of a design project. ZHACODE often develops
new functionality in existing tools to better suit
the desired workflow and project requirements.

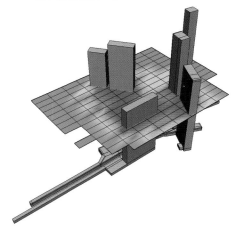

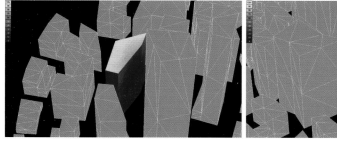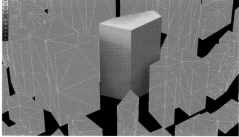

8 Zaha Hadid Architects, competition proposal
for Samba Bank Head Office, Riyadh, Saudi
Arabia, 2009: shading analysis
Due to the extreme climate, when the building
was analysed in its context using the Ecotect
tool, it was determined that solar shading
would be required on all facades to reduce the
effects of solar gain, but at different amounts,
depending on the position on the facade, and
at different times of year.

of a project. The team first works to abstract a complex design into geometric rule sets. Then it develops custom digital tools or adapts existing ones that integrate computational fluid dynamics (CFD) into the parametric geometry model. Wind analysis is important to understand how a building or a series of buildings will create conditions on the ground that people can experience, and studies are carried out at various stages to allow results to inform the emerging design. ZHACODE has been using CFD since 2007, carrying out wind simulations by utilising Maya fluids, and analysing the same geometry from different heights.[3] Visibility analysis is an important area of study in the office as it can be effectively used to model and understand lines of sight and exposure to environmental conditions on the site. The office also works with external consultants, such as the pedestrian movement consultancy Intelligent Space Partnership, which has developed a piece of software called Fathom that can assist design teams with visibility studies. Using Fathom, pedestrian routes can be mapped, and design decisions such as level changes or flows of pedestrian traffic can be considered in the early stages.

SAMBA COMPETITION
ZHA proposed a sculptural, prismatic tower with deep openings or 'crevasses' in the facade for its competition entry for the Samba Bank Head Office in King Abdullah Financial District Riyadh, Saudi Arabia. The office's proposal for the crevasses took the form of a series of strategically placed cuts or cracks in the otherwise continuous and tapered facade that allowed light in and illuminated key interior spaces. To maximise the performance of this architectural strategy in terms of daylighting, preventing overheating, and understanding the experience of the ground-floor plaza given the geometry of the entrance, the office developed new tools and workflows, which remain influential on later projects. Louvres were arranged vertically to give further architectural expression of verticality, but also as a means of providing a multi-layered facade system, with a fixed outer layer mounted vertically and movable overlapping inner layers dependent on geometry that use sensors and motors to allow varying amounts of light into the building based on the position of the louvres, the time of day and the desired performance. Bhooshan explains on this project: 'we did the analysis that we do with hacked tools or Maya, then we asked the consultants to do it in their own way'.[3] Their speedy studies with customised existing tools were used to make the feedback process quicker and more targeted. This way of working also enables the designers to have freedom to use the parts of a tool that are useful. Bhooshan explains that the 'hacked tools' in this case showed shading variations, ambient lighting and adaption of 'mental ray baking'.

SIMPLE-YET CUSTOM REAL-TIME SOLVERS
In a recent paper, Bhooshan explained the office's aim of gaining multi-stage design feedback that can be visualised, prioritising speed and user interaction in a progressive, error-reducing process of convergence. ZHACODE seeks to compare and analyse multiple account solutions that satisfy evolving design, structural

7 Zaha Hadid Architects, urban tower visibility analysis
Visibility analyses are used to show the environmental conditions for a range of heights on a site. Visibility analysis is a way of modelling what pedestrians can see and where they can go within buildings and street networks.

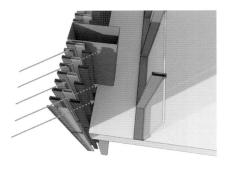
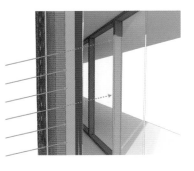

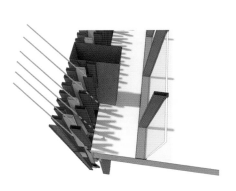
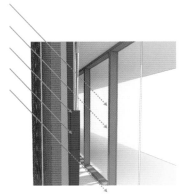

9 Zaha Hadid Architects, competition proposal for Samba Bank Head Office, Riyadh, Saudi Arabia, 2009: louvre analysis
This study shows a study of aligned (top) and unaligned (below) positioning of louvres on the facade of the tower. When the rear louvres rotate, they become more horizontal, which provides more effective shading from the midday sun at a higher angle.

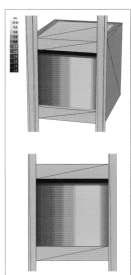
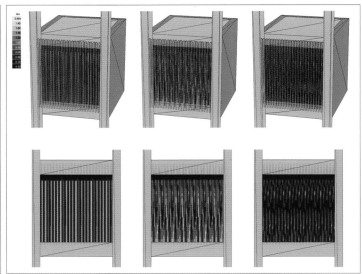

10 Zaha Hadid Architects, competition proposal for Samba Bank Head Office, Riyadh, Saudi Arabia, 2009: sunlight analysis
This typical floor plate, daylight and sunlight analysis shows total isolation and sunlight hours.

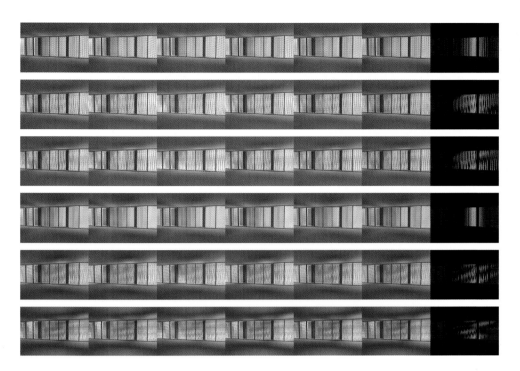

11 Zaha Hadid Architects, competition proposal for Samba Bank Head Office, Riyadh, Saudi Arabia, 2009: louvre analysis
Study showing louvre effects on internal areas on the north-east facing facade on 1 April 2009. The time of day across the columns ranges from 7am to 7pm. The rows show different designs for levels of movement, fixed positioning and alignment of the louvres, giving the designers graphic feedback.

and manufacturing constraints rather than exact solutions.[4] The workflow is multi-stage and multi-resolution to allow designers to develop an intuitive approach and to allow effective design refinement. Visual feedback from simple-yet custom and real-time solvers helps in continuous iteration and design development, more than accurate, sophisticated black-box solutions.[4]

REFERENCES
1. Shajay Bhooshan, 'Upgrading Computational Design', in Patrik Schumacher (ed), *Parametricism 2.0: Rethinking Architecture's Agenda for the 21st Century*, Architectural Design (AD) series (John Wiley & Sons, Chichester), vol 86, no 2, March/April 2016, pp 44–53.
2. Patrik Schumacher, 'Parametricism as Style— Parametricist Manifesto', presented and discussed at the Dark Side Club, 11th International Architecture Exhibition, Venice Biennale, 2008.
3. Author interview with Nils Fischer and Shajay Bhooshan, 19 February 2016.
4. Shajay Bhooshan, Mustafa El-Sayed and Suryansh Chandra, 'Design-Friendly Strategies for Computational Form-Finding of Curved-Folded Geometries: A Case Study', in proceedings of the Symposium on Simulation for Architecture and Urban Design (SimAUD), Tampa, Florida, USA, 13–16 April 2014, pp 117–24.

IMAGES
1–11, courtesy of Zaha Hadid Architects

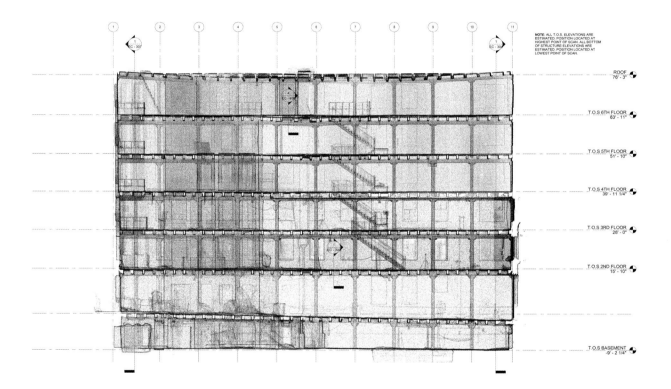

NOTE: ALL T.O.S. ELEVATIONS ARE
ESTIMATED. POSITION LOCATED AT
HIGHEST POINT OF SCAN. ALL BOTTOM
OF STRUCTURE ELEVATIONS ARE
ESTIMATED. POSITION LOCATED AT
LOWEST POINT OF SCAN.

ROOF
76' - 3"

T.O.S 6TH FLOOR
63' - 11"

T.O.S 5TH FLOOR
51' - 10"

T.O.S 4TH FLOOR
39' - 11 1/4"

T.O.S 3RD FLOOR
28' - 0"

T.O.S 2ND FLOOR
15' - 10"

T.O.S BASEMENT
-9' - 2 1/4"

DUE NORTH SECTION AT 'C'
1/8" = 1'-0"

1 WeWork, laser scan of a potential office space,
2014
WeWork's process involves carrying out scans of
the buildings and inputting the building data into
a digital model to better predict their renovation
scope, timeframe and budget, and make sure that
their prefabricated partition walls and furniture can
be a perfect fit.

18. WEWORK:
BUILDING DATA FOR DESIGN FEEDBACK

TERRI PETERS

WeWork is a real-estate company that rents high-end offices and desk spaces on demand or on a month-to-month basis. WeWork has more than 60 co-working locations, which tend to be situated in urban neighbourhoods near creative industries, such as New York City's Brooklyn Heights, Tel Aviv's Sarona Market and Spitalfields in London. The company is growing rapidly, as one of the most valuable private companies in the world, with a valuation of $16 billion in 2016.[1] It has been called the 'Uber of real estate' because it relates to ideas of the sharing economy, with a business model that builds on underused capacity. WeWork finds floors of office buildings for lease and renovates them to a high standard for on-demand co-working. Remarkably for this kind of company, key reasons for its success relate to architecture and data analysis. WeWork seeks out buildings with interesting architectural qualities, uses computational tools and digital modelling to understand the existing conditions, tracks the success of the renovations through user surveys and observational studies of the buildings in use, and deploys sensors for real-time monitoring to gain feedback from its community of more than 50,000 members. WeWork's sustainable approach of reusing and improving existing buildings while offering a creative setting for small businesses to co-work and collaborate has been made possible by its forward-looking approaches to data collection, analysis and management.

WeWork finds available floor area in undervalued buildings in desirable areas, often taking over several floors or sometimes even a whole building. Many of these are former warehouses with high ceilings, day-lit interiors and spaces for socialising. Members pay for their space and receive access to other areas that vary from building to building, including phone call rooms, break-out spaces for events and meetings, furnished lounge areas and private meeting rooms. The building's interior layouts support networking and community development. Members have free beer and coffee and spaces to hang out in. When they take a break, they can socialise with other creatives. People are connected virtually through the WeWork smartphone app, which is how members book meeting rooms, buy food and make connections with other members.[2] This is also one way in which WeWork surveys members about their satisfaction with their environment and

finds out which areas are being used the most, and which areas require changes. The company has invested in virtual and physical infrastructure for members and it has paid off. The WeWork team's success has been amplified by aligning themselves with the right people, who know about collecting and managing data about buildings and their users.

ENHANCING BUILDING DATA ANALYSIS EXPERTISE: CASE JOINED WEWORK

In 2015, Case, the building technology company founded by David Fano, Federico Negro and Steve Sanderson, joined WeWork. Case was known as an industry leader in cross-disciplinary building information modelling (BIM) coordination for high-profile design projects, including the Louisiana State Museum and Sports Hall of Fame, designed by Trahan Architects in 2014. The company's work identified and filled an important gap in the building design industry, relating to building data analysis and adapted workflows, technologies and visualisation strategies from other industries to enhance how designers can learn from building data. Case identified early on that the architectural profession was frustratingly slow to value its buildings as sources of data. In 2013, Case saw that architects were handing over that authority, potentials and risks of analysing their buildings to specialists rather than engaging with building data and reaping the benefits: 'Architects are not fully leveraging the downstream value created using these processes to increase their value in the production of the built environment. Unless computational designers and the firms that employ them are willing to step away from the keyboard and engage fully in the translation of information with the various

2 WeWork building, Washington, DC, USA, 2014
Housed in a historic row building at the centre of Washington's Chinatown, WeWork has transformed this building into a collaborative workspace.

stakeholders involved, their role and influence over this process will continue to diminish'.[3]

When Fano, Negro and Sanderson and their staff joined WeWork, they brought with them technology and systems to amplify WeWork's knowledge of their real-estate portfolio to enable better business decision-making. Rather than consult on building design and construction, they now consult on already built structures, helping WeWork to understand and then harness the potentials of empty, often overlooked buildings that can be transformed into creative hubs for freelancers and small studios around the world. While their role at WeWork is not architectural design per se, their ways of working and approaches to 'computing the environment' and using digital design tools to gather and analyse data is highly relevant to many design disciplines.

BUILDINGS=DATA

Central to the philosophy of the WeWork team is the concept of 'buildings=data'.[4] By this, the designers mean that buildings produce data, and also data produces buildings. In a recent lecture, Daniel Davis, the director of cities and spaces research at WeWork, discussed the changing role of data in the architecture industry. Davis argued that in design workflows 'only recently have we had to grapple with the production of data and understand what data is—for many architecture firms this is a real struggle'.[5] He argues that architecture firms are differentiated by their approaches to building data: how to produce it, how to analyse it and how best to use it. WeWork is keenly aware that not all data is created equal, and the scale of data production in architecture is still fairly small compared with some industries. Designers can learn from WeWork's philosophy about leveraging digital tools and computation to gain better building feedback. New computational design technologies enable the creation of large amounts of data during the design, construction and operation of buildings. In terms of computing the environment, architects could learn from some of the methods of technology companies, such as Facebook and Google, which have radically new ideas on data, its collection, and how it can be used to help shape the world around us. Buildings offer a wealth of data, and designers can harness it to enable better decision-making at various scales.

LASER SCANNING FOR HIGH ACCURACY BIM

WeWork co-working spaces are often located in historic and architecturally unique buildings in urban, mixed-use, districts of cities. While floor plans and drawings of these older buildings exist, there are often differences between what is shown in the drawing and what can be found on site. WeWork's business model depends on efficient and cost-effective interior renovations, so given their tight renovation schedules and desire to fit their premanufactured glazed interior partitions in the spaces, WeWork laser scans all buildings before renovations begin. Ideally, WeWork scans the buildings before it even commits to the lease, to negotiate better rates and also to be fully aware of all of the risks when dealing with older buildings. In order to measure,

3 WeWork, number of people observed in an eight-person room, 2015
WeWork researchers monitor how their buildings are used to inform business decisions and to know where to focus their resources in future projects. This study shows that eight-person meeting rooms are being used by groups of between one and four people for 87 per cent of the time, which suggests that WeWork's members would be better served by having more space dedicated to smaller meetings.

4 WeWork, occupancy dashboard, 2016
The WeWork smartphone app enables members of the co-working community to post messages and book shared amenities. Daniel Davis, the director of cities and spaces research at WeWork, explains: 'We have been internally exploring ways of measuring occupancy and surfacing this information to our members. This image shows a real-time dashboard of phone booths at our headquarters.'

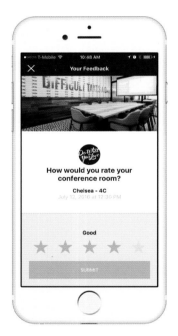

5 Feedback from users through WeWork's custom iPhone app, 2016
After members use a room, WeWork asks for feedback. As designers and managers of the space, they can use the feedback to address any immediate problems and better understand member preferences in the design of future spaces.

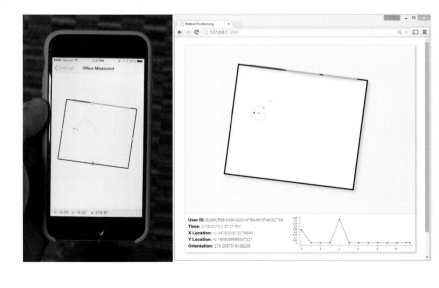

monitor and simulate the performance of the buildings, it relies on these highly accurate digital scans to gain a starting point of the building. This method of evaluating on-site measurements and creating a new set of building data is highly unusual—laser scanning is not commonly used in design practice, although the costs are coming down, and the ease-of-use is improving.

OCCUPANCY MONITORING FOR BUSINESS INTELLIGENCE

How people use their workspace, including which routes people take through a building and where they choose to spend the most time, can be rich sources of data. WeWork gathers the same kind of user data for every building in its portfolio, to allow comparison and benchmark performance. Since the company's designers model everything in BIM—the plans, room sizes and layouts, and the furniture pieces—they can correlate the spatial data with the occupancy data, which helps them to understand how the spatial layout affects the members' use of space. These insights enable them to simulate future buildings, allowing them to make design decisions that are backed by data instead of just intuition.

DATA FOR BUILDING CONSTRUCTION

The interior renovations are carefully planned and sequenced to be time- and cost-efficient. The laser scan of the building informs the BIM model, which can be continually updated and shared. WeWork studies the results of previous renovations and construction sequences, figuring out how to benefit from the knowledge of what has been the most and least successful. Often during the renovation, there are delays at the interfaces of trades and disciplines, and WeWork collects data on errors and changes, and also how they are resolved. The company tracks the timetables and drawing comments by trades and consultants over time in order to understand delays and improve the renovation process.

REAL-TIME SENSOR DATA FOR ENVIRONMENTAL FEEDBACK

Vital to the success of WeWork's co-working environments is an in-depth understanding of how members use the spaces. The company has developed workflows to use real-time and aggregated sensor data to analyse how its spaces are performing. By using machine learning, its team can understand how this data relates to survey feedback, which allows them to identify, in real-time, how particular spaces are performing. Members also benefit from the data about which areas are most used and patterns of occupation in the buildings. The WeWork app lets users know if amenities are free to book, such as private meeting rooms, and has an online discussion board for posting updates and community events. WeWork's research team continually updates these workflows by using various studies. For example, a recent study investigated how WeWork's member happiness and productivity was impacted by the availability of amenities, such as meeting rooms, phone booths and informal meeting spaces. Combining ethnographic observations from psychologist Rachel Montana, with real-time data gathered by architect Carlo Bailey, and business analysis from design researcher Nicole Phelan, the team was able to show how design changes impacted the experiences

6 WeWork, building analytics diagram, 2016
WeWork gathers building analytics from multiple disciplines, each of which has different ways of sorting and visualising data. It is interesting to note that all disciplines use Microsoft Excel, a non-visual spreadsheet program.

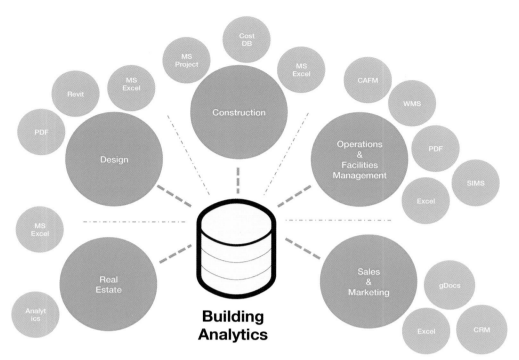

Building Analytics

7 Tracking indoor positioning using iBeacon

This smartphone app, developed by Andy Payne from Case, tracks a phone's location in a room. When given to volunteers in the office, the app allowed researchers to observe how frequently particular people used spaces in the office. The research was undertaken with Mani Williams from RMIT University and Daniel Davis, who was working for Case at the time.

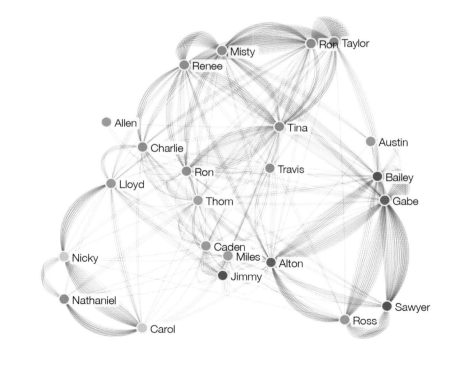

of members, leading to revisions of the WeWork design standards. Another example is a research project with architect Mani Williams (see Chapter 6), where a study using iBeacon to track people in space was conducted.[6]

BUILDING ANALYTICS: STRATEGIES FOR COMPUTING THE ENVIRONMENT
WeWork's approaches and workflows connect to key sustainable design principles of reuse and effective use of resources. The building and user data about the environment is collected on site, modelled using BIM, renovations are carried out, feedback is gathered and modifications are made in an iterative cycle. Computation and BIM have enabled underutilised floor spaces in key locations to be productive co-working environments, with their own ecosystems of virtual and physical meeting areas and communities. Perhaps most importantly, WeWork has recognised that the study of buildings in operation offers a wealth of data, and that designers can harness it to create better designs. Gathering data is the easiest part of this process, using low-cost sensors, site measurements and user surveys, but the analysis and contextualisation of the data, and interpretation of it as useful building information that can be productively analysed, is more difficult. Through real-time sensoring and feedback, WeWork gathers data on the physical and social environments of its buildings, and then uses computational approaches to analyse it, to make design changes, and to predict the performance of new designs. WeWork offers a useful and relevant model for designers, demonstrating new ways of using computation and digital modelling in building performance and management over time.

REFERENCES
1. Scott Austin, Chris Canipe and Sarah Slobin, 'The Billion Dollar Startup Club', in the *Wall Street Journal*, 18 February 2015, online at http://graphics.wsj.com/billion-dollar-club (accessed 18 July 2016).
2. The WeWork App is available through iTunes, online at https://www.apple.com/uk/itunes.
3. Case, 'Mind The Gap: Stories of Exchange', in Brady Peters and Terri Peters (eds), *Inside Smartgeometry: Expanding the Architectural Possibilities of Computational Design*, John Wiley & Sons (Chichester, UK), 2013, pp 209–11.
4. B'Buildings=Data' conference New York, USA, 28 May 2015.
5. A lecture by Daniel Davis in the Design Modelling Symposium, Copenhagen, Denmark, 30 September–2 October 2015.
6. Author interview with Daniel Davis, 15 June 2016.

IMAGES
1, © WeWork; 2, © Lauren Kallen/WeWork; 3, © Daniel Davis/WeWork; 4, © Carlo Baily/WeWork; 5, © WeWork; 6, © David Fano/WeWork; 7, © Andy Payne/WeWork; 8, © Andy Payne/WeWork

8 Case: visual analysis of occupant activity over the course of a work day
Visualisation of a study of spatial and social connections between individuals in the Case office as they move around during their day. Image credit: Andy Payne, Mani Williams and Daniel Davis

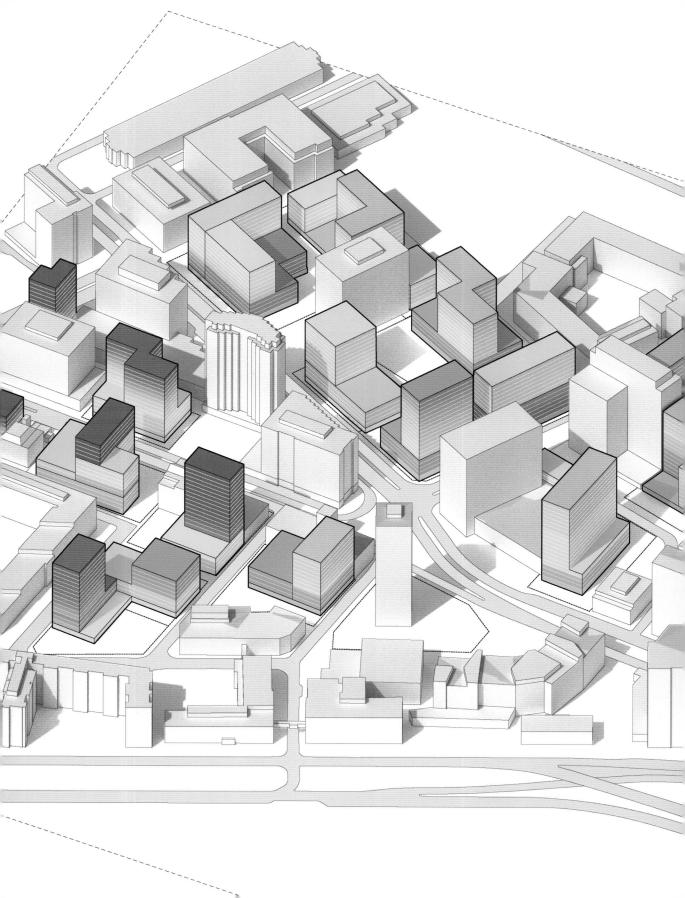

19. GLOBAL ENVIRONMENTAL CHALLENGES:

TECHNOLOGY DESIGN AND ARCHITECTURAL RESPONSES

TERRI AND BRADY PETERS

Globalisation, rising costs of non-renewable resources and extreme climate events are part of an uncertain future facing us all, including designers. In this chapter, five experts in computation and sustainability, offer different perspectives on the development of future technologies, the impacts on people, and speculate about the next design challenges on the horizon. There can be no certainty about what the future holds, but these five designers offer thoughtful and largely optimistic viewpoints about important roles that architects can take in using digital tools for effective, collaborative and interdisciplinary working.

1 Timur Dogan, UrbanDaylight tool, 2015
This urban scale energy simulation tool is a Rhino 5 and Grasshopper plug-in that allows designers to simulate and evaluate the daylight potential of large urban designs.

INSIDE, OUTSIDE AND ALL AROUND

TIMUR DOGAN

Timur Dogan offers insights into the need for simulation and comfort at a large scale. Dogan is an architect, a building scientist and Assistant Professor of Architecture at Cornell University. He is lead developer of Archsim Energy Modeling; UMI, an urban modelling interface; and Urban Daylight simulation software. His PhD research at the Massachusetts Institute of Technology (MIT) Sustainable Design Lab in urban design and early design stage energy modelling was supported by an MIT Presidential Fellowship, the leading environmental engineering firm Transsolar (see the profile in Chapter 8 pp 106–117), and the German government. The digital tools that he is developing can be integrated into established architectural design workflows by using widely available computer-aided design (CAD) software tools Rhino and Grasshopper. Dogan's new tools address the need for urban-scale environmental design tools that can be deeply and effortlessly embedded in the design process, perhaps, he argues, even offering a future independent architectural language.

HOW WILL NEW TECHNOLOGIES CHANGE HOW WE DESIGN IN THE SHORT TERM AND THE LONG TERM? WHAT DO YOU THINK WILL BE THE IMPORTANT NEW TECHNOLOGIES FOR THE DESIGN OF SUSTAINABLE ARCHITECTURE—IN 2030 OR 2050?
By 2050, population growth and urbanisation will require us to build new urban habitats equivalent to 750 times the size of Rome.

This is a worrisome development, especially since roughly one third of the global greenhouse gas emissions can be attributed to buildings. On the flip side, it can also be seen as a unique opportunity to mitigate climate change through an increased use of solar energy as well as energy efficiency improvements for new and existing buildings.

Most of the technologies required to build with a significantly lower carbon footprint are decades old, well-tested and affordable. According to a McKinsey report from 2007, carbon reductions for most buildings could even be achieved at a negative cost. However, the application of these technologies in practice is still limited. One reason is that adequate planning tools that can be deeply and effortlessly embedded in the design process are missing. Urban design is of interest, since in this phase critical design decisions are made that involve project goals, sustainability statutes, local building codes and land development plans that prescribe densities, construction standards, energy supply concepts and urban massing morphology. The urban form significantly influences solar, daylight and natural ventilation potentials, and hence largely predetermines the intrinsic environmental performance of a neighbourhood and its buildings.

At the urban scale we are facing multiple challenges, such as the lack of dedicated urban environmental modelling software and design tools, time-consuming, manual simulation set-up, as well as unfeasible computational overhead. In order to provide relevant simulation-based feedback on the energetic and climatic implications of urban form during a fast-paced design process, we need to develop faster simulation algorithms, as well as automated procedures for model set-up. My vision is that the next generation of tools will not require any extra effort to obtain information on the environmental impact of a specific design. The information would be instantly available and presented in an immersive format within one's favourite design environment. I believe this would significantly facilitate the design of intelligent, low-impact and high-comfort spaces, buildings and neighbourhoods, and hopefully lead to a much wider adoption of sustainable design in practice.

WHAT WILL BE THE IMPACT OF COMPUTING THE ENVIRONMENT ON THE LIVES OF PEOPLE, ON POLICY, AND ON THE QUALITY OF THE BUILT ENVIRONMENT?

Increasing urban density leads to a conflict between space-use efficiency and access to environmental resources, such as solar radiation, daylight, fresh air and breezes for natural ventilation. To manage this conflict, cities have traditionally relied on zoning guidelines proposing simple, two-dimensional geometric evaluation techniques such as setbacks and minimum distances. This seems antiquated at times when our capabilities to compute the environment are ever increasing. Digital tools could be used to formulate simulation-based frameworks for more nuanced prescriptive zoning rules, along with a performance-based

PROVIDING DESIGNERS WITH EASY-TO-USE, RELIABLE AND FAST SIMULATION TOOLS WILL ENABLE THE PROFESSION TO FIND NEW AND INNOVATIVE SOLUTIONS FOR LOW-IMPACT AND HIGH-COMFORT DESIGN THAT HAS THE POTENTIAL TO BECOME AN INDEPENDENT ARCHITECTURAL DESIGN LANGUAGE.

approach for developers interested in exploring innovative, high-density urban form.

Recent advances in daylight simulation software, for example, allow us to compute annual climate-based daylight performance metrics for urban environments accurately, in high spatial resolution and in a timely manner. Stakeholders in the built environment should use this technology to ensure the long-term daylighting potential in neighbourhoods and provide fair access to this resource. The hope is that being able to reliably and rapidly model the environment inside and around buildings will substantially improve the quality of the built environment with respect to comfort as well as fair and efficient use of resources.

CAN NEW WAYS OF VISUALISING AND SIMULATING ENVIRONMENTAL PERFORMANCE ENRICH THE DESIGN PROBLEM AND OFFER NEW CREATIVE OPPORTUNITIES? HOW DOES THE ABILITY OF A DESIGNER TO COMPUTE THE ENVIRONMENT AFFECT WHAT THEY DO AND THE DEFINITION OF DIFFERENT DISCIPLINES?
If we think of the design process as a three-tier approach that starts with the basic building design, integrates passive systems, and finally considers mechanical equipment, then visualising and simulating environmental performance has the potential to significantly enrich and strengthen the first two tiers. Decisions made in these tiers have direct influence on the aesthetics and the appearance of a design. Providing designers with easy-to-use, reliable and fast simulation tools will enable the profession to find new and innovative solutions for low-impact and high-comfort design that has the potential to become an independent architectural design language.

PRECISION, INFORMATION, PREFABRICATION

WERNER SOBEK
Werner Sobek is a renowned architect and engineer. A successor to architect Frei Otto and structural engineer Jörg Schlaich, Werner Sobek heads the Institute for Lightweight Structures and Conceptual Design (ILEK) at the University of Stuttgart. He founded his office in 1992 and is known for experimental lightweight structural design, transparent facade systems and sustainable building concepts. He argues that new technologies can help designers—provided we are ready to change our attitudes and our way of thinking about them. Sobek forecasts a future where designers have a more integrated vision of sustainable design and technologies, and where design for disassembly and interdisciplinary collaboration will be commonplace and required.

HOW WILL NEW TECHNOLOGIES CHANGE HOW WE DESIGN IN THE SHORT TERM AND THE LONG TERM? WHAT DO YOU THINK WILL BE THE IMPORTANT NEW TECHNOLOGIES FOR THE DESIGN OF SUSTAINABLE ARCHITECTURE—IN 2030 OR 2050?
It's not wise for me to try to predict which technologies there will be in 20 or 30 years' time. There are other people more qualified to

3 Werner Sobek Group, House
B10, 2014: diagram showing
building components
The house is fully recyclable
and has been industrially
prefabricated within a few
months and assembled on site
in one day.

01 PV-Anlage / Attika
02 Decke / Beleuchtung
03 Elektrotechnik-Modul
04 Technische Gebäudeausrüstung
05 Küchen-Modul
06 Bad-Modul
07 Schiebelemento zu Modulen
08 Trennwand Eingang
09 Trennwand Schlafen
10 Drehscheibe
11 Textilfassade / Beleuchtung
12 Flying Space / Wandbeläge
13 Boden / ELT-Versorgung
14 Glassfassade / Sonnenschutz
15 Rotationsklappe / Stahlrahmen

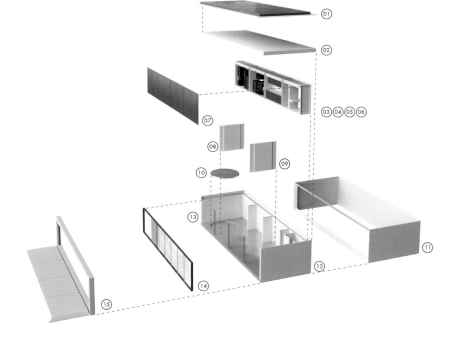

2 Werner Sobek Group, House B10, 2014: exterior photograph

New technologies such as the predictive, self-learning building control system have greatly impacted the resource use. The house generates double the amount of energy from sustainable resources as it uses, and the surplus energy powers two electric cars and the neighbouring house built by the architect Le Corbusier (home to the Weissenhof Museum since 2006). The house is the link between the user, building, vehicle and the smart grid.

do so. However, in my opinion, one doesn't have to know exactly which tools there may be in the future to be able to predict a radical change. In recent years, we have already seen the development of powerful new technologies that can (and certainly will) affect the way we design (and use) our built environment. This development took (and takes) place not only in the realm of hardware and software (that is to say, regarding planning), but also with regard to machinery and manufacture. For the time being, these technologies have only had a relatively limited impact on the work of architects and engineers. Once the young students growing up in a natural way with these technologies have come to the fore, our way of building will definitely change. There will be more precision, more information, and certainly also more prefabrication. By the way, these young students not only grow up with new technologies, but also with a changed attitude towards the importance of sustainability. For them, sustainability will be a much stronger natural ingredient of their ideas and their design than was the case in previous generations. Design for disassembly will be a matter of course, just as the awareness that it's the elimination of CO_2 emissions that matters—not energy efficiency in itself.

WHAT WILL BE THE IMPACT OF COMPUTING THE ENVIRONMENT ON THE LIVES OF PEOPLE, ON POLICY, AND ON THE QUALITY OF THE BUILT ENVIRONMENT?

Computing the environment can help us to make the lives of people more comfortable—but it will not do so automatically. It very much depends on the designers, engineers and other planners using these new technologies. *They* have to ask the right questions, and *they* have to make the right decisions. The same applies to the process of policy-making. The simple fact of having more data at your disposal will not necessarily make it easier for policy-makers to take a decision. Nor will it make the decisions taken by default any better. Despite the aforesaid, one cannot doubt that upcoming new technologies are a powerful tool and can definitely assist us in improving the quality of the built environment. As stated: young designers will have a more natural way of using these technologies as a part of their daily work than previous generations.

CAN NEW WAYS OF VISUALISING AND SIMULATING ENVIRONMENTAL PERFORMANCE ENRICH THE DESIGN PROBLEM AND OFFER NEW CREATIVE OPPORTUNITIES? HOW DOES THE ABILITY OF A DESIGNER TO COMPUTE THE ENVIRONMENT AFFECT WHAT THEY DO AND THE DEFINITION OF DIFFERENT DISCIPLINES?

The new technologies you cite do not offer by themselves new creative opportunities. In a first step, they can even be considered to make life harder for designers: they bring in yet another set of information to be considered, just as architects and engineers are already struggling to keep up with changing laws and regulations, ever-increasing financial and time pressures, and so on. We have to learn how to integrate these technologies into our work processes, and we have to understand what is really useful and important— and what is simply a gadget. For me, the bottom line is that new technologies can help us—provided we are ready to change our

DESIGN FOR DISASSEMBLY WILL BE A MATTER OF COURSE, JUST AS THE AWARENESS THAT IT'S THE ELIMINATION OF CO_2 EMISSIONS THAT MATTERS—NOT ENERGY EFFICIENCY IN ITSELF.

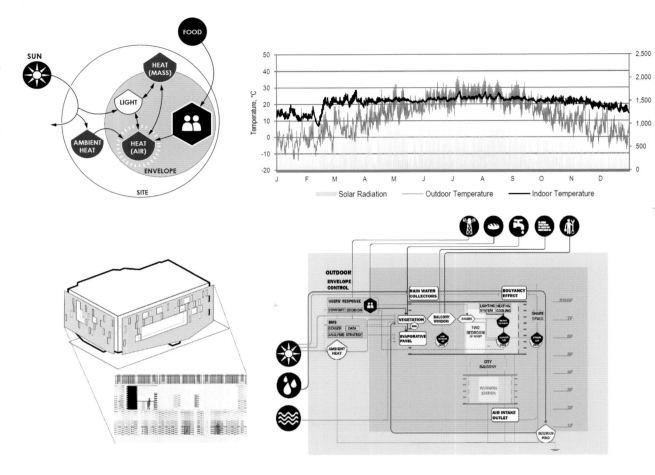

attitudes and our way of thinking. The traditional boundaries between the various disciplines will certainly be deeply affected by this. Taking an interdisciplinary approach from the very beginning of a design project will definitely and positively become obligatory.

THE (SIMPLE) MODEL IN YOUR HEAD

WILLIAM W BRAHAM

William W Braham is an architect and Director of the Master of Environmental Building Design, and Director of the TC Chan Center for Building Simulation and Energy Studies at the University of Pennsylvania. His work impacts both professional and academic audiences. He has written important peer-reviewed journal and conference papers on building energy analysis and digital tools, and also writes for a professional and specialist audience in his recent and influential books on architecture and energy, including *Energy Accounts: Architectural Representations of Energy, Climate, and the Future* (2016) and *Architecture and Systems Ecology: Thermodynamic Principles of Environmental Building Design, in three parts* (2015). Communication and collaboration are key ways of integrating new technologies for sustainable design

5 Master of Environmental Building Design Studio 2016, New Chautauqua Institute, New Orleans, Louisiana, USA, Climate Zone 2a Team: Jeeeun Lee, Mingbo Peng and Shin-Yi Kwan, spring 2016
New screen shading and opaque material adjustment, bioclimatic hybrids.

4 William W Braham, simple diagram of building thermal behaviour, 2013
Using the Energy Systems Language, this diagram shows an hourly simulation of the model in a typical year of Philadelphia weather.
© William W Braham

into practice, and Braham advocates simpler models, whose relationships can be more easily understood and explored to create more effective designs for environmental building design.

HOW WILL NEW TECHNOLOGIES CHANGE HOW WE DESIGN IN THE SHORT TERM AND THE LONG TERM? WHAT DO YOU THINK WILL BE THE IMPORTANT NEW TECHNOLOGIES FOR THE DESIGN OF SUSTAINABLE ARCHITECTURE—IN 2030 OR 2050?

For the computation of environmental building design, a term I prefer to sustainable architecture, the steady change of the last decade has been the increased availability of computational power. We are still challenged by the fact that most of the software available was developed for analysis, typically focused on including every factor contributing to a single result, such as energy use, glare or daylighting levels. The results are compared with norms or design targets, but with the complexity of factors involved, the answers often give little insight into the causes and little guidance for designers. As computing speed and power have increased, simulations of multiple parameters have been explored, giving a better sense of the underlying dynamics and helping designers to see the 'solution space' in ways that provoke the imagination. Until Kevin's untimely death, Don Greenberg and Kevin Pratt at Cornell University were exploring massive solution spaces to help designers to visualise the full range of possibilities. More recently, Mostapha Sadeghipour Roudsari at the University of Pennsylvania has developed two popular tools—Ladybug and Honeybee—using the visual programming languages of Grasshopper and Dynamo to help designers build simulations to explore the parametric space of their projects.

WHAT WILL BE THE IMPACT OF COMPUTING THE ENVIRONMENT ON THE LIVES OF PEOPLE, ON POLICY, AND ON THE QUALITY OF THE BUILT ENVIRONMENT?

The abundance of results from these parametric simulations shifts the problem from 'benchmarking' and interpreting single results to making data intelligible for design decisions. Roudsari developed a representation tool at Thornton Tomasetti's in-house research group, CORE studio, called Design Explorer[1], to chart the relative effects of multiple simulations and prevent the premature dismissal of potentially interesting combinations. This approach has been called 'filtering forward', rather than filtering out, but raises the deeper question of how much of the environmental dynamics do architects have to understand to design innovatively?

As powerful as the new parametric tools have become, my own preference has been for simpler models of building environmental effects, whose relationships can be more easily understood and explored. Most of the energy analyses performed on existing buildings, statistically correlating energy usage with weather data, for example, are based on very basic models of building thermal behaviour yet produce surprisingly accurate results. Developing simple models to explain building performance is a vital step for students learning to understand buildings and to interpret the results of sophisticated simulation

THIS APPROACH HAS BEEN CALLED 'FILTERING FORWARD', RATHER THAN FILTERING OUT, BUT RAISES THE DEEPER QUESTION OF HOW MUCH OF THE ENVIRONMENTAL DYNAMICS DO ARCHITECTS HAVE TO UNDERSTAND TO DESIGN INNOVATIVELY?

packages. As a teacher of mine often observed, it is the model in your head that has the greatest impact on the design.

CAN NEW WAYS OF VISUALISING AND SIMULATING ENVIRONMENTAL PERFORMANCE ENRICH THE DESIGN PROBLEM AND OFFER NEW CREATIVE OPPORTUNITIES? HOW DOES THE ABILITY OF A DESIGNER TO COMPUTE THE ENVIRONMENT AFFECT WHAT THEY DO AND THE DEFINITION OF DIFFERENT DISCIPLINES?
The biggest challenge of environmental computation has been to connect the many discrete kinds of analysis we perform on buildings—energy, daylighting, electricity, and so on—with the larger environmental effects we are trying to address. How should we compare energy with water usage, greenhouse gas emissions or occupant satisfaction? Architects work at multiple scales and need to think about wholes and parts together. I have found the Energy Systems Language, developed by HT Odum and his colleagues, to be the most powerful tool for helping designers to bring the many different scales and mechanisms of interactions together. The diagramming language can be used to describe many kinds of interactions, and by charting e[m]ergy (total embodied work and energy), it enables the ready comparison of materials, energy sources and equipment. In particular, it helps to make explicit the often-overlooked contribution of the environment and the mostly forgotten equivalence between human forms of work and the use of concentrated fuels.

OUR MODEL OF MODELS

KIEL MOE
Kiel Moe is an architect and Associate Professor of Architecture and Energy in the Department of Architecture at Harvard University Graduate School of Design, and is Director of the Energy, Environments, and Design research unit at the school. Moe is a leading expert on architecture and energy, and his research questions how architects and designers can and should consider and conceptualise new environmental tools and concepts. Moe is critical of the idea that digital tools in themselves can bring about more sustainable architecture or higher performing buildings. He feels that until designers begin to question their models of causation, they will continue to repeat the same mistakes of previous generations. His books are provocative and informative, and his thoughtful critiques and well-researched discussions should be required readings for designers, students and professionals who are interested in challenging how energy and performance is currently being addressed in the building industry.

HOW WILL NEW TECHNOLOGIES CHANGE HOW WE DESIGN IN THE SHORT TERM AND THE LONG TERM? WHAT DO YOU THINK WILL BE THE IMPORTANT NEW TECHNOLOGIES FOR THE DESIGN OF SUSTAINABLE ARCHITECTURE—IN 2030 OR 2050?
The blatant, unquestioned technological determinism of this question is emblematic of the many philosophical and intellectual barriers that continue to constrain the full incorporation of energy and matter in the realm of design. Without understanding the

6 Kiel Moe, interior simulation
of a simulation, 2016
Like all design tools and
methods, simulation relies on a
designer's expertise, it should
not be seen as a 'solution'
in itself to environmental
design. Moe explains:
'without robust knowledge
of the thermodynamics, fluid
dynamics, scale analysis,
and the hierarchy of energy
of a building's ecosystem
dynamics, simulation will not
enrich a designer's capacities'.

fundamental models of causation that unwittingly underlie the
determination and development of design today, designers,
building scientists and policy-makers will continue to err in
technical, social, ecological and formal ways.

'Important' technologies will only emerge in this century from
cogent and coherent conceptions of energy and environments.
In both scientific and political ways, the current techno-
managerial apparatus of 'sustainability' is unsustainable because
it routinely construes the world as a series of closed, isolated
systems. In scientific terms, closed-system thermodynamics
of first law thinking dominate. In social and political terms, a
closed discourse and cartel of expertise dominates the field of
decision-making that influences the everyday life of citizens.
Both closed-system models strain against the reality of the
constitutively open systems that shape and support life on this
planet. In this way, proponents of 'sustainability' too often lack
a general sense of irony about the thermodynamic, ecological
and social contingencies inherent in the praxis of buildings,
their environments, and what supports contemporary life.
This lack of irony is typically manifest in unwittingly adopted
technologies with inherent isolated system boundaries, and it
leads to irreconcilable epistemological problems with the stated
ambitions, claims and methods of sustainability. As such, the self-
ascribed expertise among sustainability proponents can prove to
be a form of disabling knowledge and a failed form of politics. It

is by now time to reckon with both the epistemic and ecological damage wrought by the technocratic apparatus of 'sustainability' in architecture and its unquestioned system boundaries.

WHAT WILL BE THE IMPACT OF COMPUTING THE ENVIRONMENT ON THE LIVES OF PEOPLE, ON POLICY, AND ON THE QUALITY OF THE BUILT ENVIRONMENT?

Without interrogation, the ill-considered system boundaries and procedures of 'computing the environment' will continue to limit what people consider to be the environments of architecture and what those environments could do through design. Contrary to the Calvinist ethos of sustainability, architecture should aim to maximise its impact on the environment. To do so will require designers to radically reconsider what the environments of architecture are, what the relative orders of magnitude of impact each of those environments are, and could be. Even now, designers errantly assume that the scale of the building is an appropriate scale of consideration and an adequate system boundary for design.

CAN NEW WAYS OF VISUALISING AND SIMULATING ENVIRONMENTAL PERFORMANCE ENRICH THE DESIGN PROBLEM AND OFFER NEW CREATIVE OPPORTUNITIES? HOW DOES THE ABILITY OF A DESIGNER TO COMPUTE THE ENVIRONMENT AFFECT WHAT THEY DO AND THE DEFINITION OF DIFFERENT DISCIPLINES?

In the post-digital context—in our current context in which architecture is not determined by digital procedures but is dependent on them—a more nuanced and evolved relationship between design and digital possibilities is necessary. Simulation, for instance, has no inherent significance for design. Without robust knowledge of the thermodynamics, fluid dynamics, scale analysis and the hierarchy of energy of a building's ecosystem dynamics, simulation will not enrich a designer's capabilities. As electro-numeric signalisation has silently come to subsume architectural production, simulation has served to narrowly constrain and delimit how we think about energy and matter in a couple of important ways.

First, simulation remains beholden to prior hylomorphic models of causation. In ways alternately technocratic and dogmatically 'formal', in our current model of models, architects are trained to impose intent and their will on seemingly inert matter-energy. This salient hylomorphic teleology in architecture is so pervasive and deep that it is difficult for most academics, students and architects to even grasp its epistemological command on the discipline or any alternatives. Whether it is the explication of intention through the obdurate insistence on geometry, now digital, or through the technocratic, scientist posture employed to validate a range of neoliberal energy agendas, architects continue to impose intention on seemingly inert matter and energy. More immanent models of causation must precede any technological infrastructure.

Second, the projective simulation for buildings, cities and climates is fraught with basic ontological problems that question the

UNTIL DESIGNERS BEGIN TO INTERROGATE THE MODELS OF CAUSATION IN DESIGN—WHETHER ANALOGUE OR DIGITAL—THEY WILL BE CONDEMNED TO REPEAT THE SAME TECHNICAL, ECOLOGICAL AND FORMAL MISTAKES OF PREVIOUS GENERATIONS.

knowledge produced with this technique, as the philosopher of science Eric Winsberg has eloquently and rigorously demonstrated. He asks of this false positivism: 'Under what conditions should we expect a computer simulation to be reliable? How can we evaluate a simulation model when the predictions made by such a model are precisely about those phenomena for which data are sparse?'.[2] We might ask other questions, too, especially as simulation is enacted in architecture. For example: if it is not in a pull-down menu for the architect-simulationist, does it ontologically exist for the design? What of significance is included in the model and what is externalised from it? What orders of energetic magnitudes are the most relevant, and which are mere defaults of pedagogy or practice?

Until designers begin to interrogate the models of causation in design—whether analogue or digital—they will be condemned to repeat the same technical, ecological and formal mistakes of previous generations.

THE FUTURE IS INTERDISCIPLINARY AND IN-HOUSE

NEIL KATZ, SOM

Neil Katz is an architect with extensive practice experience and a pioneer in architectural design computation. His innovative work at Skidmore, Owings & Merrill (SOM) over the past 30 years applies and develops digital design approaches that generate complex geometry and analyses it in response to many project goals, including environmental criteria and sustainability. At SOM, he develops digital workflows that enable effective optioneering, environmental analyses and optimisation. Looking to the future, Katz imagines an increased focus on collaboration and the development of tools and workflows in-house that will guide early decision-making. He identifies significant challenges in helping designers to equip themselves with enough environmental and computational knowledge to understand and interpret their often highly complex analysis models.

HOW WILL NEW TECHNOLOGIES CHANGE HOW WE DESIGN IN THE SHORT TERM AND THE LONG TERM? WHAT DO YOU THINK WILL BE THE IMPORTANT NEW TECHNOLOGIES FOR THE DESIGN OF SUSTAINABLE ARCHITECTURE—IN 2030 OR 2050?

Innovations in design and fabrication technology allow us to create building forms not previously feasible. We have an opportunity— and responsibility—to create forms which satisfy criteria, rather than create masses that are arbitrary. The criteria on which the design is based can vary among structural economy and efficiency, functional considerations, aesthetics, respect for the environment, and so on. Often, multiple criteria are considered, and sometimes they work together in the design synergistically, and sometimes we need to prioritise goals and consider trade-offs. At SOM, we are fortunate to work in an environment of extreme interdisciplinary collaboration between architects and in-house engineers— structural engineers, mechanical, electrical and public health engineers, sustainability engineers, and others—and to have

LIANSHENG
FINANCIAL CENTER

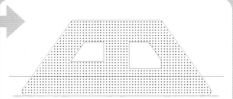

2 Office tower floor plan; the horizontal line indicates a section through the floor, a fixed distance from the south-facing windows, at which diagrams in figure 3 and 4 are computed.

4 For analysis points along the section indicated in figure 2, this diagram shows the light levels for different for different window wall ratios: 50%, 60%, 70%, and 100%, on 21 June at 12 noon.

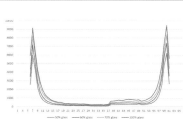

3 For analysis points along the section indicated in figure 2, this diagram shows the light levels for different seasons, specifically 12 noon on 21 June, 21 September, and 21 December; all with a window wall ratio of 50%.

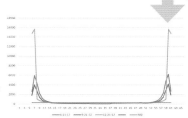

5 & 8 Perspective diagram showing the single floor that was analyzed; the cores are indicated in green, exterior columns (which slightly affect the daylighting) in pink, window glass in light blue; the window wall ratio in this image is 50%.

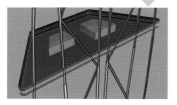

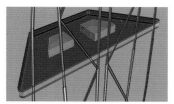

Figures 8, 9, and 10 are analogous to figures 5, 6, and 7, but for a window wall ratio of 70%; we can see an increase in the light levels in figures 9 and 10.

6 & 9 For a single analysis point on the plan, this image indicates the light levels for each hour of the year (days of the year are in the horizontal axis, and hours of the day in the vertical axis); the color range is the same as in figure 6

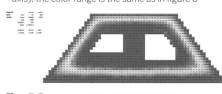

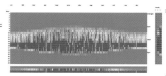

7 & 10 For a single analysis point on the plan, this image indicates the light levels for each hour of the year (days of the year are in the horizontal axis, and hours of the day in the vertical axis); the color range is the same as in figure 6.

the expertise to use sophisticated tools to design and analyse, as well as to create our own tools when necessary. For example, in the design of the Liansheng Financial Center, we carried out daylighting studies focused on a single office floor, aiming to maximise natural daylight yet minimise glare. Many design factors affect daylighting, including building orientation, window-wall ratio, floor-plate size and proportion, material selection (glass properties, opaque surface colour and reflectance), devices to block and direct sunlight, climate, season, time of day and the immediate context of the project. While we currently have an in-house team of sustainability experts, the level of knowledge among all designers in the office is being raised—from being familiar with strategies to using analysis tools. As these trends continue, considering environmental criteria as part of the design process will become second nature, and sustainability-focused design and analysis tools will become more sophisticated, easier to use and part of our standard design toolkit.

WHAT WILL BE THE IMPACT OF COMPUTING THE ENVIRONMENT ON THE LIVES OF PEOPLE, ON POLICY, AND ON THE QUALITY OF THE BUILT ENVIRONMENT?

For many projects, we use and develop computational tools, which allow us to parameterise various aspects of the design and iterate through many options. We can evaluate the effect of varying the parameters with analysis tools. The analysis process involves testing an option, visualising the results and using this to make decisions about the design. In parametric models, we often want to test the effect of varying a parameter, say the length of a sun-blocking fin, and determine what fin length is most effective. It's usually not possible to just know 'which option is best'—it will probably be true that the longest possible fin is best, however a long fin may be cost-prohibitive and may block views—also an important design consideration. We can probably learn that there is a drastic improvement up to a point, after which the benefits level off. These trends are important to derive. Multiple parameters, such as fin depth, spacing and orientation, can make the analysis computationally intense and require good visualisation techniques to understand the results, use the analysis in making design decisions, and communicate the information to others.

CAN NEW WAYS OF VISUALISING AND SIMULATING ENVIRONMENTAL PERFORMANCE ENRICH THE DESIGN PROBLEM AND OFFER NEW CREATIVE OPPORTUNITIES? HOW DOES THE ABILITY OF A DESIGNER TO COMPUTE THE ENVIRONMENT AFFECT WHAT THEY DO AND THE DEFINITION OF DIFFERENT DISCIPLINES?

An important practical issue is the analysis model. The design team will build a model best suited for their own work—to iterate and evaluate various design options and directions, and to create renderings to communicate the design to the team, project partners, and eventually the client. But when the designer is not doing the analysis, they don't know how to best set up the model for that purpose, therefore limiting its usefulness as a feedback tool. As someone who frequently performs analysis for others, I face this problem often, and almost always have spent more time either

> BUT WHEN THE DESIGNER IS NOT DOING THE ANALYSIS, THEY DON'T KNOW HOW TO BEST SET UP THE MODEL FOR THAT PURPOSE, THEREFORE LIMITING ITS USEFULNESS AS A FEEDBACK TOOL.

cleaning up or rebuilding the model than it takes to do the analysis. We're developing standards and workflows to help ensure that the models can be more useful for more purposes. Many analysis tasks take advantage of a number of tools. Often, rather than perform an analysis for which a particular tool is designed, we will decide on an appropriate analysis for a particular aspect of a project, and then either use the best tool(s) for this analysis, or customise and even sometimes build a new tool. Examples of analysis tools we currently use, and combine, are Grasshopper, DIVA, Ladybug, Honeybee and Excel. With Grasshopper, we are able to customise and parameterise the analysis model as well as the results. Excel is also an excellent tool for analysing and visualising results.

ITERATIVE PROCESSES

MOSTAPHA SADEGHIPOUR ROUDSARI

Mostapha Sadeghipour Roudsari is an architect and creator of Ladybug and Honeybee, two of the most important open-source digital design tools for architects and designers. These tools are groundbreaking due to their speed, accuracy and relative ease of use, and well-supported web community with online tutorials and examples. Roudsari is an Adjunct Professor at the University of Pennsylvania and has previously worked at Thornton Tomasetti's CORE studio. He is an industry leader in digital design tool development for environmental design, and here he argues that more collaborative and interdisciplinary workflows need to be established—designers don't necessarily need whole new suites of tools to answer fundamental climatic and environmental questions, the challenge is using the tools we have more effectively.

HOW WILL NEW TECHNOLOGIES CHANGE HOW WE DESIGN IN THE SHORT TERM AND THE LONG TERM? WHAT DO YOU THINK WILL BE THE IMPORTANT NEW TECHNOLOGIES FOR THE DESIGN OF SUSTAINABLE ARCHITECTURE—IN 2030 OR 2050?

One of the main challenges of building environmental design and building simulation has been finding efficient ways to integrate building simulation into the early stages of the building design process, where it can have the maximum impact on the design. Among all the different reasons that have been discussed, the critical breakpoint is the very different approaches in the workflow in building simulation and architectural design. Historically, the thought process for building simulation has been to study a certain problem in a linear fashion with the minimum number of effective parameters. In the building design process, multiple topics in several scales are evaluated in an iterative manner while trying to keep all the possible parameters in play. This difference in approach has in turn led to different cultures and different tools.

WHAT WILL BE THE IMPACT OF COMPUTING THE ENVIRONMENT ON THE LIVES OF PEOPLE, ON POLICY, AND ON THE QUALITY OF THE BUILT ENVIRONMENT?

The emergence of new tools that are providing direct connections between commonly used 3D modelling parametric interfaces and validated simulation engines started to bridge this gap by introducing interfaces that are being used for design and analysis. These plug-ins are particularly important because they introduce new opportunities to unify the two different thought processes. They ease the process of extracting an analysis model from the design model and by nature, and are designed to support iterative processes. Users can set up fairly advanced analysis models and iterate between dozens of possible combinations of input parameters without recreating the entire model. This is not only changing the approach to conventional building simulation, but introducing new opportunities for integrated design analysis workflows.

The popularity of these new tools is slowly changing the challenges faced by the industry from interoperability to usability. It is now much easier to set up analysis models, which in turn makes it easier to generate more results, and subsequently move from data scarcity to data overload. As a result of this shift, there is a critical need for supporting tools for data analysis and visualisation in order to help designers and engineers with making design decisions. There are several currently available technologies that

8 Mostapha Sadeghipour Roudsari, concept diagram of linear design process, 2016
Historically, the thought process for building simulation has been to study a certain problem in a linear fashion with the minimum number of effective parameters.

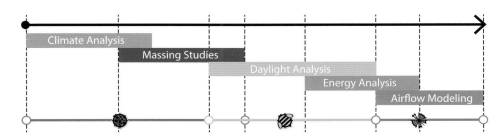

9 Mostapha Sadeghipour Roudsari, concept diagram of iterative design process, 2016
New technologies offer new workflows and building design processes that can be evaluated in an iterative manner for multiple parameters at a range of scales.

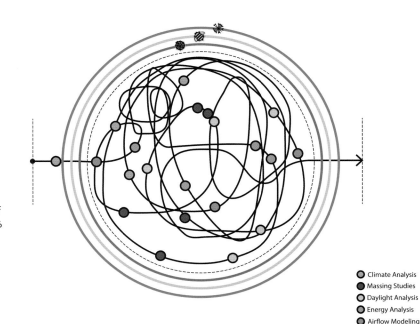

Climate Analysis
Massing Studies
Daylight Analysis
Energy Analysis
Airflow Modeling

have been implemented for a similar purpose in other industries. Among the new developments, Design Explorer is a web interface developed at Thornton Tomasetti's CORE studio that combines a number of these technologies to help designers and engineers to visually explore the results of multi-dimensional analysis. Tools such as Design Explorer make invisible design parameters visible early on during the design process.

CAN NEW WAYS OF VISUALISING AND SIMULATING ENVIRONMENTAL PERFORMANCE ENRICH THE DESIGN PROBLEM AND OFFER NEW CREATIVE OPPORTUNITIES? HOW DOES THE ABILITY OF A DESIGNER TO COMPUTE THE ENVIRONMENT AFFECT WHAT THEY DO AND THE DEFINITION OF DIFFERENT DISCIPLINES?

Prevalent thinking about the future of building environmental design is that new technologies, such as artificial intelligence (AI) and virtual reality (VR), will change the future of how we design and analyse buildings. However, the greatest change for the future of the industry will be in improved collaboration between different design disciplines. In order to accomplish this, we need a new collaborative culture, better tools and better utilisation of these tools by designers and engineers. These workflows currently exist in the current environment and there needs to be a push to utilise them. We do not necessarily need to search for the future technology as we have it in our grips now, we simply need to improve the use of it. By virtue of creating improved collaborations, we will give rise to better designers and engineers who will be able to make informed design decisions to design high performance buildings. As the science fiction writer William Gibson says: 'The future is here, it's just not evenly distributed yet'.[3]

WE DO NOT NECESSARILY NEED TO SEARCH FOR THE FUTURE TECHNOLOGY AS WE HAVE IT IN OUR GRIPS NOW, WE SIMPLY NEED TO IMPROVE THE USE OF IT.

10 Mostapha Sadeghipour Roudsari, a customised, automated design analysis workflow, 2016
Advances in digital tools that connect the design and simulation environments introduce new opportunities for integrated design analysis and simultaneous updating and feedback for designers.

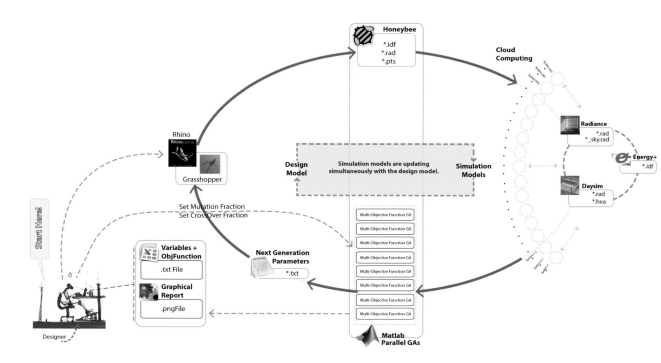

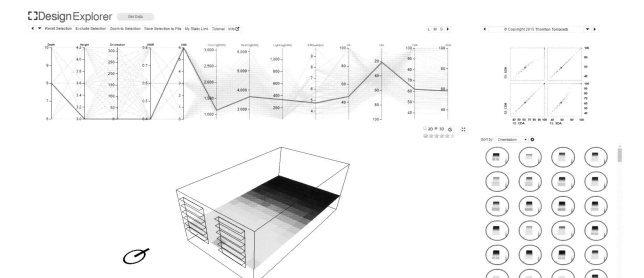

11 Mostapha Sadeghipour
Roudsari, Design Explorer web
interface, 2015
Developed at Thornton
Tomasetti's CORE studio in
2015, Design Explorer is an
open-source tool to allow
designers and engineers to
visually explore the results of
multi-dimensional analysis by
testing, sorting and filtering
options graphically.

The critical reflections by these five architects contribute to the
overall theme of the book: that there are a multitude of new
directions and design approaches for computing the environment.
Integration with design workflows and ease of use emerge
throughout this book as key challenges for digital design tools
now and in future. The question of how data is collected and input
is a challenge with many of the new tools discussed here. Not
only must designers equip themselves with new design tools but
most importantly with new ways of considering the environment,
and deeper knowledge of building science and environmental
design. Communication, interdisciplinary and collaborative ways
of working and critical evaluation will lead to designers asking the
right questions and making more informed decisions, ultimately
leading to better buildings and cities.

REFERENCES

1. Thornton Tomasetti's CORE studio, 'DesignExplorer',
online at tt-acm.github.io/DesignExplorer.
2. Eric Winsberg, *Science in the Age of Computer
Simulation*, University of Chicago Press (Chicago), 2010.
3. William Gibson quoted in Scott Rosenberg, 'Virtual
Reality Check Digital Daydreams, Cyberspace Nightmares',
in the *San Francisco Examiner*, style section, p C1, San
Francisco, California, 19 April 1992.

IMAGES

INDEX

C

C++ 194
CAD vii, 4, 25, 31, 33, 36, 47, 99, 161, 169, 189, 194, 219
Capra, Stefano 103
Carbon Calculator 65
carbon 14-27
carbon footprint 7, 65, 220
CarbonBuzz 61
Caruso St John 161
Case 81, 85, 212-13
CATIA 31, 39, 99
Cellophane House (2008) 119
Centre for Evolutionary Computing in Architecture (CECA), University of East London 193
Centre for Information Technology and Architecture (CITA), Denmark 75-7
CFX 167
Chadwick International 141
Cherrey, John 89
climate change 5, 25-6
'cloudscapes' 108-9
Clover Tower project, Mumbai, India 135
Coates, Paul 31, 193, 195
'Commonground' 185
Computational Design Research group (CDR), Aedas (now AHR) 193
computational fluid dynamics (CFD) 52-3, 87, 89, 101, 113, 167, 207
computer-aided design see CAD
CORE 185-91
Cramp, Nick 163, 165, 167, 168, 169, 175
custom software 39

D

Danish National Advanced Technology Foundation 135
DASHER project 71
data visualisation 23, 193
data-integrated design 195
Davis, Daniel 89, 213
daylight simulation 47, 49, 221
Daysim 24, 103, 189
De Kestelier, Xavier 95, 97, 103, 105
Dean, Ptolemy 169
Delos 71
Derix, Christian 31, 193, 194, 195, 197, 199, 200
Design Explorer 187, 190, 225, 234
design for disassembly 222, 223

design for sun and light 47-9
Diamond Schmitt Architects (DSAI) 23, 61, 63
Dick, Philip K. 1
digital energy modelling 17, 19
Diller Scofidio + Renfro 109, 185, 187
Dilworth Park 119
DIVA 24-5, 34, 129, 161, 167, 232
Dogan, Timur 53, 69, 71, 219-21
Dsearch group 177
DXF file 36
Dynamo 32, 39, 101, 225

E

ecoMetrics 61-4
Ecotect 24, 36, 39, 99, 141, 145, 167, 169, 190, 205
embodied energy 19
energy, definition 17
energy budgeting 23
energy consumption 7
Energy Cost Range of model 7
energy modelling 21-3
Energy Systems Language 226
energy use 141-3
    predicting 19-21
EnergyPlus 19, 24, 25, 125, 143, 145
environmental impacts 5-7
eQuest 25
eutrophication potential (EP) 113
evapotranspiration 109
Excel 141, 143, 145, 147, 232
'expressionist crisis of formalism' 37

F

FabPod 89-91
facade analysis 168
Facebook 213
Faircloth, Billie 75, 119, 125, 126
'falsecolour' maps 49
Fano, David 212, 213
Fathom 207
Feilden Clegg Bradley Studios 165
'filtering forward' 224, 225
Fischer, Alex 52
Fischer, Nils 205
'flash research' 80
Flovent 145
Fluent 113, 167
fluid flows 52-3
fog formation 125